UNDER
THE
FRENCH
BLUE
SKY

Diary of a Grand Tour

NICOLE MARIE DAVISON

**CAPRA
CYCLISTA**

Printed in the United States of America

Cover design and Capra logo by Nathaniel Navratil

Published by Capra Cyclista

www.capracyclista.com

ISBN: 978-0-692-89887-1

DEDICATION

I'm often asked how I could possibly remember so much detail about all of those thousands of miles on a bicycle. I think I could compose a response, but there is a better one to be borrowed, if I may:

Paul de Vivie inspires me daily. He staunchly defended his lifelong passion to ride often and far and at a speed much greater than his contemporaries. They accused him that by riding in such a fashion, he surely must bypass all the beauty and detail of his home country, hypnotized by such velocity. His response was this:

"These people do not realize that vigorous riding implies the senses. Perception is sharpened, impressions are heightened, blood circulates faster, and the brain functions better. I can still vividly remember the smallest details of tours of many years ago. Hypnotized? It is the traveler in a train or car who is hypnotized."

I rest my case. Thank you Monsieur de Vivie.

With his words in mind, I dedicate this book to all of you who seek to journey the earth under your own power and for your own reasons and who, despite the miles you cover or the speed with which you cover them, find joy in trying to remember every last detail of the experience.

CONTENTS

FOREWORD

On the following pages you will find the story of a grand cycling adventure. A personal story, recalled from the hazy memory of a million pedal strokes. A tale of a cyclist and her bicycle and the more than two thousand miles they spent together under the French blue sky.

My initial intentions were to write a detailed novel, remembering every second of the three week journey. Despite the relentless fatigue that plagued most of my evenings, I remained disciplined enough to scribble down a general description of the day's events in a journal before the weight of sleep became too heavy to bear. The notes are barely legible, though some words on those hen-scratched pages still pop and stir memories in my mind as clear as the day they were made. Sadly, many details still remain covered in the grime of all those endless stretches of road and they may never come clean. I'd like to think that there were just too many experiences to have any hope of remembering them all. The human brain, an impressive vessel, is still too small to hold all the wonders of this world. So I'm going to provide you, *in italics*, the daily accounts exactly as written in my journal because those words hold the most direct connection to the adventure.

Proceeding, I'll add some narrative about the stage. Until writing this foreword, I'd not re-read those pages since the last day of my attempt to ride France's greatest bicycle race course. Some have said it was the trip of a lifetime. I tell them this is just the beginning. I refuse to believe that life is only rewarded with one great ride.

My sincerest hope for telling this story is that it may encourage other cyclists to begin their own rides of a lifetime. It only takes a pedal stoke to get moving, followed by another, then another and suddenly you'll find that you've ridden and maybe written your own story of a grand adventure. The mountain doesn't have to be high; the road doesn't have to be long. Just get on your bike and start moving. Tackle the ride you never thought you could. Ride it any way that suits you and don't forget to take in the view.

Prologue

Pleasing to Remember

June 16, 2016 ~ Bicycles & Coffee, Purcellville, Virginia.

"One day this will be pleasing to remember. So says the quote firmly stickered to the top of my stem. Wise words indeed, if I can remember why I put them there – neck deep in lactic acid, kilometers clicking by, drawing steamy summer air through what feels like a straw, atop some faraway mountain, several stages already into what might prove to be the hardest thing I've ever attempted (along with saddle sores, chamois woes, torched tendons, dehydration and utter despair).

"What I hope to experience…no, what I demand of the experience, is a slow moving landscape, rolling friendships, toothy grins and the occasional secretly shed tear. Are you ready? is the constant question from customers and friends, every hour of the day for the last few weeks at least. As an amateur cyclist with a full time job, can you ever be ready for riding the Tour de France? That's one mighty big bike ride. The biggest of them all, one could claim, or at least the most recognizable."

"I got the hair brained idea from Twitter. Specifically from a post announcing an opportunity to ride the 2016 TDF route with a tour operator from the UK . In exchange for the

3

privilege of being fully supported for 21 stages, participants had to agree to a fundraising minimum per stage. While reading the tweet, I mentioned to my husband (and co-conspirator of our bicycle and coffee shop in Virginia) that I was going to leave him in charge for the summer and go on an adventure to which he replied: No way. You go, I go. Swiftly moving thumbs and two confirmation e-mails later, our deposits were taken and our minds began to swim with possibility."

"Even before we take the first pedal stroke, this trip has been life changing. I've felt every emotion known to humankind, sometimes an overwhelming mixture of them all but mostly anxiety and not a small amount of fear. The fact is, this ride is going to be hard. It's going to hurt physically and emotionally. I'm going to cry and curse and probably snap at my husband for no good reason. I'll want to quit. I'll want to get off and walk. I'm going to completely bruise my delicate pride. And so enters my self-appointed mantra: "one day this will be pleasing to remember" borrowed from the pages of an ancient Latin text."

"Each moment, each turn of the cranks, each labored breath, each bite of food, each morning I wake up with tired legs and a battered ego will be a cherished fraction of time that I will feel very fortunate to have. I've finally learned to let go of the urge to burn through my book of matches. I've got nothing to prove, except to myself, and all I care to do is finish under my own power on my own bike, at my own pace, with my best riding partner by my side."

"From kilometer 0.1 to the red kite in Paris, I just want to remember the world as it goes by…slowly… and on two wheels."

↔

How naïve some of those words seem now. How different reality is from preconceived perception. I didn't quit, but didn't make it to Paris exactly the way I imagined. I certainly battered my ego and had others do the job for me. My pride has grown bigger than its former self, but is still bruised from the process. My legs no longer ache, but my heart certainly does. There are mountains I want to ride up and down again and again, some I'd like to never repeat and some with whom I have a debt to settle. I've burned countless matches and then burned the whole damned match book. Once, I finished under the power of a train and then a bus. The very phrase "tour de force" can be defined in part as a feat of strength, skill or ingenuity. This feat required those traits and more.

I rode at a pace that found me at the front of the pack some days and at the back on others, but most days were spent in the middle. No matter where I was positioned, each stage left me feeling satisfied that I had ridden my own ride, my own way. Most importantly of all, despite his own setbacks which could fill another entire book, I *was* able to ride into Paris with my partner by my side.

First of all, I should explain what exactly we were attempting to do. To the initiated, the Tour de France hardly needs an introduction. Beginning in 1903 and in an attempt to increase readership of a sports newspaper named L'Auto, printed on yellow media, the journalist named Géo Lefèvre conceived a plan to create a bicycle race like none had seen before. Despite the course covering nearly 2,500 kilometers or 1,553 miles, his 5-stage masterpiece was created. Open to both professional and amateur racers, all men of course and overwhelmingly French, the stages were unbelievably lengthy; the bikes incredibly simple. Quite literally a "Tour of France" the event's secondary intention was for race enthusiasts to take a trip, following in the wake of their favorite cyclists (often hometown heroes) and see more of their own beautiful countryside. The Tour became ever the more popular with fans, with sponsors and with participants, many of whom came from the farthest reaches of the cycling universe to compete. No longer a French-only event, the Tour or "Big Loop" as it was locally known, soon became the world's competition and would help to change bicycle racing forever.

Today, closed to amateurs, the race is arguably the most famous of the Grand Tours of professional cycling and covers 21-stages over a span of 23 days and a distance that averages around 3,500 kilometers or 2,175 miles on any given year. That's right, modern racers are allowed a mere two days of rest in a three week period. That's far less rest overall than their predecessors but also less distance covered compared to past versions of the Tour which averaged 5,600 kilometers or 3,480 miles. Most stages of a modern Tour range from 120 to 140 miles, with "long" stages topping out at 150 miles and "time trial" stages averaging 11 to 35 miles. Stages are ridden together as a "peloton" of roughly 175 to 200 cyclists, competitively and with the fastest man at the end of stage declared the winner for the day. Those individual cyclists are all members of the same cycling team and only teams are allowed to compete, not individuals. Time trial stages can be ridden as a single cyclist on course or with all the members of the team riding the course at the same time "as one" against the clock. There are several awards up for grabs in addition to individual stage wins: points leader, fastest sprinter, best climber, best young rider, most aggressive rider, manufacturer's prize and team prize. Of course the most coveted is the overall prize, that of the yellow jersey or "maillot jaune".

The stages vary in degree of difficulty based on their length and geographic location. For example, an early "flat" stage might consist of 140 or so miles with the opportunity for a keen sprinter to take the win. A "hilly" stage might also be 140 miles but with enough small climbs to favor an all-around type of rider, the Rouleur. The stages we all love to watch, however, are the famous "mountain" stages. The mountains of France are mythical for their beauty as well as their difficulty and have been responsible for turning men into legends. A "climbing" stage might average just 100 miles but with tens of thousands of feet of vertical gain, can test the legs of the sport's best climbers, the Grimpeur, and favor those who love to suffer. That's because riding a bicycle uphill, against the very grain of gravity is a difficult and sometimes painful thing to do. Certainly a task easier to those gifted with the natural ability to climb though for most riders, getting to the top of is an exercise in determination and a battle against nature to overcome its best attempt to keep you rolling right down to the bottom.

From year to year, the Tour organizers attempt to assemble the very best of these types of stages into an overall course that will yield a single glorious victor. The Routiers-Sprinteur, a rider who has shown the determination, skill, courage and fortitude to conquer a colossal course of the most demanding landscape France has to offer will emerge as the winner. And this, dear reader, is exactly the course we intended to ride. Granted, not at the same speed, nor for glory, not even for bragging rights…just for the unique opportunity of testing ourselves over the span of three weeks on the most famous of France's hill and dale, plateau and peak.

We would attempt to ride 21 stages in 23 days, one stage per day, only two rest days, the same length stages (where possible) like the professionals. Unlike the pros, we would benefit from no special road closures, no air travel between lengthy transfers, no fanfare, no prize money and no accolades. In fact, we would be paying to ride, not race, with proceeds not going to sponsors or manufacturers but to an incredibly worthy cause.

Now to explain how this whole crazy thing actually happened. I blame my parents (don't we all?). My parents are doers. And I am grateful to have inherited their will to "do", despite the fact that sometimes that drive pushes my financial and logistical boundaries. Perhaps it's really just another form of addiction, the impulse to constantly experience life in a thrilling new way. I wonder how different it is from the need to eat more, drink more, buy more or feel more. My need just happens to be more days spent on the bicycle, traversing roads and climbing mountains I've only ever read about in books…hard cover volumes filled with black and white photos of my wool-clad heroes, faces forever frozen in a grimace as they claw their way to impossible heights. The Tour de France makes many a cyclist's heart swell with emotion. Whether you watch it on television or travel across the ocean to follow in its historic footprint, the Tour has inspired countless bicycle dreams.

I have dreamt of riding it for years, though figuring it would only ever be a stage here or a stage there. Being female, and all other pertinent factors aside, racing the Tour as a professional athlete was sadly not on my horizon. If I were ever to experience the pain, the pleasure and sometimes even the mundane miles of the historic route, I'd have to do of my own volition.

I adore the history of cycling, of the Grand Tours, of all those road-hardened pillars of cycling's past and I do not begrudge their overwhelming maleness, nor of the skewed perception of masculine ability that permeates our sport's past. The past isn't the problem. The present is. I simply cannot come to terms with the lack of a full-scale women's Tour de France or the attitude that women could not be successful Grand Tour athletes. The two events that attempted to prove that sentiment wrong have both been made obsolete. Le Grande Boucle Feminine held fast for 25 years before it fizzled in 2009 due to lack of sponsorship and other organizational issues. The La Route de France Féminine, a seven stage race held each August since 2006 was cancelled by the UCI after a ten year run due to supposed "scheduling conflicts." Perhaps that's why this opportunity was so important to me. It wasn't a race, nor in any way a competitive event. It was a chance to ride my bike along a route so revered by millions, but experienced by only a privileged few.

It was November 11th, Armistice Day. I was standing in the coffee bar at our bicycle shop, waiting for my husband Scott to finish cleaning the espresso machine. Those familiar with the retail bicycle industry will know that late fall can be a flat time of year. The summer riding season is winding down, in some cases the weather has started to turn for the worse and the holiday peak is still weeks away.

Being a small boutique shop with only two employees meant we generally stayed busy. We had a steady stream of custom work and wheel builds to keep us occupied and there was always coffee to be made. Although our shop held well-attended weekly gravel rides, neither of us were feeling inspired by our usual two-wheeled routine. The fall rain and grey skies may have been to blame.

Like a smoldering match on the forest floor, almost anything could have sparked my interest that day, so fueled was I for adventure. Any number of epic tours or charity rides or bucket-list must-do's for the modern cyclist could have flashed across the tiny lit screen of my phone but it was this collection of characters that would be responsible for lighting the fire: Think you could ride the Tour de France? Here's your chance! So I took it. The chance to ride the Tour. At that very moment, the whole plan seemed simple and I thought to myself *"I'm decent enough on a bike. There's plenty of time to train. Fundraising can't be that hard. I won't be missed at work. Besides, I really love France."* Only fools rush in, do they not?

It took the span of a fraction of a second to turn to Scott and ask if he would you watch the shop while I rode the Tour de France next summer. Most of my proposed adventures hovered well within our physical, geographical and monetary constraints. This one certainly did not. I expected his usual guffaw at my never ending stream of outlandish proposals, because you see, he had become quite used to this sort of thing. So imagine my surprise when he narrowed his eyes and with determination told me that under no circumstances was I going without him. Apparently fools come in well-matched pairs. That was as good as yes in my book and without further inquiry or discussion, using the modern miracle of the internet and a credit card, I followed the link to the sign up page and submitted our deposits.

People still ask me what we did to "qualify" for the riding the tour. Nothing. The process was and still is entirely self-limiting. Like skydiving or Everest summiting or strapping yourself to a bucking bull, you don't exactly sign up for a turn unless you have a little experience and a whole lot of can-do attitude. So it never actually occurred to me that it was something we *couldn't* do. I expressly understood that we'd need to do a whole lot of work between now and then, gain a whole lot of fitness and put way more miles in our legs and asses. I also knew the climbs in France were to be taken seriously. Despite the challenges, I believed we were just as capable as anyone to give it a try.

Our blind gumption would be the only thing I had to hold on to over the next few anxious months. It was the flimsy tether keeping me tied to the whole damn idea on the days I felt incompetent, or the middle-of-the-nights when I would wake up with my heart pounding and head swirling with all the realistic ways I could possibly fail at this; not raising the money in time, not finding anyone to run the shop while we're gone, not getting fit enough, getting sick, injured or worse. There were many, many moments when I thought we had bitten off too much to chew this time, though it was always over the enormity of the logistics and never because of the enormity of the ride. For that, I am grateful. However naïve my thinking might have been, to worry about everything would have been too much. So I worried more about the things I could control and worried less about the things I couldn't.

I worried most about the fundraising. The financial commitment was hefty but fair. Our host, Tour de Force, was offering an opportunity to participate in a charity cycling challenge. They would provide the route, the lodging, the food, the staff and logistics for 21 stages at a set entry fee per cyclist. In exchange for their support and expertise in organizing the entire event, each participant would be required to commit to a minimum amount of fundraising per stage. So obviously, the more stages you chose to ride, the more funds you agreed to raise. The cost of entry was surprisingly affordable when considering the magnitude of feeding, housing and organizing between 40 and 150 cyclists over a span of three weeks in France.

Let's say you failed miserably at fundraising (I replayed this dreaded scenario in my head over and over) and had to write a check for the total, then you'd still be getting the deal of the century. Twenty-three days in France on a fully supported bicycle ride with any other tour agency would have cost a mint. That is, if you could find someone to offer such a tour. Most of the major operators only offer two to ten days of riding the Tour de France and from what I could tell, none offered the opportunity to ride all the full length stages.

As we were not in the financial position to simply cut a check for the whole tab times two, we worked out a plan to start saving money for our entries and began a campaign to raise the required funds. We also planned to use the points accrued on a travel credit card for our plane fare. We always used a mileage card for big business purchases and after a few years, those miles really added up. Even still, we had to book our flights through Iceland because direct to Paris for two would cost more points than we had. It was important to communicate to our donors that they weren't just helping get the two of us to France to ride our bikes around for three weeks. Nor did we want them to think they were paying for our entries. Those, plus the expense of our bikes, gear, consumables or extras would come out of our own pockets.

This is a good time to explain the impetus behind choosing to fundraise for the Tour de Force and the William Wates Memorial Trust. William Wates and the story of his life and tragic death, struck in me an empathetic cord. If he were alive, we would have only been a few months apart in age. The motivation behind his attack and the brutality of his murder are difficult for me to erase from my mind. He was robbed of pocket change and left to die alone by teenagers a so-called civilized society might label "worthless thugs". But William didn't seem to think anyone was worthless and he was there in that precarious country trying to give back to the very individuals who hurt him, trying to make sense of their acute poverty when his own life was so privileged.

Had he survived, he may never have blamed his attackers, understanding first hand that they simply acted out of desperation, that they were young and impressionable and

14

crime was the only path they knew; who given direction and opportunity, might have made a less harmful decision that day. Something about William's life and desire to give of himself unto others, along with the actions of his family to set up a trust in his name so that through the Tour de Force and its donors and riders, he could continue to give back year after year, has made a permanent impression on me.

In order to meet our fundraising goals, we needed the support from a large audience and that meant relying on the digital universe. The sea of social media can be treacherous and there were days when we launched our meek little message into the churning tide of information, only to watch it disappear under the waves of more entertaining posts and more epic pictures. Initially, we had some enthusiastic supporters but no donations. Then a few of our family members chipped in. Both our mothers were gracious donors as were many of our closest friends and customers. The holidays were approaching, so instead of our usual shop party, we planned a silent auction, whereby we offered hand-made products donated by local artisans and businesses. Though the turnout was small, the generosity was substantial, and by the end of the evening there were tears of gratitude and a solid sum of fundraising accounted for. Then a customer suggested they'd buy a commemorative tee if we'd offer one, so we did. Three, actually. All the names of well-known mountains along the route of the 103rd Tour de France.

They are still my favorite shirts to wear and I'm always surprised by the number of people who are familiar with them and comment upon them when I wear one of those tees in public.

Meanwhile, we were just as desperate to tally up the miles on the bike. I had enthusiastically hand-written a training "plan" just days after signing up for the event. It outlined how many miles we'd ride each week increasing by the month plus special events we'd attend that offered long supported days in the saddle. Early winter was kind to us, with warm afternoons and little precipitation. One hundred miles a week was all we had planned for December and January. So far, so good. It still seemed like a lot when coming off of two fall seasons of cyclo-cross racing, where endurance miles are exchanged for a weekly schedule of interval work and skills training. At that point I couldn't remember the last time I rode 50 miles in one stretch and felt good about it.

We took our one day off of work to ride a "long" 50 or so miles, then tried to get out for short spins the rest of the week. Fortunately, we were a stone's throw from the Washington and Old Dominion Trail, once a rail bed, now a car-free paved path stretching 44 miles towards Washington, D.C. The "W&OD" trail would turn out to be a life-saver when the weather declined or the light waned or the traffic grew more thickly on the roads. Without it, we would have hardly found a safe place to ride and I apologize for ever thinking it mundane.

The New Year broke with a vengeance. For all the rideable days in December, we now had a debt to pay. January was plagued with heavy wet snow fall. Road riding was impossible, even on the W&OD trail. I had picked this winter to swear off riding a trainer indoors and was determined to stick to it. Not denying its value as a fitness aid, I had burned myself out riding one the season before while training for cyclo-cross. That fall, the area was plagued with early frost and chilling rains. It only took a dozen or so trainer sessions to sour my taste for them for life. Bikes, in my opinion anyway, are born to be ridden in the great outdoors. I found that by removing the indoor option, I became much more willing to cycle over the winter on the clear days despite the cold and was getting in more miles and feeling better about my rides.

When snow made the roads impassable by bike, we took to walking three to four miles at as brisk a pace we could manage. It kept our heart rates up and stretched out our hips. The first few of these walks were followed by several days of soreness but after a while, we could really hoof-it without breaking a sweat. If we were absolutely stuck indoors, we begrudgingly worked out on a borrowed elliptical machine (which was previously being used as a towel rack). By the end of January, we were suffering badly from cabin fever.

Grey days and wet snow fall had taken its toll on us mentally and we were getting restless and grumpy and losing all enthusiasm to stay fit. The two of us had only managed 12 hours and 150 miles of saddle time by the end of the month and we needed some kind of boost. Scott and I discussed signing up for a spring training camp, but turning ourselves inside-out for two weeks didn't sound motivating either. I kept my eyes peeled for last-minute package deals to some warmer cycling destinations. A bargain popped up for a trip to the Balearic Island of Mallorca, a popular cyclist destination in Spain, so off we headed to soak up some soft winter sun and test our legs on the very European-like switchbacks to be found there. The trip paid off by helping us double our mileage for the month, but we had still only managed 21 hours and 249 miles.

Whatever fitness we gained by our trip to Spain was short-lived once we returned home. It was now late February and the weather was unrelentingly miserable. The roads were either covered in dirty slush or re-frozen black ice. Any half-nice day was battered by roaring winds. The closer we got to spring, the worse the wind became and the temperatures rarely broke 50 degrees. March and April were going to be the wettest anyone could remember.

In February I was committed to spend two weeks in Oregon attending a professional mechanic's certificate program at United Bicycle Institute. Several major sponsors, along with UBI, had generously awarded 16 scholarships to women in the bicycle industry. I was thrilled to be chosen to fill one of the spots, and it was an honor to learn alongside those 15 other future mechanics. They are an inspiration and continue to do great things to encourage women to ride and enjoy the sport we all love. The skills and knowledge I gleaned at bike school did more in a two week span to increase my confidence with bikes than did two years of working in a shop…even my own. Now, the knowledge I had of bicycles was intimate and never again would I have to rely on anyone else to help me out of a mechanical jam. I'm proud to say that as the first all-female class the school ever offered, we did our instructors justice by being the first class to graduate with 100% passing grades. Self-sufficiency is an empowering tool indeed.

Though I was able to travel with a bike, we were in class for 8 hours a day, so riding time was limited. Besides, Oregon isn't known for being especially dry in the spring. After school, travel time and the temperamental weather, I had only managed 12 hours and 163 miles for the month of March. That meant we had some catching up to do. Lots and lots of catching up. Armed with fenders and rain gear, we rode as much as work would allow. The warming temperatures meant more foot traffic at the shop. The service department was filling up and new bike sales were increasing. Someone joked once that owning your own bike shop meant never riding again. While that wasn't the absolute rule, it did hold a grain of truth. You can't just turn the phone off and lock the front door, as much as you'd like to some days.

Our April efforts yielded 33 hours and 474 miles of ride time. An improvement for sure, but still a long way off from the 200 miles a week we had proposed on our training plan. Making matters worse, we were getting more and more anxious each day we missed a ride, especially with the constant inquiry from customers and friends about our fitness level. "How's your training going?" they'd ask. Swimmingly, I thought sarcastically. Then I'd smile, tell them it was going fine and try not to secretly dwell that we were less than three months away and we'd yet to even break 100 miles in a single ride.

May would be the turning point and not in the way we hoped. Just as our rides were getting consistent and we were starting to feel some semblance of fitness, Scott would make a stubborn mistake that would define his entire summer, his entire Tour experience and my experience too. Stubborn because it was as simple as stopping on the ride to raise his saddle. His seat post had slipped down about four centimeters during a 75 mile gravel ride. He still beats himself up over not stopping to adjust it. He just kept saying he'd fix it when we got back to the shop. It was wet and cold out and he didn't feel like pulling off the road and getting out his tool and making the adjustment. Riding the rest of the way home with his saddle position lower than normal put extra strain on the tendons of his right knee.

Those unfamiliar with the delicate nature of bicycle fitment, four centimeters sounds miniscule, but adapting a cyclist's form properly to his or her machine is critical to performance. Adjustments on the scale of millimeters can completely change the balance of the entire biomechanical system. It's a little like modifying computer code…changing a single one or zero changes the entire program. Proper fit doesn't just make you faster or stronger or more comfortable on the bike, it is also necessary for remaining injury free.

It wasn't apparent right away that there was a problem. He did experience some unusual soreness that he figured would pass in a few days. But it didn't improve and the following weekend we participated in one of our area's toughest gravel endurance events, held deep in the steep hills of the Piedmont. The course was a demanding 60 miles, including a nearly 10-mile loosely graveled climb with grades at some sections hitting 20 percent.

In typical Scott style, he got caught up in the competitive atmosphere and pushed hard on the pedals…the exact opposite of what his poor knee needed. It turned from a nagging soreness to a legitimate ache, sometimes sharp enough to cause a wince and troubling enough to start missing weekly spins. Now he was truly between a rock and a hard place; needing saddle time versus needing recovery time. In hindsight, he should have chosen to stay completely off his bike.

I imagine it was incredibly difficult to align his fitness expectations with mine. I also admit that I was likely putting unspoken, if not undue, pressure on him to take rides with me. For the majority of my cycling career, we'd ridden bikes together. I'd raced two seasons of cyclo-cross while he ran the shop, completed countless solo training sessions, ridden charity events a few times with friends, had plenty of miles in small

21

groups and had certainly led my fair share of shop rides without him…but had not done any training miles for the tour solo. I was capable of doing it for sure, but not necessarily comfortable, as the distances were ever increasing and the whole point was ride the tour together. Make no mistake; I was never the kind of rider who always sat in the shadow of their partner, resigned to only ever ride at the back. The sport had very quickly evolved from "his" thing, to "our" thing and I enjoyed Scott's company immensely on the bike. As the one who introduced me to a two-wheeled existence, he encouraged me to find my legs and was now a supportive and enthusiastic riding partner.

I was bummed for his lingering injury as much for him as for myself, knowing that if he didn't ride, I wasn't likely going to have the motivation to ride alone. He knew this truth and would suffer through the next several weeks of training, slow and steady, however painful, to keep me in good company. By the end of May, with Scott's loyal companionship, I had logged 47 hours and 720 miles in the saddle.

It was finally June. Time can tick by ever so slowly when there's nothing but life to be lived. Mark down something epic on the calendar and watch time truly fly. On June 19th, we would head to France, so that didn't leave much time left to squeeze in the miles. By this point, we were out of days in which to accomplish any real training and if we had followed our well-intended plans, should have been using the time to "taper" or recover our legs from a heavy schedule of long distance efforts on the bike. Laughably, there was really nothing to recover from. Scott had an excuse, I had none. While not intended, we had pretty much loafed our way through the winter and spring months and summer was upon us.

We were now more concerned with packing the right clothes and the right spares and making last minute preparations to leave the shop in the hands of our new manager. In the midst of a clothes cleaning frenzy at home, I had thrown a white graphic tee in the wash with new red cycling socks. The clean garment was now a lovely shade of pink. *C'est la vie,* the shirt read. Such is life, indeed.

Warm Up:

A Cat Named Crevette

It is absolutely pissing rain. There's no less vulgar way to describe the weather. We were shoe-horned into our rental car, Scott and I, along with two bikes, two large gear bags and two back packs. My knees were against the dashboard and poor Scott could barely work the clutch, his seat pulled so close to the steering wheel to try to accommodate both bike bags in the back seat of the painfully efficient five-door. We were bone tired and whatever pep we felt with our feet finally treading on French soil, was drained during the hour long extraction from the late morning madness of the Périphérique.

Paris traffic is a special kind of hell when you are forced to battle it post-trans-Atlantic flight, running on zero sleep and airplane cuisine. Don't dream of blaming Parisians for the trouble either. Your jet-lagged Sunday driving is the cause for clogging up their perfectly choreographed, lane-splitting, hand-rolled cigarette smoking, gesticulating, croissant and caffeine fueled quest for work-day punctuality. Free of the ring-road circus, we head towards the Norman countryside, eager to begin a week of acclimation. Our plan was to catch up on sleep, equilibrate to the time zone, plus get in some easy rides so we'd feel prepared to take on the following three weeks of business. I didn't want to take any risks with our general well-being and couldn't realistically rule out catching a bug on the plane or having to deal with an out-of-sorts digestive system. Spending a week in Normandy; the motherland of culinary delights including cheese, cream and cider, could be potentially problematic to the hard-working gut of a cyclist. Let's not forget the apple tarts and Calvados and butter and caramel cookies and salt lamb and then more cheese. Though not just any cheese. Camembert, Pont-l'Évêque and Livarot, all members of the royal family tree of fromage.

Two years prior, way before ever dreaming of riding around the entire country, I had a shirt made to read "I ride for French Cheese". That one got a lot of giggles at the shop, only I never intended it as a joke. However, I did not expect those words to ring true as they were about to do. Never doubt the power of cheese as fuel for the legs as well as the soul. My heart goes out to the dairy-intolerant.

↔

I swear I didn't mean to close my eyes that long and felt a jolting panic like a student caught sleeping in class. I was supposed to be keeping Scott entertained and therefore alert behind the wheel. Gasping for breath, I surged awake. It was still dumping out. The windshield a sheet of wet. The landscape was a grey fuzzy blanket and the visibility on the road could be measured in meters, not miles. Turning to him to apologize but finding his lids sealed shut, there was a brief moment of amused irony before my synapses interpreted the situation for what it was. Our fatigue was about to be the death of us both. Exactly how long had we been barreling down the A13 with our eyes closed? I blurted his name, sans expletives. Then suggested guiltily that we pull over at a rest stop. We still had a few hours to go and the weather showed no signs of easing. Between the din of tires on a wet road and the methodical swipe of wipers on the glass, plus the thermostat dialed just a touch too warm sleep came easily.

The French have incredible gas stations. I have a particular fondness for the pre-made (with mustard) saucisson and cornichon sandwich one can find there. I also love their paprika Pringles and I don't even eat Pringles in the States. I don't eat gas station sandwiches either, but if they were made with local mustard and AOC labeled cold cuts, I might make a habit of it. So we pulled off the motorway towards the next available station and had our fill of its interior delights.

I have since visited that very same station and still find it satisfying that we can simultaneously fill up the tank with petrol, use the impeccably clean wash rooms complete with fresh bouquets, buy an expertly made sandwich and pastry to-go and pick up a few local specialties like tiny spicy pork sausages and a bottle of apple brandy. Not to mention utilize the towering row of automated coffee vending machines. Why yes, I would love a grand crème, *sil-vous* plaît. A one euro coin in, a scalding hot double espresso with milk out. *Voilà*! Or if you prefer a human's touch, you may alternately ask the smiling Madame behind the coffee counter for a café noisette and she will deliver it *tout-de-suite*.

As it has a tendency to do, the caffeine made us feel better so we squeezed back into the car for the last push to Normandy. We still had to find our way to the small village of Genêts and get the key to our room by the time requested by the property owner. I can't remember covering those miles but we made it, exchanged pleasantries and a deposit for the key, and flopped onto the bed fully clothed, unmoved until the day broke on the morn.

↔

Day two was all about the bike. Unpack the bike, assemble the bike, torque the bike's bits and take the bike out for a shakedown. But first, breakfast. Breakfast in France, until I learned to reset my expectations, was a source of morning irritation. Forget any notion of "American" fare, unless you are staying in a tourist-heavy hotel. Some form of cereal can be found most anywhere. Omelets only are to be found on the lunch menu and bacon is merely an ingredient for a well-balanced salad. There are exceptions to these statements but in general (and I no longer complain) breakfast consists of a freshly baked piece of baguette and an equally fresh croissant both obtained from the local boulangerie.

At home you are expected to have in the fridge (and serve alongside) such things as un-salted butter, jam or honey and in some cases a piece of cheese, ham slice or a hard-boiled egg. You may opt for a pastry from the patisserie (sometimes a part of the boulangerie, sometimes not) but eclairs, tarts and the like are typically eaten as dessert. None of this is the part that bothers me. It is the fact that there is no coffee served at either establishment. Meaning, you either find a patisserie with a café next door (whose proprietor graciously allows you to consume your pastry bought elsewhere, with a few laughably small coffees bought from him while he wonders why you didn't just order the *petit déjeuner*...because his is clearly the best in town...meanwhile wondering how the hell you can stomach three cappuccinos) or you find a decent *crêperie* who does manage to have something resembling breakfast and something resembling a coffee under the same roof. Though we were soon to discover the third option and still one of my favorites, the *bar-tabac*.

As the name unimaginatively implies, the bar-tabac is where one goes to get an adult beverage, a newspaper, a pack of cigarettes and a double espresso. If you find a bar-tabac-*café*, then you may also expect a quick, well-made meal. You can almost always pick up a baguette there and find a dozen or so horse racing dailies. Harness and flat racing remain a healthy industry in the region and betting is still considered a sporting gentleman's pastime. So is drinking *pastis* at 9 in the morning, a habit especially common in the country.

Historically, this is a place where local "blue-collar" men gather at the standing bar to catch up on gossip and collect the day's necessary sundries. Women are not uninvited, just not the primary patron. Occasionally, a bar-tabac also offers a few sparsely furnished, inexpensive rooms for rent and is technically a bar-tabac-chambre *meublée*, like the Hôtel des Falaises just outside the village of Jullouville. A favorite watering hole of the dozen or so taxi drivers we routinely saw parked out front. The '60's era interior space was tidily kept and well run attended most mornings by a gruff, white-haired Frenchman.

For several days we would enjoy people watching over two *grand crèmes* and returning the under-the-table affections of a petite grey tabby. My endearment towards his pet on the first morning meant he quickly dropped the grumpy barkeep routine despite us clearly being foreigners. Having an excellent grasp of the French language, Scott asked the Monsieur "*Quelle est le nom du chat?*'. "*Quoi?*' the Monsieur grunted. The cat? Scott inquired again. What do you call her? The Monsieur looked at the ceiling for a moment then replied "*Crevette!*" with a dismissive wave of his hand before escaping to attend the register. A pretty little name for a pretty little cat, I said. You realize he just named his cat "shrimp"? Scott queried. Yep, I said beaming. It's perfect.

I decided then that I liked this Frenchman, his establishment and his feline very much.

Back at our lodging, we dressed in our kit and headed out the pea gravel drive for our first warm-up ride. Neither Scott nor I had properly ridden a bicycle in France prior to this moment, so those first few pedal strokes felt pretty special. It wasn't the longest or the most scenic, with no long climbs to speak of and no mind-blowing landmarks, but it was the first time the enormity of the upcoming event hit home. We were really going to do it. Heart and limbs aflutter, I looked over at Scott and said flippantly, hey…we're riding our bikes around France! Then we grinned goofily at each other and giggled like little kids. It was the first time in my adult life I had felt that rush of child-like enthusiasm…like waking up Christmas morning to find out what was under the tree or the first time I rode a horse all on my own…well before finding out Santa was make-believe.

↔

That evening we ate at one of the two restaurants in our tiny Norman village. Chez Francois is better expressed as a dining "experience". Part bar-tabac, part hotel and part restaurant, it is described in French as a grill au feu de bois, literally meaning to "grill on a wood fire". Neatly tucked into the main floor of his corner village house, Monsieur Francois matter-of-factly rattles off the menu du jour written upon a large chalk board which he briefly displays upon your table while you make your choice.

Don't waste his valuable time asking him to translate and whatever you do, refrain from asking for deletions or substitutions. Renowned for his pork, it's best to pick something porcine from the menu. Beef is never a bad choice either. Or just point to something that looks good. If you eat meat, prepared expertly and simply over a roaring flame in the belly of a medieval fireplace, you'll be pleased. Fair portions, locally sourced, served no-nonsense, with perfect fries and salad. The experience is intimate, the dining room warm and cozy and elemental, with the fire cracking away and the smell of searing fat in the air. We ordered the specialty of the house; crispy pig's ear potato salad, pork trotters stuffed with boudin noir and salt lamb raised on the marshes of Mont Saint Michel. France can be a frustrating place to dine for those who refrain from eating animals but for the curious omnivores of the world, this country's whole animal approach is both appealing and appreciated. It makes no sense to eat only a few choice cuts of an entire beast just because those are what make us less squeamish, when the rest of the carcass goes to waste. Here, meat might prevail but the portions are smaller and nose-to-tail offerings mean more mouths are satisfied by less livestock.

↔

The next morning, after a deep and dreamless sleep brought on no doubt by generous amounts of red wine and protein, we made the pilgrimage to Crevette's place for a coffee before loading the bikes in the car and heading to Brittany for another warm-up ride. While the forecast in Normandy called for grey skies and showers, the Breton skies looked mostly sunny with not more than a chance of a brief sprinkle. A place which still holds mystery and that has produced a fair share of cycling greats; we'd never before visited the region. With over 900 miles of delineated cycling routes, rolling terrain and a mild climate, Brittany is often overlooked by cyclists save for the flocks of families seeking tranquil summer spins along the shoreline or the thousands that dedicate themselves to completing the Paris-Brest-Paris randonnée every four years. If so inclined, you'll have the chance to enter in 2019. (Until then, I recommend you start pedaling.)

That fifty mile ride remains one of my favorite days on the bike ever. Sometimes a simple route, good food and company, fair weather and a fine mood leave you totally satisfied. We had glimpses of the green-blue sea along the Côte d'Emeraude. The current name means "emerald coast" and may be more descriptive but far less amusing than the previous one of Clos-Poulet, literally meaning chicken enclosure. *Je ne sais pas.*

Brittany may not be known for poultry, but the oysters here were worth the trip alone. Harvested a mere ten paces from the roadside stand where they are served; we stopped mid-ride to eat a few dozen. They tasted strongly of the sea from where they spent their lives and went down so well with a cold bottle of cider and the dark rye bread typical of the region. Then we continued on our way and wound through the seaside avenues of St Malo before turning south for the steep climb out of town. Not typically having a sweet-tooth, I was finding it increasingly difficult to pass by the luminous store fronts filled with myriad pastries. The pastel displays of all shapes and sizes of sugary concoctions radiated desire through the thick glass windows. I was especially interested in trying the famous Paris-Brest, created in 1910 to commemorate the colossal ride of the same name. Favored by participants of the event because of the sheer number of calories the dessert delivered.

Roughly bicycle wheel shaped and bursting at the seams with hazelnut cream, the whole pastry is then dusted heavily with confectioner's sugar. It's a hefty treat and the one Scott bought me at a small, pink patisserie on the outskirts of town disappeared in a flash. I barely paused to give Scott a single consolation bite before gulping the rest right down my gullet. It was a memorable experience, sitting under the branches of a plane tree on a curb, our bikes leaned against the wall of a 14th century stone church, enjoying a hundred year old confection honoring an amateur bicycle event one day away from launching off on a cycling adventure of our own.

If this moment even remotely foreshadowed the next three weeks to come, then we were convinced the trip would be a success. I'm thankful of the time we took before the tour to get our heads in the right place. We totally looked forward to getting started, to putting one foot in front of the other, to stop fretting over our fitness or fortitude.

Tomorrow we would head to Mont Saint-Michel, to meet our
fellow participants and be briefed by the staff for what was to
come. Our experience as cyclists would forever change in two
days' time. Maybe that's why this petite gallop through
Brittany still feels so special. It was the last ride before my life
would change so profoundly.

Miraculously we slept well and woke with only one thing on
our mind. Coffee. Being serial coffee drinkers at the shop where
there is a daily unlimited supply of American-sized servings,
several mornings of tiny cups had finally caught up to us.
I was starving for a 16oz mug of drip to wrap my hands around
and savor. Two grand crèmes at Crevette's place would have to
do. Plus I wanted the chance to say *au revoir* to Monsieur
Falaises and his tiny friend. Sadly, the cat was nowhere to be
found and the proprietor was distracted by a heated discussion
at the bar over who-knows-what. We drank our espressos and
waved our goodbyes, the importance of our relationship clearly
one sided. (We visited again several months later and Crevette
seems to have vanished though we did get a half-smile from the
Monsieur that indicated some hint at recognizing us as the
coffee guzzling Americans.)

We returned to our lodgings to load up the rental car with bags
and gear to transfer to the host hotel for the evening. Since our
tour officially started at the foot of Mont Saint-Michel, we
would be staying there and rolling out early the next morning
for Stage 1.

After leaving our things in the lobby, we returned the rental car in Avranches and rode our bikes back to Le Mont to check in. Other cyclists were starting to assemble on the lawn of the hotel, a pile of gear beginning to swell in front of the two large support vans. We expected to see the other 36 riders who would join us for all 21 stages, but didn't consider the nearly fifty additional participants who would ride along for the first few days then depart. This would be a common theme throughout the ride; one could choose to ride the entire tour, either the first "half" or second "half", stretches of stages in the Pyrenees or Alps, or as little as two consecutive stages like the Grand Depart or Grand Finale. So while there were 38 of us who chose to ride as "Lifers", that is, 21 stages total…there would be dozens of others who would come and go over three weeks' time. We would form bonds with many of the Lifers during the trip, but for now, shyness prevailed and everyone's attention was hyper-focused on getting bikes, bags and room assignments settled.

The tour mechanics were already busy with last-minute adjustments and fitting the few loaner bikes to their pilots. Scott and I had never faltered in our desire to ride our personal bikes, considering our familiarity with them and the fact that they were both custom made for us. My machine of choice was a black and white steel Waterford, designed by Richard Schwinn of Waterford, Wisconsin from True Temper S3 tubing and a carbon fork by Enve. Scott's; a handmade Bishop Bikes frame with paper thin lugs by Chris Bishop of Baltimore, Maryland using a mixture of True Temper and Columbus tubes. Scott opted for a sleek yet compliant steel fork to match his bright pink frame, also handmade by Chris Bishop. Both bikes were modern, light and perfectly designed for the task at hand. They also happened to be the only steel frames on the trip, not surprising in this carbon age, though a few riders bought along nicely outfitted titanium models. In fact, there wasn't a beater to be found in the bunch. The value of bikes stored nightly in the tour vans must have been astounding. It was a rolling parade of the best components the industry had to offer.

We left our steeds with the very capable staff (this was after all, their 10th year of toting riders around France) and settled the rest of our luggage into our hotel room and made a mad dash to Le Mont to take a tour of the impressive Benedictine abbey before closing time. Mont Saint-Michel was a significant site of religious pilgrimage for centuries. Sitting solitary and majestic in the soft light of the bay surrounded at times entirely by the gently lapping tide, it casts an unmistakable silhouette on the horizon that can be seen for miles along the lower Normandy shoreline.

Its symbolism holds a special place in my heart; though my religion is cycling. Called a "technical and artistic tour de force" by UNESCO, I was soon to embark on my own tour de force, legitimately technical and reasonably artistic. The archangel Michael sits gilded atop the Abbey's crowning spire, as he slays the dragon of evil; the dragon I wanted to slay was self-doubt.

Devotees traveled thousands of miles on foot to reach it; I would ride thousands of miles from it to reach another iconic French landmark, the Arc de Triomphe. While varying entirely in scope and nature, assumedly their journey was spent reflecting on their purpose, their passion, their motivation and most importantly, their dedication. I wonder how differently they viewed the world from the first footfall to the last. Despite the lifetimes between us, I believe we'd still have a few things in common.

As the sun set over the Bay, the time had come to join the others at the briefing. I have a hazy memory of the specifics of the meeting, but the gist of it was that the next three weeks would be hard. Very hard. The first half of the meeting was reserved for the Lifers alone, so we could hear bluntly about the challenge laid out before us. We were introduced to Phil Deeker, our fearless ride leader. I don't use the moniker "fearless" lightly. If he fears anything at all in this world, he certainly never showed it. This man is one of the most inspiring human beings ever to pedal a bicycle and knowing he'd be at the helm was a huge confidence boost.

Never having met Phil before the Tour de Force, his reputation preceded him through social media, magazine articles and his leadership of the epic Rapha Cent Cols Challenges. Adopting cycling later in life, his mastering of the sport was an inspiration. To me anyway, he was an icon. A real life Saint Michael, slayer of mountains, not dragons. Phil would continue into the evening by giving advice on all the topics we hadn't considered in the months leading up to this; nutrition, hydration, group riding, pace lines. All this time, I had pictured Scott and I riding alone, the two of us, on a nice spin around the French countryside. Sure, there'd be mountains here and there but never in my mind's eye had I imagined us embedded in pace lines and echelons and the like. Nor had I bothered considering the trials my poor body might go through…not like Phil was describing. This damn meeting was actually starting to make me feel worse. I was getting increasingly nervous about tomorrow, not less, especially when I glanced at the other faces in the room and all were bearing the same mask of despair. But the longer I stared, the more I began to see that those faces were not that different than our own. Of course they *looked* different with ages ranging from early 20's to late 60's, some tall, some short, some more fit than others, but all seemingly normal folks. No professionals, no career racers, no super human athletes. Just average people who must have the same above average affinity for riding their bike as we did ours.

Dinner was an awkward affair. It was a heavy serving of omelet in the style of *La Mère Poulard*, followed by duck confit, then Camembert cheese, then tarte Normand. A fine meal for a tourist spending their days burning off all those calories taking in the sights, but it did nothing to help procure a restful sleep. At least our table could share a laugh over the weight of the meal. That seemed to break the ice and introductions soon followed. The proffered hand I remember most clearly was that of a shy individual named Indy, a Londoner and brand new cyclist, as in, only been riding for several months brand new. He was soft spoken and gentle but his courage was immense to take on such a challenge. He would be riding the three week tour alone, with all of us of course, but without anyone from his personal life to accompany him.

That was a common theme among the group. Nearly the whole lot of them came alone, including the only other woman to ride all the stages. A handful knew each other from previous tours and some had ridden three and four years in a row. Scott and I were the only "couple" the Tour de Force had ever hosted and were two of three Americans to participate as Lifers. The third quickly found the event too taxing and would follow along in a car for the rest of the trip. I think he rather enjoyed himself anyway and it was encouraging to see him make lemonade out of lemons, so to speak.

Laden with duck fat, milk fat, butter and sugar, we dragged ourselves to our room to lay out the next morning's kit and pack our day bags. It was the beginning of a routine we would learn well: eat, organize, decompress, and sleep. Tomorrow, we would ride.

STAGE 1:

One Kilometer in a Lifetime

June 25, 2016. ~ Mont-Saint-Michel to Utah Beach. "What is one kilometer in a lifetime?" Sign posted in Normandy, denoting the completion of the first kilometer of the 3,529 kilometer 2016 Tour de France route. Author unknown.

"123 *miles and 4,131 feet climbed. No sleep last night. Anxious. Wild dreams. Good appetite this morning. Uncomfortable in the chamois all day, likely because of the slow pace of the group to feed stop 1. Fun section through the woods. Nice stretch of road to Joulloville from Genets, right past Crevette's place. Almost felt like my "hometown" after a week there. Beautiful herd of Normandy cows. Lots of local pride in them. Many shouts of encouragement and waves as we ride through villages, plus one "Allez!" through a loudspeaker atop a sedan. A dozen or more typical Norman churches with their tall square tower and low chapel. The gilded "Coq" atop each one.*

"*Cloudy skies and much cooler temps on the coast than I expected. Turned inland and found plenty of sun filtered by clouds. Watched Saint Michael's Mont fade away into the morning haze. Temps never broke 73 degrees. A stiff, cool wind blew us sideways in the afternoon. Perfect roads with fresh pavement, a benefit of the Tour coming through in a week. Tidy villages everywhere. Steady traffic but polite drivers.*"

"Most roads have a shoulder about two feet wide. Plenty of space and never felt danger from passing cars. Short, steep descent towards Utah Beach. Got into the drops and had a go at the pedals. Was surprised at the power still left in my legs. Felt pretty good all day. Plenty of local cheese for lunch (camembert and boucheron) and forced adequate amounts of water down. Knees are a bit sore (maybe a pedal stroke problem) and sit bones were throbbing by the end of the day. Enjoyed standing up on the pedals to give them a stretch. The Beach was packed with tourists and riders from a local cycling club who rode the entire 1ˢᵗ stage of the Tour. Families, teens, moms with kids, retirees, etc. in droves, on the lowliest of cycles, most with desperately squeaky chains. Five wide, holding up a line of cars for miles. Not a single one honked. Vehicles passed one at a time. We passed them too when we could, waiting for a safe gap."

"Seeing all those generations of locals, out for a nice ride to Utah Beach, makes me wonder about the now-peaceful beauty of the place and the horrors it witnessed in 1944. Are the deepest layers of sand still stained with the blood of all those soldiers? They are the ones responsible for this peace."

"Quiet, easy pedal to the hotel. Lane barely wide enough for a modern car. The hedgerows held off the headwind but made the air stuffy. Appreciated the pockets of coolness as the road dipped every mile or so. Stopped at a small, roadside Ranger memorial to pay our respects. Dad would be proud. Caught a glimpse of the Sainte-Mère-Église church. Regret not stopping."

"It is soothing hearing the village churches chime away the hours. Makes me glad there are so many hours in the day. 125 miles was easier than I expected. Tired for sure but not beat.

Found so much joy during this relatively "boring" stage (so says a fellow member of our group). Nothing boring about today. Can't wait for tomorrow."

↔

On any other occasion, riding over 120 miles would have been a big deal. This was the longest I had ever cycled in one stretch and at the end of the day both Scott and I felt pretty good. We wanted to celebrate but were cautious, not wanting to jinx ourselves so early on. One "century" down, another 8 to go before our first rest day, with several of those days edging closer to a century and a half. Thinking about the stages in a collective manner was overwhelming, so we needed to force ourselves to only consider one ride before we started to worry about the next.

We rolled in to the hotel parking lot where one of the support vans was already loading the bikes of the riders who had arrived before us. Before handing our bikes over to the staff, we washed them at the provided stands and lubricated the chains. Then we collapsed onto the grassy front lawn and helped ourselves to a post-ride snack. Dinner wasn't until 7 pm and it was important to give our legs the fuel they needed to start the repair process and be fresh for tomorrow's efforts. Eating promptly after the completion of a stage would be one of our most important responsibilities along with proper hydration.

There were other cyclists enjoying the end of their long day in the saddle with a nap in the sun, some were having a quick massage and others were joining us in maintaining their bikes. It was only late afternoon, so there were many more riders still out on the stage. The pack had gotten rather strung out over such a long distance, as we were essentially allowed to go at our own pace throughout the day.

There were only two hard and fast requirements each stage. No rider was allowed to depart the first feed stop of the day until the last rider arrived, signed in and had a chance to refresh themselves. Also, each rider must pause at every feed stop in order to check their name off the daily roster of starters so the staff could account for every rider. After that, our pace was our own. We were encouraged to ride in groups, to share the work load, but were not required to do so. We could spend as much time as necessary at the remaining feed stops, though it was generally understood not to linger, so that we could get the day over with during daylight hours. We were also at liberty to stop along the route, if we felt so inclined, for a coffee, ice cream or a restroom break and there would be days to come when we indulged in all three.

Following the day's route was simple; we just had to adhere to the arrows. Despite riding in an age where tiny plastic boxes flash and beep and dictate our every turn, the most efficient way to keep us on the right track was to display neon green signs with big black arrows, laminated against the weather and affixed to posts or trees along the assigned route. The hardworking sign master started his day bright and early to demark our path, placing an arrow (or several if there were important turns ahead) at regular intervals during the long stretches of road and again whenever there was a turn, split, detour or tricky section to navigate.

Thanks to the generosity (or good manners) of the French, these arrows always stayed put and were removed promptly by the crew after the last rider no longer required their guidance for the day. We would get rather dependent on these green markers, so much so that they were also used at the hotels to guide us to our bags, our room and to dinner. If you paid attention, you might catch the tongue-in-cheek placement of an occasional arrow pointing in a ridiculous manner.

The only hiccup was that the arrows sometimes appeared on the left hand side of the road instead of the right and we could only assume it was because UK motorists drive opposite of the French (and the greater part of the world) and it seemed perfectly natural for the crew. There was some grumbling initially about not having GPS files to upload every day, but imagine the nightmare that would ensue if there were construction zones or detours, blockages or road closures. For example, there was one stage in the Alps where it was unclear if the road was even traversable due to a landslide. The crew needed the flexibility to manipulate the arrows on the fly. This low-tech approach provided a convenient solution.

I appreciated the heads-up, un-plugged riding the arrows offered. While Scott rides with a Garmin and is generally responsible for not getting us lost on the road, I never bother with one. I disregard metrics of any kind and would rather rely on a soggy, crumpled cue sheet than a navigation aid squawking away for hours. I made one technology allowance for the tour (two if you counted my iPhone without which there would be no photographs of the trip) and that was a mid-range model Garmin, tucked away in my jersey pocket, faithfully recording the mileage and feet climbed.

The basics of how far and how high interested me much more than the how fast or how strong or even the how-to-get-there. Plenty of riders brought power meters and cadence sensors and the like and I'm sure the data they collected was fascinating. I was only concerned with staying upright and getting to the finish without succumbing to the following: breaking, bruising, spraining, pulling, rubbing, blistering, dehydrating, bonking, etc. So with the start button mashed, we turned the cranks and set off to face the day.

I was so full of nervous energy. This was not a race and there were no winners or losers but I had the same race-day jitters as if I had shot off the start line with a number pinned to my back. I wasn't alone. Everyone was ready to stretch their legs and fill their lungs with the morning air though we'd stay reluctantly throttled for the first 25 miles. I relaxed a bit after passing the first Tour de France related sign, with hundreds more to come.

Posted at precisely the one kilometer mark, it read: "What is one kilometer in a lifetime?". It was a sage message from an unknown messenger that really hit home. That sign reminded me that each kilometer was a gift, whether good or bad, pleasant or uncomfortable, wet or dry, cold or hot. That the goal of our journey, Scott's and my own, was to take in the view and enjoy the ride no matter what came our way. That sign reminded us that this was our story to make. So, I took a deep breath and slowed down and all the anxiety disappeared.

Riding slow is actually easier said than done. Especially when the road is flat and straight and there are miles upon miles of it. By mid-morning my sit bones were singing and my crotch was devoid of feeling. Most of the discomfort abated once I stepped off my bike and walked around a bit enjoying the bounty of feed stop 1 (bananas, jam and bread, brioche, juice and water). Though the complaint would plague me the rest of the day and increase in intensity over the next few stages.

I hadn't experienced any saddle issues over the last year of riding, so I was surprised that it was happening now. I can only speculate that it was from the slow, straight roll for the first few dozen miles, probably ridden more tense than usual. We were warned that each consecutive day would feel worse before our bodies finally adjusted to the task and then we'd gradually start feeling more fit with small aches and pains going away by day three or four, so I tried not to dwell on my current level of discomfort knowing relief was on the horizon.

The issues weren't unbearable, just annoying, and there was plenty to look at along the route to keep my mind distracted. Like the giant grinning hay sculptures or the bicycle-laden art in village round-abouts. This was the Grand Depart, so every town and village along the route, all 66 of them, had dressed for the occasion. Blue, white and red streamers, banners and flags lined the shops and streets. Store windows were decorated with cartoon images of famous riders complete with messages of encouragement for the professional peloton. We were riding each stage exactly one week ahead of the official race, so much of the finery was already set in place for its arrival.

We also benefitted greatly from the condition of the roads for the majority of our tour. Most were freshly paved with flawless tarmac, though in some regions we would find that last minute road improvements were still underway or hadn't yet been carried out. Those were the tricky stretches but for now the way ahead was smooth sailing. Normandy was a bright and cheerful place, despite the occasional clouds, with generous smiles and ample *bonjours.*

Feed stop 3 was officially lunch and was a delightful and filling array of pasta and whole grain salads, fresh greens, cold cuts and lots of local cheese. We also had our choice of juices and fruits and of course, dessert. Near the end of the day and for a stretch of several miles, we would pass riders of all ages completing their own Stage 1. Members of a local cycling club (not a racing club but bicycle enthusiasts) including families and children and plenty of seniors had organized an impressive full-stage event, complete with volunteer crossing guards at busy intersections and a celebratory carnival at the finish. What was heartening was the behavior of motorists, as the some-hundreds-strong group pedaled five wide and slow as they pleased along the busy motorways. Had anyone been bold enough to hold such an event in the mid-Atlantic region of the United States, providing they'd even have permission to be on the roads in such numbers, they might be subject to a cacophony of honks and an outpouring of profanity not fit for the ears of children. Likely, there'd also be a number of cyclists reporting close passes and brake checks. This isn't the case everywhere but happens enough in our neck of the woods to bear mentioning. Here in Normandy, not a single horn was honked in anger. The long line of cars waited patiently for their chance to pass with many drivers waving out their windows as they drove around cautiously. There was both a strong sense of community and an apparent regard for the riders' safety.

Stage 1 was unique in that it terminated for the first time in history at Utah Beach, bypassing the small but historically significant village of Saint-Mere-Eglise on its journey. For those lacking any familiarity of this place or of the events that occurred in the Manche, I implore you to take the time to learn about the drama that unfolded here. We are many generations removed from the horrors of World War II but that does not relieve us of our responsibility to know what happened here. We owe it to the men and women, soldiers and civilians alike, victors and enemies, to remember their bravery and sacrifice. The D-Day beaches, as they are collectively known, witnessed one of the most consequential and destructive acts of war the world has ever seen and was a major turning point towards the liberation of France and the victory of the Allies. Scott and I had visited this region once prior to this year's tour to visit the beaches (and again since with my father, a retired Army officer and 101st Airborne Ranger), the museums and the American cemetery. It is a moving, humbling experience and puts the very notion of war, sacrifice and liberty into perspective. So we paused for a few moments at Utah Beach, unmounted our bikes and walked up the steps past the memorial to gaze out at the wind whipped waters of the historic bay.

STAGE 2:

Thou Shall Not Be Dropped

June 26, 2016 ~ Saint-Lô to Cherbourg. "Rolling coastal roads today, with a little sting in the tail" Route information as provided by ride leader, Phil Deeker.

"117.3 miles and 6,886 feet climbed. Good sleep but early morning. Inexpensive yet comfortable hotel in Sainte-Mère-Église. Pride of ownership shows. Had the best croissant of my life to date. In a hotel! Light, flaky, oven-darkened exterior just enough butter to taste rich but not greasy. If they tasted like this in the States, I'd be in trouble. They don't. It must be something in the water or the air, no doubt in the quality of the ingredients. But enough about croissants…"

"The plan was to go steady today, i.e. "slow". That never happened. Not even when I barked repeatedly at Scott to slow down. He wasn't having any of it. It was more about the notion that we "should" be going slow and not that we needed to. Just worried about burning through the match book so early on. Section 1 was a pleasure. We sat in with the first group to roll out. A nice bunch of gents, all with an easy demeanor and carrying a steady pace. Was able to lead for a good stretch which felt satisfying. We rolled into the first feed stop together, though I dropped off the back trying to get photos of the medieval abbey

*at the bottom of the hill. Winding down the narrow road with
the ruin over my right shoulder bathed in sunlight... so peaceful,
complete with a photogenic herd of Normandy cows grazing the
morning away. What a postcard moment."*

*"Second section we burned a fair bit of fuel pushing with
Phil. Lots of wind again. Yesterday the breeze was a novelty but
today we're starting to take notice. Overcast skies put me in a
mood. Not bad. Not good. Made me determined not to get
dropped from Phil's wheel today. He would start putting down
power and open a small gap, then check over his shoulder. I'd
close it and smile back at him. I'm still here. Certainly he could
leave me in his wake but I think he's feeling generous letting me
hang on and I'll gratefully accept the kind gesture. Legs felt so
strong in those big ring pushes. Coming into this, I didn't think I
could ride that way. Didn't used to be able to. Think I was too
afraid to try."*

*"Third section Scott and I sat in with another group of
men from the UK, all Lifers. Chatted away with Jaime also
from the UK, but lives in Barcelona. What a wonderfully
positive human being. Friendly, skilled, steady wheel and really
fun to pedal with. Rode all the way to the last stop with them
and the time just flew."*

*"The pleasure of group riding was short lived. Pick the
wrong group and everything goes haywire. Too many nervous
pilots and unreliable wheels. Some poor riding etiquette and
unsolicited cycling advice. Deep breaths keep me from telling
them off. Rode alone with Scott for a bit. Rode a screaming
downhill section of pavement, dropping us into Cherbourg. Top
gear, tiny cog flyer! When Scott jumps, I have to pay attention or
I'm dropped. Risked a quick glimpse of some medieval ruins near*

the harbor. Would like to explore them. Caught up with Tom, who we rode with earlier. Had his good company for the trifecta of pesky climbs through the city. The Tour organizers utilized what seriously looks like someone's private driveway. Narrow and impossibly steep. Thankfully short, but dumped us directly into the busy commercial center."

"Interesting place, Cherbourg. Huge ships docked here. Industrial in flavor. Dinner was a relief. Last two have sat like a stone in my stomach, so light salads and cold cuts, fish terrines and local pâté, went down easy. Best cider yet. A bottle from the Cotentin. Dry and effervescent without too much sweetness and floaty bits at the bottom of the bottle. I'm so sad to be leaving Normandy though looking forward to tomorrow. Legs feel fine, but for how long? Knees and hips ached until the first rest stop. Sit bones are sore. Phil told us tomorrow we can expect more wind and possibly some light showers in the morning so it's another good day to go slow."

"We were passed by a car today that slowed down as the passenger began to yell out the window. I thought it was going to be an angry, profane message. It was an emphatic shout of encouragement. There were, however, a few close-fast-uncomfortable passes. The plates were overwhelmingly British."

↔

By stage 2, our "one day at a time" approach quickly morphed into "one feed stop at a time". It was a lengthy day in the saddle, but nothing like the rides to come, ramping up in distance until the dreaded 150 miler later in the week. We found the stage easier to get through once we compartmentalized it even more. As the feed stops were generally placed 25 to 30 miles apart, focusing on the stretch of road from one to the next meant that we could put the enormity of the event out of our minds and enjoy the ride until it was time to take a quick break, satisfy our grumbling stomachs and relieving ourselves of the contents of our bidons.

As quickly as day two, our systems were wise to the schedule and at 25 mile intervals would begin to make demands, starting as a distant grumble and if ignored, intensifying until our insides were simultaneously burning and wrenching. We'd roll into the feed stop ravenous and grumpy, irritated by the already formed queue at the mandatory sign-in easel and hand-washing station.

Stop one was all smiles, cheerily and mannerly waiting our turns to choose a small jam and butter sandwich and banana. Stop two was still polite but more determined to quickly ingest a welcome savory snack of pâté and butter sandwiches and French-press espressos. Stop three was when we ate a proper lunch. Chaos ruled and the hungry masses descended upon the buffet like a plague of ravenous insects. Stop 4 was back to civility but only because we were drained of any motivation to muster a cohesive thought, much less to jockey for position to be first in line for corn chips and candy bars.

Sugar, salt and fat dominated the menu at the last stop, as well as the devil's bitter invention…the black caffeinated nectar that "Coffee Ian" as he would come to be proclaimed, would dole out graciously from his own personal stash. I only hope I thanked Ian properly for always offering a steaming, attitude adjusting, body warming, brain stimulating cup of goodness with an out-stretched hand and genuine smile before the request for one could even leave my lips. Like the white light at the end of death's long tunnel, he was the peace we knew we'd find no matter how hard the struggle of the day would prove. I think the staff enjoyed this stop the most, as all the riders were putty in their hands, completely incapable of putting up a fuss. By the last few kilometers, we simply did what we were told.

It was this early stage when the women of the group began to realize that we'd be facing an additional challenge for the next three weeks. Despite the best intentions of our organizer extraordinaire Sarah, the rest stops hardly ever coordinated with the location of a proper toilet. Men have an uncomplicated and un-hindered relationship with taking a leak. I realize there may be exceptions, but humor me. Despite having several sets of ingeniously designed "drop-seat" bibs, where the entire derriere unzips, most days would provide no cover behind which to facilitate a nature break.

Having somewhat of an iron bladder, I managed for the majority of the first two stages to just hold it until a reasonable screen of foliage could be found or better yet, a toilet magically appeared at a feed stop. They almost never did and if we were so lucky to find one, they would certainly never have toilet paper. A side note regarding French toilets; they can be lavishly modern or shockingly rudimentary depending on their environment. I'll give you two words and you can guess which version we were most likely to find: roadside and rural. I could write an entire guidebook on French toilet varieties and the wonders and horrors of each. However, I'll just mention that I am very proud of the ladies in the bunch and of myself, for very quickly become comfortable with letting it all hang out. It's something you just have to get over because 140-plus miles with a full bladder is nothing to joke about.

This was also when we began to sort out the temporary pack of riders, called "Tour Tasters" from the Lifers, those of us committed to all 21 stages. Some we remembered from our pre-tour dinner, though most still blended into a rolling assemblage of unfamiliar bikes and jerseys. More than few already began to leave an impression, for their welcoming demeanor and their steady wheel. We would spend at least a portion of each stage for the remainder of the tour riding with these standout fellows, most of which I'll mention in chapters to come.

Stage 2 offered our first opportunity to ride some with Phil. We even got to push the pedals a bit with him, expending watts in a reckless manner for so early in the ride. Despite what I felt were good-natured efforts to bounce me off his rear wheel, I managed to cling there for a kilometer or two.

Notwithstanding the occasional rain and throbbing of my sit bones, riding in such a way was a huge ego boost. Maybe I could do this after all. I had never had the confidence to sit in the big ring and really crank out the miles. There was some alarm in my head that started to chant "You'll burn out if you keep that up. You'll bonk. You'll end up dropped and alone on the side of the road. You don't have the fitness or skill or power so sit up and soft pedal". Climbing hills was a different story thankfully, and there was no lack of confidence once the road pointed up. In fact, I seemed to have a natural knack for getting to the top. But there was something keeping me from believing that I could put power into the pedals mile after mile on an undulating stretch of road without completely coming apart at the seams. Mental fitness was the hardest to gain, but I was making a bit of progress.

The stage was now more than half over and riders had really begun to string out. Scott and I would pass several lone cyclists along the way. They would hang with us for a while and we would either tow them to the next small group or they would unhitch and fall back into a solo rhythm. A few would strike up a conversation covering the basics; we would exchange how-do-you-do's, comment on the weather, inquire where each of us were from, etc. Some however, especially when I was riding far enough away from Scott to be out of earshot, thought I might need some totally good-natured but undoubtedly unsolicited cycling advice.

56

My favorite was the suggestion that I not ride so close to the edge of the road, namely that I should stop riding to the right of the solid stripe, in case I should falter and find myself careening onto the flat wide shoulder or worse yet, the grassy patch beyond. Scott was around to hear that one and chuckled then politely inquired of my fellow cyclist if he'd ever heard of cyclo-cross. Undeterred, my white line advisor insisted that a jaunt across the green stuff would surely mean a crash. His opinion was that we were safer riding to the left of the white line, regardless of any off-road skills, because cars were more likely to see us and respond in an evasive manner. Each to their own but I would learn to feel safest as far from speeding metal as possible, with an eye on an escape route, no matter how close that brought me to the edge of the tarmac. It sure improved my ability to ride in a smooth, straight line. And smooth and straight is usually the safest way to ride no matter what part of the lane you have your wheel planted. This particular patch of impeccably maintained French byway (manicured roadside maintenance is standard across the whole of the country) offered a favorable escape route in the case of a wayward vehicle, something I would habitually become cognizant of. Not a bad plan since we were going to spend over 2,000 miles riding in the close company of cars.

Much of stage two was spent in the drops, shouldering the wind, taking pulls, passing one tidy village after the next. Horses and cows in every field, calves and foals frolicking in the wet grass and cool air. It made me miss my own young horses back home, whom I wouldn't see for many weeks. They weren't yet trained to ride under saddle, but I enjoyed spending time in their company watching them graze and play and nibble at our clothes and hair. I missed their horsey smell and the feel of their warm, soft spotted coats. The cows in Normandy were spotted too, with big brown patches on a white base and most had a unique brown ring around both their eyes, which made them look like goggles. They would lift their heads and follow my progress as I pedaled past their pasture. They seemed to appreciate being spoken to and I was calmed by their gaze.

The countryside gave way to signs of city life as we approached the bustling port of Cherbourg. There was a wide, downward sloping boulevard along the waterfront and catching all the green lights, Scott and I blasted through block after block enjoying a game of chase. We were finally stalled by a red light where we caught up to Tom and had the pleasure of his company and his steady, high cadence riding style all the way to the hotel. Between us and the day's final destination we'd have to navigate a few ugly bumps in the road.

I think Ian Yost's TDF preview article in Bicycling Magazine said it best: "The final 50km of the stage are quite lumpy, and several climbs could have been categorized had the organizers chosen to do so." Lumpy indeed. Had the organizers felt like categorizing the climbs at the end of this day (or the dozens of others throughout the rest of the Tour) there would have been a handful of short fours under our belts by the time we got to the

official category three of Glacerie Hill. This was no scenic climb
in the middle of postcard France, but a wall smack dab in the
center of a bustling industrial zone. With evening commuters
darting around us while we struggled on the narrow lane to
even get the cranks turned over, it felt irritatingly
claustrophobic. I burned a match to get to the top in front of my
two cycling partners, only to realize there would be two more
"bonus climbs" back to the hotel. Dejected, I dropped behind to
pout over my poor planning. My legs were toast and I was
looking forward to a snack and a cider. This was a routine we
would learn well…struggling through the extra miles tacked
on to the end of the stage. Occasionally these "bonus" miles
would occur at the beginning of a stage but seemed to bother us
less on fresh morning legs.

There is a difference between the *départ fictif* (false start) and
the *départ réel* (real start). The official stage start can sometimes
differ from the point where the timer begins. Départ towns pay
a substantial amount for the honor of seeing off the riders for
that day's stage. So the start is often in the center of town,
where the crowds can gather and the fanfare is thick, giving
spectators a chance to glimpse their favorite riders and perhaps
catch a souvenir or two tossed from the gaudy publicity caravan
(though I do admit to enjoying the sight of a giant chicken on
wheels). The riders are asked to slowly lumber through the first
few kilometers, dutifully smiling and nodding and exposing
their sponsors' names to the cameras. Once safely away from
the throngs, the riders pass the actual start line to the point

where the clock officially starts ticking. The watch stops of course at the finish line, where the mass of media, fans and tour busses await the riders for interviews, autographs and to tote weary riders to their hotels. With no such fanfare the stage end was our *fini fictive* aka "false finish" and often saw us pedaling many more miles and the occasional climb or two, to reach the *fini réel* or "real finish". No matter, the long day was done and we were rewarded with a nice dinner and a good sleep despite Phil's warnings at the briefing about more wind and more showers tomorrow.

STAGE 3:

Shadow of a Thousand Swifts

June 27, 2016 ~ Granville to Angers. "I'm not the first man to be wrong about the weather" – Ride leader, Phil Deeker, commenting to a water-logged audience at the evening's dinner briefing.

"141.1 miles and 6,680 feet climbed. On to the Pays de la Loire. Leaving Normandy. Despite Phil's assessment of early drizzle followed by clearing skies, we got very wet. Rain jacket was inconveniently stashed in the support van. Legs felt fresh, brain felt foggy. Needed some solo time, so slowly made my way to the front of the pack and just kept the pedals turning, concentrating on my pedal stroke and the white line on the soaked tarmac. Kilometers floating past. Pedaling felt slow and deliberate, yet a peek back revealed an empty road behind me. I was struck with an overwhelming sense of sadness. I knew I would cry during this trip but expected it to be on top of some mountain. Began to sob uncontrollably. I was grateful for the rain. My gratitude would not last."

"Maybe it was the soundless sleep or the next-to-nothing breakfast. Dinner was fine, but I could only choke down half a croissant and a tiny cup of coffee. Screw it. Keep pedaling. And then the miles worked their magic. Sadness abated."

"Not much to report for the rest of the day with the constant drizzle and fog. Heads down the whole distance to stop 2, overtaking one small group then the next. We tried to settle in to a pack but found we were too fast for one then too slow for another. Fresh morning legs felt like sacks of concrete after stop 1. I was grumpy at myself, my husband and most of the other cyclists. At times, for good reason. The rain does not tend to bring out the best handling skills. It dumped on us from 5 minutes out to 5 minutes in so everyone was miserable today. So many beautiful herds of cattle here. If I keep focusing on the cows instead of the rain and everything will be alright."

"Sat up, had enough of the disorganized pace line. Too fast, too erratic and too confusing with guys who are used to riding on the wrong side of the road. Still passing along the eastern border of Brittany, then we see Vitré. The town has beautiful ruins and narrow streets, lined with half-timbered houses. Must return here to sightsee. Having something to see made our mood better and then the rain relented to a light drizzle. Soft pedaling side-by-side, taking in the sights. Even stopped for a picture. No TDF fanfare here. Phil calls it a through-zone. Not a stage start or finish. Then we entered the Loire. More handsome cattle. Different breeds in different regions, these likely Maine-Anjou? We also passed through Marans; the village sharing a name with a heritage breed whose dark brown eggs are their signature trait. Chicken trivia."

"Lots of rush hour traffic heading into Angers. Getting cranky with cars. Understand though that we are in the wrong place at the wrong time on the wrong roads. The bigger the city, the more carelessly close the drivers get. Still, nothing intentional. The evening commute is just serious business."

"I just hope "close" never ends up "too close". Speaking of close, I couldn't unclip at a stop light today. I screeched at Scott to catch me and thankfully he wasted no time in asking questions, just grabbed ahold and held me in place until the light turned and I could pedal away. Phew. Probably due to dirty cleats. A good reminder to stay out of the mud! Staying on the edge of town with a cloying view of Angers Castle. Sad we won't get to see it up close. Remember to come back for a visit. Felt wiped by the finish. Emotionally and physically. Phil tells us during dinner to expect more wind and rain tomorrow. It will be a good day to go slow. I'm starting to sound like a broken record."

↔

Like a saloon door, the French weather swings. And so did my mood on Stage 3. We were up early for the bus ride to Granville from Cherbourg. Unlike the professionals who finish their stages with time to spare and get the transfers out of the way in the evenings, we took so long to finish the day's route that we had to do most transfers in the wee hours of the following morning. The buses were large and comfortable and I didn't mind them so much, as the drive gave me time to digest my breakfast and wrap my brain around the day ahead. Most of my fellow cyclists took the time to catch up on sleep. It was our last day in Normandy and I woke with an underlying sadness about leaving the region. I should have been excited to see the Loire, as I had never before visited. I was excited, but after spending a week in Normandy and having previously spent time there, I had a strong connection with the place as somewhere I could settle down, raise a pretty herd of dairy cows and drink copious amounts of fizzy cider. Maybe I was Norman in a former life or maybe I just really liked their cheese. Whatever the case, I didn't expect to start sobbing uncontrollably upon my bike, while cruising down the motorway. I'm going to blame it on the fatigue.

Physically, I was tired but functional (aside from the searing pain in my left sit bone and some minor soreness in my hips and knees). Mentally I was feeling the effects of a year's worth of anxiety and worrying. I upped the tempo a bit to take a pull at the front of the group I was riding with and before long found myself completely alone. I didn't blast off…just got in the drops and started to focus on my pedal stroke. Around and around, nice and round, not stabbing, not squares, just big easy circles. Then I looked back and there was nothing behind me but empty wet road. And that's when I lost it. Total water works. I've never been more thankful for rain. The clouds weep and my thick wet tears rolled together down my face to forever quench the land I loved. It was a poignant moment and I felt better for the good, old-fashioned cry.

I managed to gain some composure by the time I spotted the arrow for the first feed stop and t was a welcome sight. I was the first one to arrive to the surprise of the staff, no doubt wondering what had inspired this heroic effort. But I was only motivated by, in order of necessity: the loo, a proper bite to eat and my rain cape. Then I realized there was coffee. Sarah had secured the use of a parking lot of a café who had also generously offered to open their doors to us early thereby providing our peloton with a flushing toilet and a hard-working espresso machine. They probably didn't expect the associated dampness of dozens of dripping cyclist who bee-lined from the front door to the bathroom door to the coffee bar, in that order precisely. Scott and I tried our best to smile, apologize, thank profusely and over tip. Then we proceeded to soak the seating area. We were turning into a bunch of misbehaving animals.

Between stop 2 and lunch, the rain came hard and fast and relentlessly drenched us all. It wasn't cold, but there was a moment where two things happened that turned the experience of riding in the rain into a big wet blanket. The first was when the splash from the road breached the shoe-sock barrier. A steady rain will splash back from the pavement and onto everything, shoes, legs, bike, etc. But the tiny vents of a well-made cycling shoe are decent at keeping air moving through and road-spray out. Mostly. Like a dam breaking, the droplets got too plentiful and it was all over. My shoe instantly filled with rain water and my socks became a soggy mess.

The other situation was just as unpleasant. Rain was falling on my helmet, my shoulders and my thighs and because I was moving a decent clip, started to funnel its way from my pumping legs down my saddle in a tiny rivulet right towards my lap until it hit the mark. My blasted chamois.

Modern cycling bibs do a spectacular job at absorbing moisture but they don't discriminate between sweat and drizzle. It only made me squirm for a minute, before my body-temperature warmed the deluge in my bibs to a nice 90-something degrees. Then it just felt like a wet diaper and there was nothing to do but keep pedaling thinking longingly of a dry change of clothes.

After lunch, the skies cleared but the whole group was riding franticly. Like pouring a pitcher of water over an anthill, movements and decisions were erratic and thoughtless. I sat up, more interested in slowing down and taking care of my line, considering the wetness of the road and decline in traction. We'd join a group, try to organize with someone taking the lead and shouting directions and get to work. The rotation was opposite of what we were used to and it took a lot of brain power to stay properly engaged.

In the States, the lead rider would take their turn before pulling left into the lane of travel, allowing the trailing group to pass through along the shoulder, with the former leader taking their place on the tail end. This only exposes one rider to traffic, with all of the other riders hugging the outside of the lane. These guys rotated in the opposite manner, with the leader pulling off to the right, while the entire train passed on the left. Done in this manner on French roads, exposed the entire string of over-taking riders to be out in the lane of travel, while the single rider dropping to the tail was protected on the outside of the group. I'm sure the approach made perfect sense to them, but it was not one I was familiar with or had ever taken part in. It was confusing to say the least and unsettling to say the most. We would sit in and take our share of pulls, but were not convinced someone wouldn't be flattened by a passing lorry.

Towards the end of the day, when the rain wasn't pelting us, we had the chance to sit up and take in the sights. We had left the marshes of Normandy behind, along with the swarms of circling swallows and their daring acrobatics above the village squares. Those were replaced by the streamlined swifts of the Loire with their shrill song and when the sun shone briefly through the dense clouds, I enjoyed seeing their shadows play over the road ahead. The pavement became rough here. Our tires not wanting to roll as smoothly along as they did on the fresh asphalt of the previous days' roads.

Instead of long-legged horses and gnarled old orchards, the fields bordering the road were thickly sown with barley and wheat, knee-high corn and the bright yellow flowering canola plant. Sadly, there was an uncountable number of flattened roadkill. Their tell-tale brown and white spines clearly proving that hedgehogs and speeding cars don't make good companions. I saw thousands of their tiny squished bodies along the roadside, but never managed even a glimpse of one in a three-dimensional state.

Travelling along a main artery, away from the great Loire River and quieter country roads, we saw no châteaux here. Though we spotted two outdoor velodromes along the route, one in a small village in the department of Maine-et-Loire and one in the finish city of Angers. The latter, a well-known and well used facility made of concrete, spanned 300 meters in length. The other, much smaller and not well documented, was clearly a labor of love built by the community and fans of the sport. Upon further research, I would discover that in addition to the major velodromes of France, there are roughly 110 municipal tracks with several more across the country in the planning phase. What another striking difference between a nation that reveres its relationship with the bicycle and one that unfortunately finds it burden.

STAGE 4:

The Birth of Baguettes

June 28, 2016 ~ Saumur to Limoges. "At least there's a tailwind." —Scott Davison remarks after starting the longest stage of the ride in the pouring rain.

"150.7 miles and 6,601 feet climbed. Finally, we see some hills! Tough start to the day. SO saddle sore. I've finally succumbed to using chamois cream. I found this part of the Loire boring. It looked too much like home for the first part of the stage, but then gave way to a rolling green horizon. Drivers passed too fast and too close. Beautiful cows were the same shade of golden red as the wheat in the fields. Add the pouring rain and voila! The birth of all those tasty baguettes. Then more rain. Not cold, just impossibly wet."

"Very, very uncomfortable body is still managing to churn out the miles of undulating roads. We crossed the river Vienne. That was a treat. A few picturesque villages to break up the monotony including St. Germain, over the river Gartempe, via a lovely 11th century stone bridge in view of a medieval chateaux on the river bank. In the water are a lovely green plant with many white flowers, rippling in the flow near the surface. Enter the Limousin. I could live here. It's beautiful with huge oaks and chestnut trees and a smattering of conifers. Lots of small lakes."

"In Texas, they'd be called "tanks" and would be used to water the cattle. It's a sea of grass and grazing cows. Gorgeous specimens they are too. We were detoured from the main road to a single car-width rustic lane, winding around and around a hillside. My favorite road so far. Passed a farm with a huge old barn, proudly displaying dozens of metal plaques for prize winning animals. Then the climbing begins. Funny, as this stage was called "flat". Phil caught us up and we felt fresh enough to give chase…foolishly burning more matches. We might regret it in time, but it felt good to stretch our legs and burn the funk from our minds and body. Down, down, down we go, around and up again. The kind of up that suits me. 5% and rolling. I hung on tight. I'm still pushing and I feel strong. Scott's right behind me. We had so much fun and ended the longest stage fresher than the last three."

"We ride into Limoges from the top of the valley above a shimmering lake, glinting with an almost forgotten sun. Sweeping views from our line of hills to the next layer, then a layer beyond. Somewhere over there, tomorrow's story is waiting."

↔

Cheops aka "Khufu" is the oldest and largest pyramid of Giza. It was also the name of our strange lodgings in Limoges. As you might expect, it was an Egyptian themed affair complete with pharaoh décor and paintings of pyramids adorning the walls. The facility was built originally to house teams of young athletes visiting Limoges to train at various Olympic disciplines, mostly gymnastics, wrestling and the like. The hotel was clean and clinical and we dined cafeteria style just like we did in elementary school, plastic tray and all. Except this cafeteria had free beer. I had been allowing myself one post-stage alcoholic drink to help wash down dinner and rubberize my tired legs. One sometimes turned to two, though no one but me was really counting.

Tonight we would say hello to a new group of Tour Tasters joining us for tomorrow's stage and riding along only until we reached the Pyrenees. By now most of the Lifers felt like old pros. Heck, some really were. Both Tom and Sylvain, a powerhouse cyclist from Montréal, had ridden the Tour multiple times in a row. The rest of us were quickly becoming road wizened and rain weary and must have looked rather unapproachable. We had a tendency to cluster together at meals and generally exclude the new recruits. It wasn't intentional; it was just that after four long days of riding together, we had already developed a certain bond. So much so, that we were mildly chastised by the staff to be more inclusive of the new faces and make more of an attempt to act like welcoming hosts. This exclusion would only get worse as the stages wore on, but I rather think we earned the right to behave with a certain degree of haughtiness towards the newbies. Besides, the road would have its way with us all equally in time.

Because the world is actually quite small in the grand scheme of things and we do all seem to be connected by six degrees of somebody or another, we were not terribly surprised to meet two cyclists from the United States that we had met before. A father and his college-aged daughter, that recognized us right away. We had briefly ridden together at a Chris King Gourmet Century event in Asheville, North Carolina the year before. Scott recognized his high-quality titanium frame (leave it to him to remember bikes but not faces). His daughter, however, was memorable for her skill in the saddle. She was fit and light and quick up the hills.

With the longest day done and the proper mountain stages still a few days off, there was a sense of relief in the air. We cautiously allowed ourselves to exhale. Then along comes Phil, with his hand drawn profiles complete with graphs and warnings and crude drawings of stick men on bikes. Ever the buzzkill, he warns us not to relax just yet. Tomorrow we would meet our first vertical challenge, the often underestimated climb of Puy Mary in the Cantal.

Phil also doled out the nightly awards; one for a great act of heroism or accomplishment on the bike and the other for a great act of stupidity. At each rider briefing, one lucky recipient throughout the Tour would either receive the honorary chapeau or the ridiculous squeaky elephant horn. The current holder of each prize had the responsibility the next day to pay the honor forward to the most deserving participant. These were the only two "official" awards of the event and one was given only with the faintest grain of salt. In reality, there were untold acts of heroism, bravery and determination every stage, by every rider.

Whether you finished first or last, fastest up hills or slowest down them or didn't finish at all…the stages were long and filled with difficulties and one rider's trial would prove to be another's whim and vice versa.

We all had our challenges and our victories and many went un-noticed or un-mentioned, but it was a nice gesture nevertheless to highlight a standout individual and their daily accomplishment. It brought sheepish grins, hearty applause and reminded us all to look for the good in one another. Our tour was beginning to be more than just a series of miles linked together by a chain of mountains across a beautiful landscape. It was also an exercise in decoding and understanding the full spectrum of human persistence, struggle, relationships, emotions and how differently each of us managed those things.

It's interesting that on the longest stage, I wrote the least in my diary. Perhaps it was because we spent nearly twelve hours in the saddle, or because I spent over an hour cleaning and lubing my bike before dinner. Or maybe I was just finally too exhausted to put down any more words. We'd ridden over 530 miles in four days, most of them in the drenching rain, and we were all starting to feel their effects. Long gazes, drawn cheeks, slow moving but still there'd be laughs and smiles and good humor. Unfortunately, Scott was beginning to really suffer. His painful knee, which had been plaguing him for the months leading up to the trip, was a consistent companion. More concerning though was the thickening of both Achilles tendons and the soreness he was starting to feel both on and off the bike. Fortunately, the staff included several physiotherapists and masseurs, all specifically trained to offer relief by way of massage, acupuncture, physical therapy, stretching sessions and sports tape. There was also a cycling physician, Dr. Julian, appointed to treat more serious afflictions and dole out any necessary over-the-counter pharmaceuticals. Scott finally decided enough was enough and had the first of many consultations with the doctor and physios about providing supportive therapies to help get him to Paris. I believe he was cycling in more pain than he let on. He didn't want to admit to himself that this stage might have been the beginning of the end of his tour and he certainly didn't want me to know that because he knew I wouldn't want to ride without him. We'd already made the tentative plan that if his body raised the white flag we'd rent a car and drive the rest of the way, enjoying the wonders of France from four wheels instead of two. Not ideal, but neither was needless suffering. The mountains would be right where we left them, to be climbed another day.

I seemed to be holding up fine all things considered. Sure, things weren't entirely peachy. No specific injuries, just discomfort and at times, a whole lot of it. There are many insignificant patches of flesh and parts of the body that that you never really dwell on because they typically don't cause a fuss. That is, until you sit on them in the rain, use them in a repetitive fashion, expose them to the cold and the wind, pressure and friction in a manner they are not accustomed to.

Then they sing to you like a loud, lonely caged canary; shrill and persistent and you are their captive audience for hours with nothing to do but focus on the very source of your discomfort.

I have no children, so don't quote me, but I imagine there are similarities to endurance cycling. The body is capable of experiencing immense discomfort and then conveniently distracts you from remembering such pain by way of a heavy duty endorphin rush. I bet if you asked any mother (or any endurance athlete for that matter) to think hard enough about the process, they could tell you just how badly it felt. That doesn't mean they weren't happy to go through it or they weren't willing to do it all over again.

Scott can remember all his pain, sharp and lasting as it was. I have a harder time recalling every specific ache, but I do remember them being present. I remember better the day they all went away. Phil assured us the worst physical discomfort would be felt over the first three days. This was day four and my body felt like a furnace; burning in some unmentionable places, flesh hot and limbs heavy. My sit bones were constantly throbbing and finding a comfortable spot on the saddle was now impossible. I could only manage a minute or so of sitting before I had to pedal standing. Holding my place in a pace line was torture. I could hardly offer a steady wheel to those behind me, constantly squirming as I was. It was starting to make me anxious, so Scott and I spent the next few stages relatively solo where we could both suffer freely.

Such is the magic of the Tour that we didn't have to suffer all the time. There were stretches of lane and landscape that were so beautifully distracting that nothing could devalue the moment. Riding a bicycle can be so simple and riding a bicycle in the quietude of rural France with the person you love, so gladdening. One such stretch was near the end of the stage, a departure actually from the official route due to road construction. It was a detour we were grateful to take, as it remains one of our favorite moments of the trip. We veered left from the main two-laned, rural road and climbed briefly to the top of a squat plateau before winding back and forth along a narrow strip of pavement, barely wide enough for a horse-drawn cart. The track was sunken from centuries of use and the surrounding hills were gently rolling and deeply verdant, an occasional hamlet and soaring stone barn all the civilization we'd see. I'm not sure if I could ever find my way back there and sadly, have no photographs of it. So enamored I was of being in the moment, I didn't dare ruin the illusion by reaching for my iPhone. Some memories live their best lives in our heads alone.

Shortly after the detour reconnected us with the official route, did we find ourselves overtaken once more by Phil. He had a knack for magically appearing on your wheel without a hint of him there the last time you looked over your shoulder. Nevertheless, we always enjoyed the brief stretches of road we shared with him. His love for France was second only to perhaps my own and he certainly had an intimate knowledge of each region through which we passed.

I really began to cherish his insight into the land and its customs and curiosities. I don't think I saw him happier than when he was talking about his adopted country. He had made the Ardennes his home, an environment that seemed to suit him perfectly. Remote and hardy with a touch of the mystical, full of cycling history and lore. That was Phil alright. He had a knack for being the perfect guide and for the most part delivering each guest exactly what they needed from him, exactly when they needed it. He was always there for us when we needed to be inspired, to be energized, to rev up our engines and blow out the exhaust of a laborious day.

When Phil starts to pedal, you have two choices; watch him shrink into the horizon or wind yourself up for the chase. The latter is far more satisfying and we had a spectacular ribbon of road on which to use all our gears, from big ring to small, every cog in the cassette had a chance to do its duty. The road was really beginning to roll and dive and as soon as we'd crest a short hill, it would disappear below us and our speed would swell. Down in the drops, we'd carve out the contours of the knoll, the leaf heavy chestnuts and oaks whipping past. Then the land shifted up and we started to climb.

By this time Scott had grown tired and the gap between us was increasing by the pedal stroke. I reluctantly nodded farewell to Phil and cut the throttle. Now ascending at a pace more appropriate for tired legs and torched tendons, we climbed our way slowly to the top of the last hillock and over our right shoulder was a sprawling lake, basking in the rays of sunshine that had stubbornly broken through the day's dense clouds. It was a picturesque view and well worth our efforts. Much to our delight, across the road was the final feed stop of the day and there was the waving, grinning face of Ian, dancing with abandon to the techno blaring from his stereo. The faint smell of espresso wafted over the road and we were drawn in to enjoy the waning moments of a damn good day.

STAGE 5:

A Dance with Lady Mary

June 29, 2016 ~ Limoges to Le Lioran. "This really caused a stir in Paris." – Phil Deeker, ride leader describing the announcement by the Tour de France organizers that Puy Mary would feature in stage 5, breaking tradition that no climbs above 1,500 meters appear in the first week.

"137.8 miles and 12,963 feet climbed. Whoa. Again, the region around Limoges was incredible. The steep, unpleasant climb this morning in rush hour traffic was not. That stretch of road was a nightmare. All was forgiven once we entered the Cantal. Holy shit. We are leaving everything behind and eloping with this place. Rolling fields gave way to the richest green hills I've ever seen. Baby mountains blanketed with grass and stone. Beautiful villages, each one outdoing the last. All putting their best foot forward for the soon to arrive Tour fans and caravans. Then we climb past herds of big-eyed, bell-wearing Salers cattle, who according to anyone you ask here, make the world's best cheese. They are textbook perfect, big and round with thick tufts of rich brown coat. Their substantial bells are deeply toned and have a mesmerizing effect. But they also seem to be announcing the climbing to come, as if they are tolling the hour until we arrive at the foot of the Tour's first true test."

"*We descended madly down into a hidden, densely vegetated ravine towards a river, spanned by a huge steel suspension bridge, then climbed atop a long ridge that funneled us into the heart of the Auvergne.*"

"*Flatted then fell over. Bent derailleur. Spent too long at lunch. The sun had already begun to dip in the sky and we hadn't even started climbing yet. I was anxious about the delay until we rode through the village of Salers. Must return and eat the cheese. Great view from the busy main square of the valley below, which is the regional park of the Auvergne volcanoes. Second natural park of the day, the first being the Millevache en Limousin. The park of a thousand cows? My kind of place.*"

"*Up and up we go. The grade is mellow but persistent and I'm grinding it out in the big ring for a while, then it pitches another degree and it's all about the 34 now. We're getting close to Puy Mary. The forest is growing dense, almost hiding the river on our left. She teases us with a gentle approach then appears out of the trees like a monolith. You can see all the way to the top, watch the riders clinging to her sides, way up there in the sky. It looks like a long way to go. The road swells to 10%, turns, then swells again. Scott has fallen back to climb in his own rhythm. I lost him at the first switchback but got to see him crest the summit just as the incoming cloud engulfed the whole mountainside and everyone on it. She really made me hurt but my reward was descending down her gentler backside, free of cars with a cool tailwind.*"

"*The sun comes out again and there are more Puys to climb, most with 8% average grades. Seems to be a popular shape for extinct volcanoes. The roads here are near-perfect and passing cars are few and friendly. More cows with bells, huge brown hawks and I think I saw a weasel. Hamlets with small, stout stone houses are dwarfed by cavernous stone barns with huge slabs of raw slate for a roof. Then a never ending bonus climb that was less than amusing. Almost 13,000' of pedaling up and my legs are feeling it now. Sit bones are a mess, especially the right one. Need to remember to talk to the doctor about it. Can hardly sit on my saddle anymore. Also feel nauseated and had trouble with dinner even though the hotel was proudly serving up the local specialty of mashed potatoes and melted cheese. Not exactly sure what tomorrow brings. Way too tired to care."*

↔

This was the first day of "proper" climbing, the kind that really leaves a mark turning muscle and mind to a whimpering mush. It was a long day in the saddle by anyone's standard and was punctuated by a seemingly endless bonus climb to the hotel, perched precariously to the mountainside and felt about as far away from the stage finish as possible without being in another département altogether. It was only about 2.5 uphill kilometers, but when translating that to a worn-out, bonk-bordering, bleary-eyed pair of cyclists it sounded like pretty bad news. Plus, the newly laid asphalt was far from being cured and riding up the grade felt like pudding. Any small, sharp pebble not ensconced in tar became instantly embedded in our tires resulting in several dismounts to brush them off by hand. Then, the left pointing arrow showing us the way to our lodgings sent us careening down a pot-holed, forlorn jeep trail which we were certain was the wrong direction and would only result in us having to climb back out the way we came.

I tried hard to put on a pleasant face for the camera crew that would follow us for the first week. They were making a short promotional documentary for the organizer and were exceptionally nice fellows, always smiling and shouting encouragement from their chase car. I could hardly be grumpy at them for wanting to get a good shot of the face of suffering. But as I tried in earnest to answer their inquiries about the stage, my stomach was hurling hunger pains with precise aim and I was finding it difficult to even form a coherent sentence. Plus, the sun was setting which added a layer of anxiety when I still had to get the bike attended to, body washed, muscles fed and brain unencumbered by complicated thought. This is why the pro peloton has handlers. To do the thinking for them. They aren't over-paid prima donna's. After a hundred miles at race pace in the hills, they literally can't function. We were appreciating their accomplishments more and more as the stages wore on.

I hurriedly settled bikes and bags and checked room assignments, then ushered Scott off to wait in line for the physio. Each participant was responsible for the cleaning and basic maintenance of their own bicycle then unloading and loading their own luggage from van into hotel room and vice versa, plus making sure day-bags with all required necessities were loaded into the proper support vans for the next day's stage. It wasn't so bad once you learned the routine but make a mistake and you were up the proverbial creek without a paddle, as there was very little room for error. Physios and masseurs were first-come, first-served and also over-worked, so if you were late to finish the day and still needed their services, you'd be in for a long wait. Since Scott was now requiring daily therapy, it was my job to get the day packs sorted, bottles rinsed and filled, kit washed and hung to dry, bags re-packed, tomorrow's outfits laid out, work emails answered and social media updated. Then showered and at dinner on the nose, with no time to spare. One blip in the routine and we'd find our whole brief evening gone. We could quickly run out of time to unwind, re-organize, eat and earn a good nights' sleep. Massage wasn't really my thing (a glass of wine at dinner was a decent alternative) so I didn't mind handling the chores. It gave me some time to process the day and to go to sleep unfettered by a disorganized room.

Our quirky hotel was quintessentially 70's era French ski chalet and the shoebox sized chamber was finished with floor-to-ceiling wood panels and mauve shag carpet underfoot...even in the washroom. The shower water was hot and plentiful, so the 40 year-old décor mattered little in my exhausted point of view. The small dining hall was splitting at the seams with a hundred ravenous bodies and the staff looked understandably overwhelmed by the curt requests for more food and beer. Most evenings we were expected to behave civilly through a multicourse seated meal service, served in a professional and traditional manner. Tonight though, because the stage had taken the majority of the day, we filed in and helped ourselves to the bowls of cold starters while the skeleton staff (summer is off-season for the Auvergne ski resorts) hurriedly delivered plates of gooey aligot, the heavy local specialty of whipped potatoes and melted Cantal cheese. I had two servings of cold Puy lentils and two glasses of kir but had to reluctantly turn my nose at the potato fondue due to the instant onset of nausea that lasted the night. I was feeling guilty for leaving it untouched since the staff clearly went through so much trouble preparing it, but Scott cheerily ate both our servings.

Despite his ailments, Scott had enjoyed a decent day of climbing and described his ascent along the Pas de Peyrol as "no big deal". No big deal? I guffawed. It was wall after wall of tarmac separated by switchbacks. I liked it, he repeated. Thought it was pretty easy, he mumbled nonchalantly. I'll remind you soon enough that you said that, I grumbled as I drained my glass and dragged off to bed. I still had to write in my blasted diary.

Pas de Peyrol is the name given to the road or pass leading up the volcanic cone known as Puy Mary (pronounced pwee mare-ee). The road is the highest pass in the Massif Central, the collective name of all the volcanic mounds and plateaus in southwest France. Rather than a proper chain, most of the mounts are solitary formations, the remnants of long-dead magma spewing cauldrons, their summits softened by the hand of time. Part of the Auvergne, this province is lush and elemental with plenty of lakes and deep rivers to keep things densely green and the variegated horizon creates a sense of immense scale. It is awe inspiring and a region often overlooked in favor of the iconic ranges of the Alps or Pyrenees. Without the modern conveniences of a GPS device, this is the kind of place a cyclist could get lost in, the siren-song of a thousand cow's bells drawing you deep, a network of roads disappearing between the folds of peak and gorge.

Thanks to the efforts of the arrow master, we didn't get lost but we did let the day get longer in the tooth than planned. Lunch was served in a quiet park on a sun dappled spot of soft grass and was a generous spread of local cheeses and charcuterie, watermelon and fresh greens, freshly baked baguettes and savory pasta salads. We were enjoying the appearance of the late afternoon sun and sat down with legs outstretched, helmet, shoes and socks peeled off for a brief respite. After that we'd need to attend to my tire, which had gone flat earlier in the day.

Sometime before lunch Phil happened upon us again (how *does* he do that?) staring blankly at my deflated tire filled with sealant which was supposed to have kept rolling despite any small punctures. Ever the gentleman and gracious tour leader, he generously offered to stay and help with repairs and despite my protestations, neither he or Scott would let me lift a finger and deftly got me rolling again. Then in the most unbecoming fashion (and because my chain was ungainly stuck between chain rings) I collapsed onto the pavement in heap while a high pitched squeal left my lips. Sorry, but once you realize you're going over, you know it's going to be both embarrassing as well as unpleasant. It was such a slow fall that I ended up laying there, laughing in the middle of the road. Yes, yes, I'm fine I ensured both members of my immediate audience as well as a passing car slightly impeded by my single-bike accident. The derailleur wasn't so fine but there wasn't much I could do about it then and there, so repairs would have to wait.

After lunch, I pulled out the tube and re-filled the tire with a spare bottle of sealant in my day bag. I was giving it one last try before ditching the tubeless setup altogether. After running a different brand of tubeless tire successfully for a number of years, this brand had already troubled me with two punctures and had an irritating habit of not sealing as designed. Scott also helped me bend the derailleur hangar back into reasonable alignment. It was integrated into the frame, so we couldn't just pop on a replacement but the beauty of steel is that it tends to be forgiving to ride as well as work on. It just took that one adjustment and never bothered me again. In fact, aside from another round of tire trouble, both bikes and their components would perform perfectly for over two-thousand miles.

Back on the road, we sailed through the interim kilometers blissfully distracted by the scenery and enjoying a rare dry day. I think I was nervous about the mountain, because as soon as the road began hinting of the impending climb, I leaned into the bridle with a little too much oomph. It felt good to churn out the miles, to push a little harder than necessary because for once in a long while I knew I could. Then I settled, sinking down into the saddle for the long-haul, a slow burn beginning in my legs from the effort. I had left Scott behind, but he had waved me on needing his space to tackle the mountain whatever way his injuries would allow. I was enjoying using riders the ahead as bait. Just reel in the guy up the road, easy does it. Then the next one. Then the next. This would prove a useful technique in the stages to come, helping to set a rhythm and a means of diverting me from dwelling on the toil of much longer climbs. For now, it was distracting me from the weight in my tired legs and view of the support van ten stories above the rock face where if you dared to look, you could see tiny moving figures inching their way to the top.

I remember the first left hand turn and subsequent incline of what I assume was the beginning of the official recorded "segment" of the Pas de Peyrol. For racing purposes, whether to award points or record fastest ascent times, climbs don't just refer to arbitrary bits of road or whole blocks of mountain. As it turns out, there is an official starting point and ending point (though who decides these things is a mystery to me). These points could arguably have wandered over the decades, but with modern recording applications such as Strava, cyclists have a cut and dry understanding of where on the road the challenge begins. Not that any of this really matters to the non-pro populous, though many find it fun to look back through the electronic annals to see how they "rank" among all other cyclists up a particular climb and this friendly bit of self-imposed competition may be just the spark they need to put some effort into it. Conversely, for those with a competitive nature the quest for segment royalty namely QOMs or KOMs can be a serious business (*Queen of the Mountain or King of the Mountain. I'm still holding out for the creation a SOM; Supreme of the Mountain, though sadly none exists*). As there are literally millions of segments to chase all over the cycling world, obtaining these digital trophies can be a frustrating exercise of self-flagellation or harmless fun, depending on your tendencies.

Computerized accolades were hardly on my mind as I continued to claw my way up the pass. My speed had slowed to a trundle and I was focusing more and more on keeping my breathing steady and my heart rate manageable. Even at my escargot's pace, I was starting to overtake slower riders. Only they were now walking, heads down and back bent over their frames, pushing them along the incline. This sight really chips away at your resolve and as misery loves company, your brain starts making excuses for you to just get off and join them. I started hearing myself, somewhere from the depths of my psyche start saying "well hell…if these guys are walking, surely it's ok for you to walk too." Then, another thought, stronger than the last, says don't you dare. And that's all it took to not ever get off my bike and walk. Each time I passed another trekking cyclist, I thought I'd have to fight the same battle but every person I passed graciously offered an encouraging word, a tiny verbal push up the hill. Despite their own losing battle with the mountain, they chose to vocalize their support in the success of mine. I can't express enough gratitude for their selflessness and because of their collective positive voices, I was able to quiet my own self-doubt and pedal on.

Perhaps it was because of the cumulative miles in my unprepared legs or because it was the first major mountain test we'd faced but I remember this climb as being really, really hard. It certainly wasn't the hardest we would ride on tour and when I match her profile against those of bigger, steeper climbs, she looks like a cakewalk; but as many of you know well, climbing is more than just a chart of percentages. It's more about perception than anything else. I perceived that I was barely able to turn over the cranks and so it came to pass. I perceived that it was nothing more than a never ending series of impossible ramps, and so it came to be. I made the rookie mistake of forgetting where I was in the cassette, somehow expecting there to be one last easy gear back there, just waiting for my command to bail me out of this misery. There wasn't and when I jammed the right lever, all I managed to do was move the chain to the next harder cog and nearly bring myself to a standstill. I got out of the saddle, hovered slightly on the pedals to ease pressure on the drivetrain, clicked the lever and pushed the chain back onto the 28, my largest and easiest cog.

The brief loss of momentum made the easier gear feel no easier at all, so back out of the saddle I climbed. Up five strokes, willing the bike forward. Thighs and arms and abdomen began protesting, so I sat and let the burn subside. Slowing, I stood. One, two, three, four, flumping onto the saddle, legs again having their say. Too many of these and the burn stops dissipating, leaving you in a near-powerless state, completely unable to produce more force without which gravity wins and you roll to a wretched stop. Please Mary, I whimpered, just let me get to the top. I look up and in an instant answering of my mountain prayer another rider appears on the switchback ahead. Focusing only on his own laborious pumping, I used his position up the road to slowly help tow me towards his wheel.

Miraculously, I passed on his outside and he looked over and we shared a pained, tight-lipped grin. He nodded as if to say "up you go and make it stick". Out of respect, I intended to because there's nothing more distracting than being in the depths of a torturous effort only to have someone else play leapfrog. (*The same goes when passed by someone; humming, whistling, singing, smiling or generally looking unfazed while you toil away the kilometers.*) It takes just as much a toll to pass on a climb as to be passed. A respectable cyclist, I would learn, could do both with composure and grace. Finally the top of the climb was in sight and beyond the final rise of the road was a right-hand panorama of the valley below. A dense grey cloud was thundering our way, roiling with wind and wetness. I pedaled across the white line on the pavement demarking the end of the effort and over to the feed stop van for a reviving cup of Ian's coffee. The few of us assembled there remarked on the beauty of the view and the swift decline of the weather. Rain was coming to the summit and fast. I wouldn't start the descent without Scott, so I waited for him to crest, camera at the ready to capture the shot before we both got drenched. He seemed pleased with his ride, all discomforts considered and only wanted a brief reprieve to down two small espressos. He barely managed to swallow before the curtain of fog and mist engulfed us all. It was time to go, *tout de suite.*

The way down was well worth the trouble of going up and the lengthy, winding descent was a thrilling way to outrun the rain. We left the worst of the weather behind us and the light sprinkle did more to reduce our traction than to make us wet. It was slower going over the remaining two climbs, both because the track had grown slick with drizzle and Scott had less oomph in his stroke. I found the next climb, Col du Perthus, also a category 2, a far easier effort brought on by the infusion of caffeine in my veins and the photogenic surroundings. Alas, my jubilation would be brief and the final ten kilometers plus add-on adventure in search of our time-capsuled hotel, would feel like a whole additional stage of ups and downs and are-we-there-yet inquisitions, ending the long day just as the summer sun settled around the Plomb du Cantal, once a fiery Queen of the Massif Central, now a sleeping beauty of basalt and solidified lava, casting a long shadow over our weary silhouettes.

STAGE 6:

The Hardest Day

June 30, 2016 ~ Arpajon-Sur-Cère to Montauban. "The birds don't seem to care." – Author, with a newly adopted Gallic shrug after being told it had started to rain, again, and simultaneously discovering she'd been pooped on by a passing swallow.

"121.3 miles and 6,217 feet climbed. I seem to be attracted to sharp French rocks. While riding today, just ten minutes off the depart fictif, BANG! Ventoux in miniature poked a hole in my sidewall. Brand new tire at that. Hopefully not a foreshadowing event. Phil, the omnipresent and ace roadside support expert, was there to help sort me out...again. Then alongside pulls Scott.. as well as the support van. I was causing quite the rubber-necking over an embarrassing fender bender."

"Relatively uneventful stage after that. More beautiful views but am noticing a drastically changing landscape. Some punchy climbing on high-traffic roads this morning. They are leading us up and steeply away from the volcanic plateau and all of its wild country. Then we wound along a dense stand of trees to our right and a deep, rocky cliff on our left before plunging down an eye-popping, hand-cramping screamer to a swiftly moving river below. A nice feed stop in a park. Another Turkish toilet misadventure. My shoes got soaked."

"*Then more rolling roads. And more rolling. Scott and I alone, cruising down a quiet lane of stately plane trees graciously planted more than two generations ago. Now, we are enjoying their shade. Thanks for your selfless act, whoever you were.*"

"*Our soft-pedalling morning and the mostly tame roads come to an abrupt end at what looks like a granite wall, with a busy river churning away at its foot. The whole scene looked like a movie set. Cue the picturesque village houses and tall church spires, with the dramatic soaring canyon backdrop. We turned right, then climbed up a barren lane, opposite the slab of rock into the blazing late June sun. At the top of the steamy climb was our feed stop and those with the gumption could peer over the canyon wall into the gorge below.*"

"*Back on the road, new sticky asphalt is radiating heat so well and so early in the summer. Lots of rosy cheeks tonight at dinner and my cycling tan is a deeper shade than yesterday. My ears are also burning and not because I'm talk of the town. That'll teach me to forget to put sunscreen on them. We had so much sun today and a strange feeling it was, after so many days of rain. And so many miles of descents, it's hard to imagine we've got any further down to go. After the rest stop, we took a hard left, got a rolling start, then descended like mad on a rough gray road for what felt like miles.*"

"*For the first time ever, I completely let go of the brakes. Like, really let go. In the drops, without my hands pre-squeezing or covering the levers. It's time I learned to trust the road. Trust my bike. Trust myself. Then despite the voice inside my head raising the alarm, trust that my tires won't explode, or that I'll hit another rock, or a car will veer into my lane. I just let go and didn't touch the levers for an eternity. Talk about freedom.*"

"The route eventually stopped its gentle free-fall and began an easy roll once more. I sat in Scott's draft while he shot off like a rocket, in the drops, cutting through the air with his back flat and eyes ahead. He felt a rare moment of painless peace and jumped at the chance to really spin it up. I hung on tight to his rear wheel and enjoyed the free ride down the lonely road surrounded by thick forests of oaks. Then another right turn, onto a busy four lane road and we were blasted in the face by a stifling wind and the evening commute. The fun ended there. Flat and arrow straight and uncomfortable in every way possible."

"We pass fields of fresh herb crops, then wheat and corn but all we can smell is heat and exhaust and desperation. We took turns as best we could, then started to pick up singles, adding them to the back of the pace line. Pulls were short because everyone was beat. There wasn't anything scenic about this stretch of road or the surrounding countryside, so hopes were not high for tonight's hotel. But, in a country full of irony, it happens to be the poshest and most comfortable place yet despite the lackluster run into the finish."

"A converted Benedictine abbey and monk's quarters, modernized with care given its historical importance. Total luxury. I almost felt too salty, sweaty and covered in road grime to deserve even walking in to such a place. I'm looking forward to a hot shower, a nice dinner, a comfortable sleep and to getting back on the bike tomorrow."

"It's a small miracle."

↔

All of that happened except for the comfortable sleep. See, my normal routine was to trudge through any organizational packing duties, keep my lids propped through the evening meal, then scratch a few words in my journal before lights out. Since there was a long wait for Scott to get his post-ride physio plus the announcement that we'd have special guest speakers at dinner, no doubt prolonging the evening. I figured I'd knock out a few pages of the day's events before we ate. Recordation brief but complete, I turned on my phone's WiFi to check work emails before hopping in the shower. The myriad texts and missed calls blasting from the device would bear dark news.

Sparing the details because they are both painful and personal, the intent of the distraught caller was to inform me that one of my young horses had to be euthanized after falling down, fracturing a vertebrae and becoming paralyzed. The pain of loss is always devastating. The pain you feel from losing a pet is a special kind of terrible. I have always struggled with the loss of pets, as everyone usually does, but my deep emotional connection with horses makes their demise even more shocking. Especially the ones that entered the world before my eyes, from a mother who also took her first breath in my arms, whose mothers-mother was my very first horse. Three generations of four-legged love was gone in a single voice mail.

Scott arrived to the hotel room just as I was hanging up the phone. His timing was impeccable because he was there to put his arms around me as I broke down. I was sad for my beautiful filly and her pointless demise but it was magnified in spades by my exhaustion. So the sobs and shudders came in crashing waves; some for her and some for other losses many moons ago, finally breaking on this day's shore. Red faced and cried out, I let Scott have his freedom to get back to his own daily regimen. Determined not to add to his stress load, some switch flicked inside me to pull myself together and get on with the show. There was a lot of road in front of us that wasn't going to get easier with me being a wreck about an animal.

I decided to mention it to very few fellow riders as it was my bad news, not theirs. Needless to say, it still took an emotional toll. Her name was Rapide, the French word for "quick", because as a baby she ran like greased lightning. Adding insult to injury, her name was everywhere I looked. Quick mart, quick wash, quick meal, and the like. Passing signs like these, especially if I were out of earshot of anyone else, I'd hang my head and start to sob. As the weeks wore on, the crying subsided but I'd still get a painful lump in my chest anytime my thoughts drifted her way. I miss her still and think of her often.

The evening felt like a time warp. Eyes raw and head throbbing, Scott and I headed down to the outdoor courtyard to have a much needed drink. We sat in a corner table in the waning sunshine with a few of the other riders, including a family member of the Wates, riding to support his family and their exceptional foundation. Monty was a charming fellow, accomplished cyclist and a keen conversationalists; we found his company welcome and easy. One glass of rosé helped me shift to an easier mental gear plus being surrounded by jovial companions and the laughter from the roaring 20's costume party happening in the courtyard, revelers bedecked in perfect period costume. Somehow the French manage to do everything better. The women's dresses and headwear, feathery boas and satin shoes could have come straight from the epoch itself...and probably did. No cheap dime store costumes for these bonnes dames. Their enthusiastic laughter was difficult to ignore and helped in spades to melt my dour mood. We'd find downy reminders of their late-night *fête* lining the corridors early the next morning.

↔

I was presently sitting in a beautiful banquet hall, once a refectory, still decorated with original frescos though now lined with large round banquet tables instead of long wooden slabs. Dinner was being carefully laid out on a raised stage at the far end of the cavernous space, buffet style, and the offerings were copious and smelled as heavenly as the ghosts of so many years of pre-meal prayers. No grace for us, just a heathenly stage rush once the servers indicated we were free to help ourselves. In three minutes flat the spread was bare. Not a speck of protein in any form was spared from the ravishes of a clutch of hungry cyclists. It was near embarrassing or would have been, if I wasn't so famished myself. Instead I buried my head in my plate and shoveled perfectly cooked salmon with fresh lemons and parsley into my mouth. I followed that with potatoes dauphinoise. And that with a homemade ratatouille. Then a few mini savory tarts. More salmon. Then a small plate of local cheese, two plates actually. And finally, dessert.

Over the span of the three week tour, the group would have the pleasure of the fellowship of several members from the Wates family, including the ever-sunny Rick Wates, another Wates brother, as well as Mr. Andrew and Mrs. Sarah Wates. Devoted parents to the late William Wates, the namesake of the Trust, their presence on the tour was an inspiration. Monty and Rick would ride the majority of the tour with us, neither a slouch on their machines and Mr. Wates himself would ride several stages, bespokely attired and well mounted on an electric-assist bicycle (he's of a particular age where one has earned the right to a bit of battery back-up).

It's hugely beneficial to have the Wates family so committed to the tour. They are a down-to-earth family doing a very noble thing to help those less fortunate. Not only do they get to stay physically involved in the event that helps to fund their charitable trust, the participants who have worked hard to both complete the colossal task of riding the 3,300 kilometer course, and also raising a considerable sum for the honor of doing so, get to put a face to the name of their benefactors. It humanizes fundraising on both the giving and receiving ends which incentivizes future donors and is the very goal of a well foundation.

That evening we also had the special opportunity to meet one of the beneficiaries of our fundraising. They were the first of our "charity visitors" and not only did they get the chance to introduce themselves, they also got to spend the day riding or volunteering along the stage. The William Wates Memorial Trust supports more than a dozen youth-based charities, including Access Sport, the recipient of the Trust's largest ever grant. Their mission is to build as many community hubs as they can in some of the most economically depressed boroughs in London, a model that US cities could emulate with much return on investment. They focus heavily on BMX and cycling clubs, including the construction of parks and tracks, but also support climbing, boxing and programs for disabled youth.

Johnny, a young member of one of the BMX Legacy programs, talked a little about how his program and the Trust have made an impact on his life. It was a touching moment and we were all impressed by his bravery and poise to stand up in front of a hall of strangers and give a speech. His heartfelt thank you to the room of riders for raising money so he and others like him could continue to ride their bikes, was a touching moment. My eyes didn't stay dry for long and a quick glance around the room told me I wasn't alone. It had been a day full of emotion for everyone.

The stage had been a challenge and ended with an exhausting encore, thanks in no small part to the weather and bad news. We went from relentless morning drizzle to scorching afternoon sun to a headwind strong enough to give the impression we were pedaling in place. Add to that our group of Lifers had already totaled almost 800 miles and nearly 43,500 feet of climbing in six days...and these were the "flat" stages. So much for easing into things. While Phil may have over-estimated the time it would take for my own body to start agreeing to the idea of endurance cycling, I was genuinely feeling less like a radiator at night and was able to get out of bed easier each morning.

I still had lingering soreness in my knees and hips for the first 25 miles of each stage and my sit bones had not yet forgiven me. Plus, my clothes were starting to get tight so either I was building muscle or doing a better job than I realized packing in the calories. Scott could only ever talk about his knee and ankles, but who could blame him. He limped when he walked and bore the permanent grimace of a man in continuous pain. He was also looking fitter and slimmer by the stage, damn him.

I may not have been looking the part of the epic cyclist but I was sure starting to feel like one. I had come to France fairly sure of myself and my cycling abilities, at least in the sense that I could reasonably picture making it to Paris in one piece. I had done some racing, mostly cyclo-cross and gravel road events, ridden plenty of rough miles and technical courses. I knew the basics of bike fit and set-up and felt pretty dialed-in, reflected often about my position on the bike and how to improve it, understood how to get to the top of climbs without coming completely apart, had a handle on nutrition and grasped the fundamentals of group riding and pace lines. I felt competent and confident on the bike from day one. But as any of the best cyclists will tell you, pro and amateur alike, there's always more to learn and the only true teacher is the road. Every day, every mile on this country's incredibly varied terroir and infinitely diverse terrain was a lesson in cycling. If you want to get good at it, you just have to ride your bike. If you want to be great, you have to ride for a lifetime. I only ever wanted to be accomplished. Here was my chance to ride a lifetime of roads all at once, with France as my teacher and you better believe I was paying attention. Today's lesson was about letting go. In a sense, both literally and figuratively. I had voluntarily decided to let go of my inhibition, fear and self-deprecation on the bike and somewhat rather forcibly to let go of my pain, sadness and sense of loss in my heart. I'd hoped this was the hardest day. Tomorrow was a new month. A fresh start. And the only way to get to the finish was to put one pedal in front of the next.

STAGE 7:

Finding My Legs

July 1st, 2016 ~ L'Isle-Jourdain to Lac de Payolle. "It won't be as hard as that." Phil Deeker, ride leader, answering the valid question about the difficulty of climbing the Col d'Aspin when compared to Puy Mary.

"101.6 miles and 7,533 feet climbed. I'm tired. I feel emptied but not defeated. Restless sleep with wild dreams. I was starving when I woke up. Today was about trying to refill my batteries. It was a good day to be on the bike. I was reminded to find wonder in the little things. Like the archetypal Frenchman who smiled at me, wearing his striped shirt and felt beret, baguette in one hand, newspaper rolled under the other arm, ashy Gauloises hanging from his lips."

"Except for the straightness of the roads and the early headwind, section 1 of today's stage was not too shabby. My legs felt decent but right from the start I knew it was going to be tough going on the chamois. Section 2 was a struggle to find my legs but whatever we ate at the second rest stop did the trick (pâté and butter sandwiches plus Ian's coffee) because we had a good section 3 push to the lunch stop. Awfully steep category "4" climb, which I suspect the next time it shows up on Tour will be a category 3. Followed by an equally steep collection of descents. The bike is running well today."

"We somehow missed an arrow after lunch. We went straight when we should have gone right. I must have been taking photos of Scott and rolled right past it. It took about 5 or so miles before something started to feel wrong. It was a gamble to turn around and backtrack without knowing for sure if we were lost. We'd been riding solo for hours anyway, so it was hard to tell. We joked about just riding along on our own adventure if we never saw another green arrow. Back on track soon enough though the landscape is beginning to change again. Less lush vegetation and more white stucco and grey stone with tile roofs instead of slate. The swifts are back. So are the Tour de France decorations."

"Our morning and mid-day sun has retreated and the air is cool and cloudy once more. We started to see roughly hewn mountains rise up sharply from the horizon. Lumps of green hidden by low slung clouds. Signs for ski resorts gave hints of the impending climb. We followed a busy two-lane road, mirroring a shallow river. Then took a right hander onto the road leading to the summit of the Col d'Aspin. I'm certain the view to the top was stunning but as the clouds had rolled in by the time we started our ascent, we couldn't see a thing but grey."

"I'm starting to appreciate the very helpful signs that provide all sorts of pertinent information to the toiling cyclist. Like how many kilometers long the climb is, at what kilometer you happen to be riding, how many kilometers left (they conveniently count down and not up), the average grade of the next kilometer, etc. It gives your idle mind something to do while your legs are pumping away. I found a delightful rhythm on this climb. Maybe it was the womblike experience of being enveloped in a low, damp cloud or maybe it was because I could see only the *slick rotation of my front tire, but I found the effort pleasing and the rise of the road beautifully gentle. Unseen are the jagged snowy caps of tomorrow's mountains. Then I turn up the road and pedal into a wall of fog. Thunder clapped ominously. It began to rain. Thick drops splatted on the pavement. A cold wind started to blow against my wet core, slowing my enthusiastic progression."*

"Another switchback and the rain pelted me sideways. The conditions became disorienting. I was soaked and starting to shiver and I had no idea how far it was to the top. I hadn't paid attention to the last sign. I pulled over to put on my wet jacket just as Scott came around the bend. He can layer-up, no handed, pedaling uphill. I'm not that skilled. I warmed up plenty pushing hard on the pedals after that, feeling a drive to make up lost time for stopping. Somehow I found another gear and left Scott in the greyness behind me. I crest the summit and can barely see the sign demarking the occasion. The video crew was there, so I asked for a hand in getting a picture, then waited in the freezing rain for my partner to come over the rise. Made him pose for a picture as well, though he didn't seem as keen."

"The relentless rain made our drop down to the other side slow and deliberate. We were soaked and shivering, but the support vans were waiting with blankets. While waiting for the buses, I took a video of free-ranging cows. Lovely and tawny with soft, full tails at the tips like horses' tails. The tune they make is a welcome melody when the day was devoid of any other sense except the sound of your own breathing. Must stop having two glasses of wine at dinner. Can't be good for the legs. Be sure to look up that fragrant flowering crop we passed today...was it garlic?"

↔

It's amusing now to read such journal entries, most of which I
hadn't laid eyes on since I wrote them during the tour. I had
intended to build this story from those pages, using them only
to spark memories without including the passages directly but I
think it would have altered my voice as it sounded in the thick
of things; influenced not by the passage of time back in the non-
cycling world, but directly by the long days of riding, the
impact of the weather, the physical and emotional demands,
what I ate, how I slept and how many glasses of wine I drank
before lying in bed to scratch out a few paragraphs.

Perhaps my biggest anxiety came not from the giants on the
horizon, not the slippery descents that followed, not even the
endless line of speeding cars that would graze their way past
but the idea of not being able to remember everything. I
worried that I would let the fatigue cloud my memories and
that I'd be unable to recall the days, save for the most epic of
situations. Or worse, I'd only remember how hard the climbs
were, or how tired I felt, or how brutalized my body became.

My fears were not unfounded. Memory is a fickle device,
inefficient at best, fleeting at worst. I am thankful now for my
decision to keep notes, which is not habitual. I never even kept a
diary as a kid. But it felt like my best defense against the very
human nature of forgetfulness, especially during times of
stress. The journal has kept its promise by providing both
direct evidence of the day's events as well as the tiny breeze

105

needed to fill the sails of my memory when there was barely a ripple on the glass-flat surface. With one exception. This stage, stage 7, eludes me. No matter how many times I have read the paragraphs in my journal, even looking through photographs from my own camera, I can't seem to remember much about this stage. So that speaks to two great suppressive forces of nature; the weather and fatigue. Most people these days have flown in planes. Remember what it feels like the instant that plane flies right through the center of a cloud? Then you'd have a sense of what it might be like to ride your bicycle that way, hour after hour bereft of the depth of any landscape or presence of horizon. Then think of the most tired you have ever felt. Now multiply it seven times. Then throw in sadness and joy, elation and depression, smiles and frowns, laughter and tears plus buckets of rain, a sunburn, windburn, some saddle sores, sore joints and muscles, a few bruises and constant thirst and you've got a fair handle on how riding seven stages of the Tour de France might leave a person feeling. Pretty dog gone good. And I'm not being facetious. The point I'm trying to make is that despite the bombardment of factors, man-made and au naturel, I was still getting out of bed every morning with the desire to get back on the bike and do it all over again. I just seemed to hit the point where I was overloaded with exertion, emotion and the elements, leaving little room for recall.

I suppose I shouldn't beat myself up too badly over it. Of the nearly 2,200 miles we rode all at once, it seems plausible to not remember each one of them. I'm still surprised that I have no recollection climbing the Col d'Aspin except for the few moments it took me to pull over and put on my rain jacket. And I had to think really hard to extract it. I do remember being pissed off. One, for having to stop in the middle of what felt like a spirited effort and two, because I wasn't skilled enough to put my jacket on while still pedaling. Technically, I only had to stop to zip the damn thing. I could remove layers and replace them one-handed but when it came to taking both hands off the bars to work the zipper, I just couldn't manage. I still haven't mastered it. I can envision the patch of mountain around me, a small stretch not surrounded in fog. The road surface was wet and smooth and the air smelled earthy and clean, the sound of rain fall on leaf and tarmac alike rhythmic. There was a break in the cloud off my left side, where the slope fell away towards to valley and I could see a little patch of green down there and maybe the silhouette of a lake. On my right, the land rose sharply and there was a streamlet forcing its way through some loose rocks and wildflowers, funneling over the road. It may have irritated me then to stop, but now I'm happy I did or I may have remembered nothing of the climb at all.

I still recall the ride feeling easy, the weather notwithstanding. I remember passing other riders, their fuzzy forms, hunched over their bikes in a protective posture from the cold rain. A few muttering attagirls but most saying nothing at all, preserving their calories for staying warm and propelled. I don't remember summiting but I have the photo to prove it and another one of the videographer filming Scott crossing the summit himself.

I've already put this Col on my "to-do-over" list, preferably on a sunny day, as I hear the views from the top are spectacular. For now, I'll just have to take everyone's word for it. The only thing I remember about the descent is the very bottom, where Scott and I took a left into the wide gravel lot, nestled between the slope and a narrow stream, now churning brown with slope-side flux. The support vans were there, the staff waiting to wrap us with the packing blankets usually reserved for transporting our bikes between stages. They were a welcome sight.

We had a long wait for the bus to collect us from the soaked finish line and drive us to our hotel, several miles away in Pau. The bus was currently ferrying the first of the riders to finish and we had missed it, meaning we'd be waiting until all the remaining riders got off the mountain. Which also meant waiting in wet, cold kit and an over-worked chamois. Mistake #1: not storing a dry change of clothes in the support van. Mistake #2: wearing a soggy set of bibs for hours on end. Never, ever will I make these mistakes again. The consequences are cumulative and dire.

Scott headed off to the make-shift physio tent and I to the only source of heat, the souvenir shop/bar/café combo across the pea gravel parking lot. A dozen or so other riders were already camped out there, dripping clothes hanging from every chair back, packing blankets wrapped around their waists like kilts. I should have done the same, but sometimes the best lessons are learned to hard way. The grumble from the barkeep when I

walked through the door was audible. Here comes another
sopping cyclist, drenching my establishment with dirty water,
demanding coffee and beer with no regard to my tile floor and
no grasp of good manners. I can't say I blamed him so I offered
him to warmest smile my frozen face could muster and an
enthusiastic sing-songy *bonjour*.

The simple act of saying hello never fails to garner at least a
trace of civility in France and as a small business owner in a
country where there are increasing numbers of customers
walking in on their cell phones without so much as a wave of
the hand to acknowledge your presence, eye contact and a basic
greeting are highly valued. Therefore my subsequent request
for a *café allongé s'il vous plait*, was met with a nod of the head
and a hint of smile. Only then did I feel entitled to drip dirty
road spatter on his floor as I made my way over to the tiny
radiator around which gathered the rest of the crew in various
states of dampness and disarray.

Still wet, but now warmish, I drained my micro coffee and
settled into a chair by a back window already fogged over by
the collection of humid beer-drinking bodies in the room.
Something large and pale moved beyond the glass. Then came a
faint but resonant sound. Then a low rumble and another shape
moved in the distance. Then the unmistakable bellow of a cow
to her herd mates. I was out the door in a flash, blanket trailing
in my wake like a cape, camera at the ready. Behind the building
and over a swollen muddy stream was a vast rolling pasture, its

outer reaches disappearing into the soupy mist. A stone's throw away was a herd of off-white cattle, ambling along the waterway, bell-clad and tingling their ethereal tune.

I made a mess of my road shoes and my cleats would never function the same again, but a little muddy walkabout was worth catching a few minutes of the scene on film. What I captured was surreal footage, a micro moment in the ancient lifecycle of the haute Pyrenees. The cows, a hardy, sure-footed breed known for their high quality meat and milk. Used as draught animals in past lives, they are now free to roam the sloping pastures as they please, gorging themselves on the thick summer grasses and rare wildflowers of the region. Probably belonging to the modern breed known as Blond d'Aquitane, though these cows had upturned horns more common of the rare medieval race of Lourdais or even some mingling of the two, existing under the catch-all name of Blond des Pyrenees.

Even if you view bovines as nothing more than a steak on the hoof, the sound their bells make as they lumber along, chewing idly streamside triggers something deeply instinctual in your gut. Our survival, especially in these unforgiving environments, has for eons depended on their sacrificial offerings of milk, meat, hide, labor and companionship. That they are given the freedom to live their own lives with little human intervention on the rugged slopes of the Pyrenees is a wonder of agriculture.

↔

Dry clothes and dinner were our sole desires during the uncomfortably long bus ride back to the hotel. It was slow going down the circuitous road. Plus, we had waited for an eternity as the last of the stragglers inched down off the climb. The rain and treacherous road conditions made descending the winding road a white-knuckled experience even for the brave at heart and especially slow-going for the apprehensive.

Fortunately, our evening meal was at a neighboring café instead of the hotel restaurant which meant we could come and go as our schedule permitted instead of having to be prompt and present for a single service. Scott and I squeezed into a corner booth in the main dining room. We both picked the poulet with house made frites. Alcoholic drinks were always on our dime, but at 4 bucks a glass, we could hardly complain. I had two glasses of local Jurançon, dry and pale and satisfying.

Phil was there with his usual hilarious pictogram and loads of insight into tomorrow's playdate with the Tourmalet and Friends. He knew these giants better than anyone else, so I should have paid his speech closer attention. But in the warmth of that restaurant and the two-glass buzz in my head, I didn't much care how hard tomorrow would be. We finished up and went back to the room and slept deep and dreamless, better than we had in a week.

STAGE 8:

Terrible Mountain

July 2nd, 2016 ~ Pau to Bagnères-de-Luchon. "Don't worry, you're all quite capable of climbing Cat. 1 before breakfast." Phil Deeker, ride leader, speaking to the stone faced Lifers before the start of a major climbing day, beginning actually with a Hors Catégorie and not a "mere" Category 1 after complaints came pouring in from the lack of sufficient morning fare at the hotel.

"115.9 miles and 14,360 feet climbed. Mon Dieu! What a day. No breakfast to speak of except for a day-old croissant and a pilfered banana. Assassins! No transfer this morning thankfully but we're joined by a slew of new cadets. Forty eager climbers with fresh legs to be tested straight away by the Bad mountain. The infamous Tourmalet. I actually found her rather pleasant. Not so terrible after all. I fell into a nice sustainable rhythm, locked onto the riders ahead of me in the distance and reeled them in one by one by one. I found this approach an entertaining way to climb. I plugged away at the grade until I was climbing all alone in the vast grey nothingness. Then pedaled on, up and around and up again. Breathing steady and humming a little tune. Too bad about the weather. So much drizzle and fog. Not a view to be had for 360 degrees, except for the road directly in front of my tire and the occasional roadside cow attraction. Bonjour Madame Vache! Au revoir Madame Vache. More rain and then the wind came. Then suddenly, I was at the top."

"It was surprisingly crowded for the conditions, although it is a rather famous attraction and well visited in the summer. I waited my turn for a photo next to the summit sign, then Le Geant, the finally the Jacques Goddet plaque where I placed a memorial pin for Paul. He would have really loved this climb."

"By the time Scott made it to the summit, took more souvenir photographs and paused a few moments at the feed stop, any heat we built up during our uphill effort had dissipated. Time to get off that rock and soon. The descent was incredibly cold. I'm told its beautiful, but I wouldn't know. Nothing but cloud around every turn. My teeth were chattering so violently it was travelling down my arms. Then I began to shake and I had to concentrate on not death-gripping my bars and causing the whole bike to shudder. I wanted to get down that pass as fast as possible, just so I could start the next climb. It was the only way to get warm again. Bring on the Hourquette."

"I think this is the loveliest climb of the entire Pyrenees. Maybe because it's the only one we actually got to see due to it not being completely socked in by fog but it sure left a good impression. Easy on the legs and the eyes. Blanketed with pines that fragranced the cool afternoon air. Herd after herd of lazy jingling cattle. Their big soft eyes blinking, their wet muzzles chewing away. Then we passed small groups of voluptuously round horses, stout as the mountains they call home, beautiful babies by their sides. I smile at them and tears begin to well."

"The valley opens up before us and we're riding through a deep green paradise, lined on both sides with fast moving streams. There are huge birds of prey soaring in the sky, scurrying ground-dwelling mammals, their fur soft and thick. Around a bend and we come face to face (and face to ass) with *donkeys! With the richest brown coats I have ever seen. Right in the middle of the road. Sleepy, splay-eared and unflustered by our advance or by the rain that has begun to fall. I slow down to snap a few rolling photos. I pity the pro peloton who will not have the chance to slow roll along this pass. This is not a stretch of road I could ever imagine racing. There is so much to see. The pavement is so narrow. I stop at the highest point of the climb to take a photo of the marker plus the two foals enjoying a mutual scratch. They eyeball me with caution but equipped with teeth and hooves, they know I'm no threat. Finally the safari ends with an incredible descent, best of them all. The ribbon of road was engineered perfectly for a bicycle. Even in the rain, there was plenty of grip and a reliable camber around each of the corners. We took our time to be safe, going much slower than we cared to. We'll come back when the sun is shining and the roads are dry and Scott has two healthy legs with which to pedal."*

"The third climb of the stage was a real slog. Mount Whatever It's Called. Col de Cranky. My sit bone pain had come back with a fervor and I had a serious case of lunch legs. Scott was really hurting uphill and leaving me in his afterburners on the down grade. I was squirmy and irritable both climbing and descending. The rain had been falling steadily for hours and I was getting colder and colder by the kilometer. Plus, the gray curtain had fallen again I was getting bored with nothing to look at but the three feet of road ahead. Felt like the starring role in a documentary about fog. We got to the top, where thankfully feed stop 4 was stationed. The coffee stop. If it weren't for Ian and his French press to warm up my insides, I'm not certain how I would have finished the stage. That and the spare jacket the lovely human Heidi loaned me. I was shivering in the most uncontrollable manner, so hard I was spilling my espresso."

"I was sure the descent would kill me by rendering my popsicle fingers useless to squeeze the brakes, ending in my careening off the slippery road into the rocky abyss. It could have happened. I heard at dinner that a few of the tail-end riders had to sit in the support van to warm up. Another few took that van to the hotel. I hardly blame them. The road down was treacherous. Phil had warned us about the cow poop. Fresh cow patties, thinned into a soup by the rain, leached down the track. That's some slippery stuff."

"Three down, one to go. Col de Peyresourde. The last climb was supposed to be a nasty Category 1 but for a reason unbeknownst to my brain, was a forgiving test of my legs. The heavy rain had chased away the low lying fog and we could see the landscape again. It was another visually appealing climb, with surreal villages perched steeply aside the road with the mountain at their backs. An average grade of 8% but not a long effort and I would have enjoyed the spirited descent into Luchon (my fingers had finally thawed out) but the bone chilling drizzle started again as soon as we bettered the summit. Frozen limbed and beyond amused by the time we rolled into the hotel parking lot. This hotel is a grand old thing and our room is spacious and comfortable with plenty of hot water in a generously sized tub. Nothing like a perfectly cooked duck breast to help you forget the woes of your long day. The carafes of red wine on each table didn't hurt either. Please remember to visit again. And ask for the same room on the top floor with the great view of the mountains."

↔

This day was so full, it felt like three had passed instead of one. Many of the stages to come would feel like that and I still have a hard time believing the whole experience was only three weeks out of my life. It felt like months. And when it was over, by the time winter arrived in six quick months, the summer trip felt years ago. Long days on the bike were beginning to get addicting. We were slowly becoming machines, or melding with our machines…strangely half-human-half-bike; our only duties to eat, pedal, sleep. Sleep was still coming easy. Well-fed at dinner, properly hydrated, a glass or two of wine to soothe the legs and we slept like bricks.

One of the most relieving things about being supported with feed stops is that you never have to squirrel away snacks or rely on anything to sustain you but real food. That is, no gels, no chews, no protein bars and no bottles filled with glow-in-the-dark sticky liquids. Neither Scott or I ever had those things in our pockets and aside from the occasional "emergency banana" eaten in motion when our stomachs wouldn't stop rumbling between rest stops, never needed modern supplemental cycling nutrition. It was liberating.

We had become efficient at providing our engines the calories it needed to get the job done and in exchange our legs kept turning the pedals without too much protest. It was a delicate relationship and one that could come apart if we didn't keep our end of the bargain. There were stretches were I could feel fatigue building but I could ask for one more push or another few kilometers and my legs learned to trust that if they provided the power I was asking for then I would fuel them soon enough. And I learned how to keep my promises. Not to say that my legs and I didn't have a disagreement from time to time. While I never cramped nor bonked, I did suffer for a few stages from "lunch legs". This was probably due to the sheer amount of food we consumed at the third stop of the day, which was always lunch. For the first ten or so miles after, my legs felt like two sacks of horse feed were strapped to them. I'm certain every blood cell in my body had rushed to my stomach to put all that fromage to work, a sensation that left me sluggish and lightheaded. As the tour wore on, things began to equilibrate. I stopped craving so many calories and my legs stopped requiring a very French two hour lunch break.

Unfortunately, my sit bones were on labor strike. Something was wrong. Something beyond just saddle discomfort. My chamois was in a delicate state thanks to the last week of riding in wet bibs but there was also a deep and agonizing pain around my left sit bone. I thought in the days leading up to now that I had just bruised it but a quick chat with Dr. Julian confirmed that I was likely suffering from bursitis or more elegantly nicknamed "weaver's bottom", an inflammation of the sit bone bursa. Think of it as a small cushion between the end of the pelvis and the tendon that runs over it connecting your thigh and gluteal muscles. Irritate it enough by, I don't know, riding over a thousand miles in eight days and you make it very, very mad. It's like a blister that you get to sit on, one that gets more agitated with every pedal stroke. The only option I had was to gobble down super strength ibupropen and hope it burst on its own. It would, the nasty little bugger, but only after another 12-hour day of misery.

On the bright side, there was plenty to see and do to keep my mind off my backside. Almost immediately after departing Pau, signs of suburbia fell away revealing hour after hour of abundant green. Deep green forests, high green meadows, wide but shallow blue-green rivers tumbling over grey-green rock. There were trees everywhere. Maples, oaks, chestnuts and a few pines. Plus, the ubiquitous rows of plane tree lining the street through every village. Favored by the Greeks and imported to France by the Romans, legend has it that the Trojan horse was carved from the wood of their mighty trunks.

History tells us that Napoleon ordered the planting of millions of stately planes to shade his marching troops. Given the right conditions they can live for nearly 4,000 years. Whatever their true history, only the trees know, but they soften a sunny day and brighten a dreary one. I was fond of riding beneath their colonnaded, leafy archways.

On the outskirts of the town of Lourdes, we would turn south and march steadily towards the start of the day's four climbs. The fascinating town of Lourdes has somewhat of a dual personality. On one hand, it's a hotbed of outdoor recreation; hiking, downhill mountain biking, hot springs and paragliding (the sky was dotted with parachutes).

The town is better known as a major holy pilgrimage site because of a the miracle that happened there in the 1800's. A young girl named Bernadette heard the voice of Mary, no less than 18 times, in a grotto while collecting firewood. Today, nearly 6 million visitors a year come to Lourdes to see the grotto and visit the cathedral and pray to be miraculously healed. Even from the ring road above town, we could see the throngs of tourists. The place was jamb packed. My curiosity piqued, I'm motivated to visit to see what all the fuss is about. Some of the other riders have been and say it's nothing more than shops selling trinkets and tiny bottles of miracle spring water. From where we were riding, the town looked pristine and white and inviting and I suspect it receives so many visitors because it is beautiful and historic and more than just a place to buy tacky souvenirs.

We had managed to ride under a partly-cloudy sky for the first half of the day, but as we left the safety of the last rest stop, could see the clouds building a small army and knew the rain was imminent. From the gravel lot to the first hairpin of the D918 was about five pedal strokes, then the pitch of the road began to build toward the crescendo of the Tourmalet. Not quite the "circle of death" as the similar 1983 Tour de France stage 10 was termed, we only missed repeating it by leaving out the Aubisque and tackling the Col d'Aspin the day prior. No matter, we would climb the category 2 Hourquette d'Ancizan and the category 1 Col de Val Louron-Azet instead to keep us honest.

The road leading to the summit of the Tourmalet wasn't difficult, it made us pay attention, but wasn't draining and we had the company of a turquoise river billowing photogenically over time-polished boulders and the soothing sounds of water finding lower ground. Up ahead were long pillared snow tunnels, built of steel and concrete, designed to keep the roadway open during heavy drifts. The road through them would flatten for a bit and despite the reprieve, you sensed suffering cometh.

The Tourmalet has a bad reputation. Dubbed the "terrible mountain", it is a legend among its Pyrenean peers and legendary by cycling standards due to the sheer number of times it has been used as a torture device by the Tour de France. Eighty so far. It is more accurate to say that it's famous *because* of the Tour, or because rather the bending of the truth about its very nature resulted in it being added to the roster of new and untested climbs. The telegram sent to organizer Henri Desgrange in January of 1910 read "Crossed Tourmalet stop. Very good road stop. Perfectly feasible". In reality it was a snow packed, slippery animal track, barely passable by car at the height of the summer much less the winter. Now somewhat softened in its old age thanks to pavement and electricity, in 1910 the Queen Col was as raw and as wild as they come. After not exactly spending a jaunty day in the mountains, the first man to cycle over the summit famously shouted at the Tour officials, *"Vous êtes des assassins! Oui, des assassins!"*

The grandiosely mustachioed Octave Lapize was no doubt grumpy at having to ride his single speed machine over 326 kilometers (in one day), including 7 mountains; many of those miles being unpaved and several of those summits being snow covered. I'd be a little testy too.

Another rider to have a bad trip over the mountain was Eugene Christophe. The tough as nails Frenchman was famous for many feats of cycling prowess over his lifetime of professional racing but most notably for the "Tourmalet Incident", whereby he was penalized time during the 1913 race for allowing a boy to work the bellows of a forge while he repaired a broken fork incurred on the menacing descent. This, the judges concurred, qualified as receiving outside assistance and was strictly forbidden. The time it took to get himself back in the race, plus his penalties, cost him the lead. I'd like to mention that in addition to being the French National cyclo-cross champion many times over, he also kept a meticulous diary of his races throughout his career. Perhaps that's how we know so much about this mythical rider and his never-give-up attitude. There is a plaque commemorating Christophe at the site of the former forge in the village of Sainte-Marie-de-Campan where one could pay a visit and hope to glean a bit of gumption for when the going got tough on the surrounding terrain.

Not long after we exited the snow tunnels, the fog grew dense and the rain began to fall once more. A light rain, but it was consistent accompanied by a bit of a breeze. Whatever view we

121

had of the landscape was gone. Looking back now through pictures online and in books of the Tourmalet, the scene looks both stunning and totally unfamiliar. I heard it was a beautiful climb, but I wouldn't know. I couldn't see a damn thing but the occasional sign reminding motorists to adhere to the 1.5 meter passing law. The sign is so pleasant too...a happy motorist giving a smiling cyclist a wide berth. It really should be that simple.

The roadside tombstones begin clicking off the kilometers of the official climb. Not actually tombstones, they're lovingly if not morbidly nicknamed that because of their traditional shape. White with yellow crowns and originally stone or concrete, they are slowly being replaced by modern metal road signage to better withstand the elements and provide more information on limited real estate. The Terrible Mountain when approached from the west is 19 kilometers long, so you get 19 chances to see her famous markers, each one counting down and supplying you (whether you like it or not) with the average gradient of the proceeding kilometer. I won't bother telling you what that is in miles, trust me, it's better to remain blissfully unaware and just keep pedaling from one marker to the next. Kilometers go by much faster than miles anyway.

From the start of the climb to the summit, you'll gain 4,606 feet (there you go, you imperialists) at an average gradient of 7.4% with a maximum gradient of 10.2% near the top (it only hurts for a minute). If you don't speak French, here are the basics on what the new metal signs read, top to bottom, left to right; the mountain you are currently climbing, maximum height of the summit, current altitude of the sign, distance to summit from the sign, stick figure of a cyclist on an impossibly steep road, and average gradient of the kilometer to the next sign. You can thank local businesses for these signs, as they are the ones who essentially fund them in an effort to increase cycling tourism to the area. Spending your euros in their shops, restaurants or hotels is an easy way to do just that. It's a nice feeling to be wanted and enthusiastically welcomed and have an entire network of roads and climbs so elegantly demarked for your cycling pleasure. *Merci beaucoup la France.*

Considering the weather, I was surprised to see so much traffic on the way up to the summit. I passed several riders in our group, making their way up in their own time, plus a handful of unrelated riders who nodded the nod of cycling kinship. There is a certain comfort of another human being on a bike on the same climb who understands what you're going through even if one of you is having an easier time of it. It's the same nod you get from riders passing downgrade, except theirs is to say, "you're nearly there, keep it up".

I don't remember being overtaken by any cars on the climb, though saw many heading down as we were going up. Lots of holidaymakers and passenger cars with bike racks and one spectacular '60's era Citroën 2CV, the tiny mighty "deux chevaux" and a matching mini-caravan hitched to the bumper.

Sitting behind the wheel was surely the original owner, her grey hair in long braids and a look of satisfaction across her lips. I'd be proud of those two horses too for making it over that infamous pass. I gave her the thumbs up and she returned with a wave. Another few decades and that could easily be me. But for now my world was on this bike, in the rain, on a stretch of road high on a mountain, buried in the dense grey landscape and listening only to the turn of the cranks and the filling of my lungs. I would look up the road and see it disappear into the fog. It was surreal. Then a turn, a sign, sometimes a cow. There'd be the occasional rider ahead and my cadence would increase as I locked eyes on their wheel and reeled them in, meter by damp meter.

The wind picked up and I knew that meant the top was near. A slight right hand bend and there was the summit. A café on my right, a souvenir shop on my left. Small schools of cyclists gathered on both sides of the road, layering up, taking photographs, smiling and congratulating one another. Before I could begin my own self-celebration and then be back at the summit to celebrate Scott's arrival, I had one small piece of business to which to attend. Many months ago I made a promise to the friends and family of a cyclist named Paul van Delst to leave a memento of his life at the top of Tourmalet. Paul had visited the shop to drink a coffee mid-ride with friends a few times each year since we'd opened. A tall, handsome and jovial native Australian, Paul and I always loved to talk about climbing France's famous Tour mountains and he was

124

particularly supportive of Scott and I getting to do just that. I think those chats sparked something in Paul to do the same and he would often mention about getting over himself someday. Sadly, while on a ride with a friend in the Blue Ridge mountains of Virginia, Paul collapsed while riding his favorite single speed road bike up a climb he knew well. Despite immediate attention from his riding partner plus that of a nurse who happened to be driving by, Paul's life ended on the roadside, next to his bike with a friend at his side.

We had been contacted to see if we might be willing to help re-home his beloved bicycle with the proceeds to be donated to charity in his name. We would help, of course, but that didn't feel like enough and my heart was heavy at the thought that he'd never get to climb the mountains we so recently discussed. So I emailed, asking his friends for a small token of Paul's life that I could carry with me on the climb, something that could be left at the summit in his honor. He had proudly become a US citizen some time ago and to celebrate, bought and wore a small pin bearing one American flag and one Australian flag. It was the perfect symbol of his pride of both countries, his two homes.

I thought of him often that day. He and I shared a love for single speeds and I considered how the effort would have felt with only one gear. It would have been a piece of cake for him honestly and told him so, my words dissolving into the atmosphere. I like to think he was responsible for the breeze that day on the mountainside which lucky for me always felt like a tail wind. I doubt his pin still sits where I placed it, blown away by wind or snow or carried away by a curious visitor. Hopefully it goes on another adventure but nevertheless for a while anyway, it sat above a marker on the right side of the summit, bearing the year 1927 and the altitude of 2,115 meters. A nice quiet place at the top of the Tour's most heroic climbs.

I felt a sense of relief having the Tourmalet behind me. It was one of the three mountains that bothered me the most out of the entire tour. So much, that I would make her the subject of a tee shirt we sold to raise money for the trip. The other two were Ventoux and the Grand Colombier in the Jura. Those mountains also had shirts, one printed in purple and one in blue, white and red respectively. Tourmalet was in yellow. They were the giants that really gave me pause when I scanned the route map, studying the list of categorized climbs over the three weeks of stages. I didn't do that anymore once we were in the thick of it. It was too overwhelming at that point, but in the months leading up to the start, I would scour the internet studying profiles and ride reports, watching old grainy television coverage of the glory days of the Tour. It's never a good idea to compare the suffering of an over-taxed world-class professional road racer to your enthusiast-self. It's just not as hard as that in real time. So with one big bad wolf tamed, there were only left two to go, and those were still days away. This little red riding hood foolishly began to relax.

Turns out the terrible mountain wasn't so terrible after all. *Au contraire*, as I would find out soon that as far as mountains go, there'd be worse. So with a false sense of repose, I carved down the road into the chilly mist towards the next climb of the day, the Hourquette d'Ancizan.

The "fork" of Ancizan is not a mountain itself, but a 6.4 mile mountain pass that runs roughly parallel to the Col d'Aspin. It starts out with a bang then mellows enough for one to take in the spectacular sights that surround it, when the weather is clear. Just as we reached the pass, the rain stopped and the clouds parted enough to expose the wide, verdant valley. It was incredible and was the kind of landscape you might reasonably expect an herbivorous dinosaur to come lumbering out of the woods. It was primeval and untamed and the terrain of legends.

In fact, as the story goes, the very word "Pyrenees" comes from a Greek legend as old as the hills themselves. Hercules, the so-called hero, made a drunken and unforgivable mistake by raping his gracious host and King's daughter during a visit to Gaul. The daughter, Pyrene, delivers unto the world a serpent and afraid of her father's wrath, confides her fear to the deep woods of her homeland. Her lamenting brings forth the hungry beasts of the forest who viciously attack and kill the poor girl. Now sober, Hercules hears of her fate, buries her and with much remorse, bellows her name across the mountain tops and through the valleys. The land rumbles with the sound and echoes back her beautiful name for all time.

Though no mythical serpents fill this mountain pass in our day, the fields are brimming with wildlife and more noticeably herds of free-range cattle, horses and Pyrenean donkey. The ancient practice of transhumance is still routine here where these animals are seasonally moved from lower pastures in the winter months to higher pastures in the summer month to take advantage of the rich diversity and plentitude of grazing on the mountain slopes and passes. There are literally animals everywhere, including along and routinely *on* the road itself. You may occasionally get the sense that you are but a speck in the vastness of the landscape, but trust me, you are never alone.

The presence of all those untethered animals was felt on the next climb, or more precisely on the descent. The rain had come again, along with the fog, the wind, and falling temperatures. We had a final rest stop before the road fell away from the summit of the Col d'Azet and I couldn't have been more grateful. It was a proper climb, with a consistently steep chain of switchbacks and while the pictures I've seen of it are incredible, our view consisted only of the road surface and the rain spattering our glasses.

Once we reached the top we were sweat-drenched at the core but our extremities were numb. We were also starting to tire and were badly needing Ian's magic brew. By the time we sufficiently refueled at the rest stop, we were both starting to shiver. I was having serious doubts about my ability to continue on. I knew a steep descent was imminent, which meant I'd be exposed to more wind and cold before tackling the last climb of the day in the steady rain. Fortunately, Heidi, one of the very talented physios attending the feed stop with Ian, offered me her spare coat. Her selfless decision saved the rest of my stage and who knows what condition I'd have been in if I'd attempted to finish underdressed. She very likely saved my trip. She was certainly doing her darndest to save Scott's. She attended his injuries every evening and was an expert at taping his knees and ankles so he could keep pedaling.

We left the comfort of the feed stop and began the tedious navigation of the descent. Phil had made it a point to warn the group about the dangers of this road in particular. Between the tight hairpin bends, the narrow road, the rain and the slimy animal excrement, it was a mess. There is absolutely nothing more treacherous than a ten-foot wide strip of wet tarmac lacquered with liquid cow poop. Downhill. At speed. On 25mm wide tires. Despite the danger, I remember it being one of the most satisfying stretches of the stage. Thanks to Heidi's emergency jacket, I was warmer than I had been for hours and able to focus on the challenge. It was like a live action version of the classic '80's video game Frogger. We had to dodge the poop, then the pothole. Brakes! Corner ahead, then pedal, pedal, pedal. Caution, more poop, then rocks in the road! Car coming. Uh oh now we're slipping..slipping..slipping, shit..shit..shit. Brakes! Now turn, then pedal. Phew. The road flattened and we sat up, pleased that us both had stayed upright, and we shared a grin at the adventure.

The last climb of the stage, the Col de Peyresourde, went by in a welcome flash. Like the Tourmalet, it was first used by the Tour in 1910 and the leader over the summit was again Octave Lapiz, though he apparently had no nothing colorful to say about it. Maybe he was too fatigued, like we were, and just wanted to get to the hotel for a warm shower and a hot meal. Such were our dispositions this late in the day and while the view of sturdy stone farm houses hanging over the edge of the narrow road with the slope falling dramatically away was spectacular, the hours spent in the saddle were starting to numb our enthusiasm for sightseeing.

A category 1 climb should feel like a climb, but truth be told, I found it rather forgettable. Chalk it up to the accumulation of all the day's mountains, the panorama of grey clouds and the dire situation of my sit bones. The pain had become so severe and specific, it was hard to concentrate on anything else. Climbing was especially torturous. I could only find relief when I stood on the pedals and got out of the saddle though I was only strong enough to do that for short stretches. For the remainder of the effort, I was sitting, spinning away *tout à gauche*, grimacing all the while. It was time to find out what was really going on. I couldn't spend another day squirming about, dreading any contact between my backside and the bike seat. Until then, I managed to enjoy the run into Luchon upon the gentle road under the setting sun with the brief respite in the weather.

We had passed a true test on this stage and completed a string of notable climbs in one of the cycling world's most revered regions. We should have been proud of ourselves but were too tired to notice. It was a big day on the pedals by anyone's standards and so full of elemental wonder it was nearly too much to take in. And that was in the dreary drizzle of a summer storm. I can only imagine the power of a sunny-day experience in this place. A comfortable room in a grand old hotel, a toothsome meal and a limb-melting carafe of wine helped to soften the edges of a hard day and despite our discomforts, we both looked forward to one last push before a well-earned twenty four hours of rest.

STAGE 9:

A Long Way Down

July 3rd, 2016 ~ Vielha Val d'Aran, Spain to the Principality of Andorra. "Be careful what you wish for." Author muttering to herself while baking in the Spanish sun after announcing at breakfast that a warm weather forecast would be a welcome change.

"109.4 miles and 11,854 feet climbed. This day was hell. Whether the last 8 days have finally started to catch up to me or the bus ride in the morning sun made me drowsy, either way I did not feel like riding today. Fortunately the morning climb was agreeable. Long but not steep and the views went on for miles. We almost got an escort back to France because of permitting issues but fortunately Jaime has both a lovely Spanish accent and an authoritative air about him and managed to sweet talk our passage despite the group's detainment by the Spanish police. But we were allowed to continue our morning slog and were rewarded with a satisfying panorama of Catalonia."

"I was temporarily revived by the fastest, most harrowing descent of my cycling life. Empty, wide open highway pointed downward mile after mile after mile. It would bend, eventually but so slightly as to not require any braking or slowing to make the turn. I've never gone so fast on two wheels without a motor or sped downhill so long without touching the brakes. I would have thought that kind of speed impossible. So fast, I started to

scare myself with unintentional thoughts of disaster. All kinds; blow out, speed wobble, brake failure, pot hole, broken bones, road rash, complete annihilation. Dude, get a grip. I had to force myself to shut out the urge to panic. Instead I concentrated on being smooth and deliberate. Towards the bottom, I finally risked sitting up slightly to scrub some speed so my brain could catch up to the blurred landscape. It was at once terrifying and epic."

"Adrenaline was still pumping long after we left the feed stop by a teal blue lake, then the real work began. Another huge HC category climb, Col de Cauldron, freshly paved with the blackest tar. Radiating asphalt fumes and searing heat. The dry, sparse vegetation provided scant amounts of shade. The road in some spots was literally melting. My no-good tire was spurting sealant in my face with every rotation."

"Hot, dry wind blasted us in our sun-burned faces all the way to Andorra. The parade of cars entered the mountain fortified country through a tunnel but we went around and were waved through the border gate without a second glance. Then all hell broke loose. Horrifying, gaseous traffic! It was like cycling on a live NASCAR circuit while a Moto GP race is simultaneously going on. Hot, stagnant, choking air. From the looks of the fumes bellowing out of chopped tail pipes, exhaust regulations can't be too stringent here. So much noise. So opposite of the peace of the last few days. We have a feed stop on a hot sidewalk next to the busy road. Stayed too long changing a tire. We navigate the snarl of the dense city center then grind our way up an urban climb with a direct blast of the afternoon sun. The signs say 8% average but Scott's Garmin read 15-20% in places. I'm in terrible pain and say so. Scott wills me forward.

So is he, so I stop sniveling. For the first time I wonder what it would be like to quit. Then we rolled along a ridge above the chaos and made a long loop around the tiered suburbs towards the Beixalis. Dreadful bugger. So steep, I can barely turn over the cranks. Passed a few riders who couldn't and were pushing their bikes up the climb, one staggering step after the next. No choice but to pull over to let a van squeeze by on the narrow lane and it took all the power I had to get started again."

"Our last feed stop was waiting at the top and we were greeted by Ian and his cheers and the encouraging thump of his signature techno. Scott grabs a Coke and a Snickers candy bar, a sure sign he was in trouble. I ate half a bag of roasted chicken potato chips. I was clearly not thinking straight. It was so late in the day, we were given an update about the route. At the bottom of the descent was an option; left arrow to the hotel, right arrow to the HC giant, Arcalis but we'd have to hurry to reach the summit before dark and would most certainly descend after sunset. We had no lights in our day bags so we opted out of the climb. No love lost. Don't really care if I ever see Andorra again. As payback for my hostility, I'm almost obliterated by a red sports car on the way to the hotel."

↔

Some days you wake up knowing it's going to be a rough one. You can stand up and take the blows with as much humor as you can muster or bury your head in the sand and wait it out. I had over a hundred miles in the Pyrenees to pedal by day's end that negated the second option. It all started with breakfast. The lack of it to be exact. There was a movement happening among the bunch. You've heard of the term "early bird gets the worm", well it turns out that the earlier the cyclist is to the breakfast buffet, the more carbs they get to inhale before the rest of the herd arrives to mow down the field. Get there ten minutes before official breakfast time and you had your choice of fresh pastries, croissants, toast and jam, honey, yogurt, muesli, cereal, hard boiled eggs, cheese, cold cuts, fruit and their juices, coffee and milk. Get there two minutes after the breakfast room is supposed to actually open and it looks like a plague of seven-year locusts dined and dashed.

This phenomenon was contagious and by day nine, the Lifers had all gotten wise to the outbreak of breakfast war. Which meant if we wanted a full belly in the morning, we'd have to get up earlier and earlier, cutting into an already limited amount of sleep. I ate my sad looking baguette-end with a pat of butter and honey and headed to the bus. I was already well-versed in the art of seating strategies, so as soon as I heard the call to board, strode energetically in pursuit of the front row of the bus. Scott has always suffered from motion sickness and since he could only manage to hobble around, I took it upon myself to secure him a seat with an unencumbered view. I was too late and had to settle for a middle row. I may have lost today's battle but it would only make me more vigilant in my pursuit of the prime seats and the choicest croissants.

It was a silent bus ride. Everyone was beyond tired and trying to catch a wink on the way to the start of the day's stage. Despite the claustrophobic fogging up of the bus windows from all the hot, sleepy breathing of my comrades, I found the ride relaxing. The view outside was magical. We departed the belle epoch beauty of Luchon and snaked our way above the spa-town slow and steady, the road's width just enough for the bus to traverse without a wheel rolling off the edge. What a catastrophic mess that would make. No shoulder, no guard rails, just a sharp edge of pavement between us and the bottom of a sea of ferns and pines.

As we climbed out of the valley, the shoulders of the mountains were so steep, there were narrow waterfalls splashing out of crevices in the rock face around every turn. Our driver, like all the ones before him and all the ones after, was an expert at his craft and remained unfazed by the delicate procession. The bus seemed to climb the whole hour drive but when we arrived at the expansive empty parking lot on the Spanish border that would be our departure point, there were still peaks soaring around us in all directions. They were incredible yet I was unenthused.

It was going to be a long day in the saddle no matter if it was the last day before a break. Having an exam on Friday doesn't make the questions easier. It just means you get to sleep in on Saturday. This exam had four questions and big ones at that.

The 13.7 mile long category 1 Port de la Bonaigua, the 11.7 mile long category 1 Coll del Cantò, the 11.6 mile one-two punch of the category 2 Côte de la Comella and the category 1 Col de Beixalis and finally a crown jewel of Andorra, the HC giantess Arcalis. In true Tour fashion, both the Bonaigua and the Canto are routinely regarded as *hors catégorie*, but in an effort not to steal the spotlight from a summit finish on a notoriously difficult climb, were unceremoniously demoted to give the top honors to Arcalis. Not that it made much difference. Each mountain, no matter how it was classified, was still a bloody big rock between me and my rest day.

As would happen sometimes in the mornings, we all started out as a bunch, eager to get on the clock while the sun was still shining its gentle rays. Phil had warned us to wear our sunscreen and we were well aware by now that he had the tendency to under report the severity of forecasts. If he said it would rain a little, it would be a deluge. If he said it would be hot, well, then prepare for a roaster.

Riding in a big bunch has never been my cup of tea, but climbing in a bunch was the pits. I was squirmy and uncomfortable from the first pedal stroke and needed some space to slow down or sit up as my discomfort required. Plus, I'd always been a bit claustrophobic in a pack and hated being pinched between unfamiliar wheels or worse, against the guardrail with no exit route. So to escape our rolling road-block formation, I made my way to the left, downshifted and put some power to the pedals. Scott, ten riders or so back, understood my intentions to find some clear tarmac and deftly bridged his way to my back wheel. We were both struggling to get the lead out of our legs, especially with a morning climb right from the start. Ahead was a mile or two of wide open road and we fell into a steady cadence before cresting the rise to find a small group of our guys stopped on the shoulder. They had been ordered to halt by the *Guardia Civil*, Spain's version of the *gendarmerie*, or known in the States as the highway patrol. According to Jaime, who spoke fluent Spanish and was currently living in Barcelona, a group of our size was supposed to have possessed a permit to cycle through this particular stretch of highway.

It was difficult to understand the nuances of the conversation between Jaime and the officers but unbeknownst to any of us (or the tour organizers) groups of cyclists greater than 10 were required to apply and be granted a permit. That would have given us express permission to ride these roads as well as provided a police escort for safe passage. It appears we were being detained indefinitely, or at least until Phil could arrive to help sort out the predicament and it was possible that we would have to back track and take the bus across Spain into Andorra. Jaime explained that while our detainment seemed drastic, Spain was simply a country that expected us to follow the rules. It had nothing to do with us being cyclists, or foreigners, just that we had not followed the proper procedure. It was for our own safety and the safety of traveling motorists on this high-speed mountain pass. It was difficult to disagree with that logic. It didn't help our case that none of the 80 or so riders present had no form of identification, no passports and didn't speak Spanish.

Ever the gentleman, composed and polite, Jaime apologized profusely for our ignorance of the local laws, explained our situation (we were riding for charity after all…) and confidently negotiated our case. After a half hour of calm exchange and gesticulations indicating that the officers would show mercy on our motley bunch, an agreement was reached for our continuation. Since groups of ten or less were allowed to cycle without a permit, that's what we would do. We were instructed to leave ten at a time, wait 15 minutes, then another ten could depart. By the time the whole peloton was back on the road, staggered as we were, the sun was blazing high in the sky. Without Jaime's presence and diplomatic conduct, we would have likely been escorted directly to the French border and given a friendly boot across. I wondered if he'd ever considered running for office.

It was tough getting the pedals turning again after the delay. Plus, my stomach had already begun to repeatedly remind me that it was way past time for food. Shut-up stomach, I grumbled, forgetting my legs, as they were still half asleep. The road swept right and on the high, wide horizon was the top of the climb and the ski station of Baqueira-Beret, with the imposing stone restaurant Cap del Port. Complete with turret and slate roof, it looked quite picturesque standing guard at the summit. It was surprisingly empty up there, no line of traffic snaking around the final hairpins, the hot wind whipping across the empty lots of the resort. Our first feed stop of the day was posted in the furthest lot from the ski lifts and offered an expansive view of the region beyond. Unlike the tightly packed peaks of the French Pyrenees, this part of Spain's Pyrenean range was reminiscent of Montana, with its big sky and infinite views. Scott and I rested for a while on a quiet bench, enjoying the sound of the birds and the wind before the sun got too hot and motivated us to get a move-on.

What came next, or down rather, was the highlight of the day. The experience of descending from the pass at la Bonaigua was once-in-a-lifetime. I say it that way because I'm not certain I'll ever go that fast on a bicycle ever again though I'm not ruling out another attempt. It was impossibly fast. We hadn't seen a car for hours and the road both directions of travel was gloriously wide. There must have been four lanes at least and they didn't skimp on the quality of the concrete. The road surface was smooth as black glass and free from any debris. The face of the mountain was to our right and a deep wide canyon to our left. Without a cloud in the sky, the scene was perfect.

Once over the pinnacle of the summit, we pointed our wheels downward and in three pedal strokes were beginning to pick up steady speed. We kept pedaling and our speed increased fivefold. I was turning over the 50x11 with all the cadence I could muster. And just like that, there was no more pedaling. The only proper thing to do was tuck in tight and hang on for the ride. Yet our velocity was ever accumulating. Usually the road begins to level and so does your speed but not here on this tarmacked luge, sheltered between the swell of two giant Spanish mountains. The road was engineered beautifully, with its gentle sweeps and constant pitch and it seemed to go on forever. My bike was surefooted and glued to the ground and I simply had to look where I wished to go and it took me there, smooth and steady as she went. After a time, it began to feel almost too good. I hadn't touched my brakes in a very, very long way and I seemed to be gaining still.

For most of the descent I was tailing Scott for a few bike lengths, until I closed the gap and would swing out of his draft and catapult around him. He would do the same until he overtook me and then would jump ahead. It was a good game of slingshot and kept my mind off the obvious dangers of high speed descending. We started to decrease the distance on riders down the road and Scott took the chance to slip into their larger and more effective drafts. They began to sling shot off each other and left me several bike lengths behind and trailing. Size and weight had the advantage here and I was happy to watch them enjoying the opportunity to go even faster. And that's when it happened. No, nothing terrible. No catastrophic tire failure or speed wobble or wayward small mammal darting across my path.

The thought of the possibility any of that happening at any moment was nerve wracking but I also realized as soon as the dark thoughts left the folds of my brain that they were completely unreasonable and willed myself to think about something pleasant. Though I *had* been having tire trouble earlier in the day. Then I *did* hit a rogue rock a few stages back. Dammit. Stop that and get a hold of yourself.

The urge to decelerate was growing strong. I was losing the ability to concentrate on the road. I just needed a minute to reset. At these speeds it was safer for me to just raise my head and shoulders into the wind and my body would act as a sail, increasing drag and scrubbing just enough pace to let my overworked neurons catch up. Then I feathered the rear brake a smidgeon for peace of mind that they *were* still attached to my frame and *yes*, they still worked. Nice and easy, smooth and deliberate. Just a ten count was all it took and my eyes and brain were back in sync.

The slow rising tide of panic subsided and I dropped my chin back towards the bars and let the bike regain a bit more speed, but by now the road had begun to level out as we wound our way into the approaching village. It wasn't the first time I had spooked myself downhill but never when the conditions were textbook for descending. Nevertheless, our instincts are there to keep us from doing terribly stupid things, so if mine said to sit up and turn the volume down, there wasn't any harm in paying them heed.

For all the thrill of that fast morning decent, however much it recharged our batteries, the second climb of the day tried in earnest to drain them empty. El Cantò was up next. The name in Catalan means "the song". It was a cauldron and the only thing singing was the melting tarmac as it popped and squealed under our tires. Yes, it was that hot and no, I didn't believe it either that roads could literally melt before your very eyes. It had been mentioned over the years by Tour commentators; a condition I only thought possible in the magical television realm of professional road racing through steamy foreign lands. The sticky black tar was radiating immense heat and overwhelming fumes the higher we climbed towards the noonday sun.

It was slow going and despite the lovely view of the valley behind us, this climb made me grumpy. Plus, I was dangerously low on water. Some way up the climb we passed a pair of riders lying in the grass on the side of the road, taking what little shelter there was from the intense heat. The low slung shrubbery and sparse smattering of trees made this tiny pocket of shade a veritable oasis and I made the hasty decision that we'd pause in our labors to join them. It was Jaime and one of his usual companions, Tim. Tim was a jovial Australian cyclist big on presence and short on words (and occasionally clothes). Our company was not unwelcome and our companions shared our distaste for the current state of the weather.

From feast to famine, wet to dry, the pendulum had swung a

wide arch indeed. After a much welcomed rest stop awash in food and drink, the rest of the afternoon went by without fanfare. Scott and I took alternate pulls into the hot wind. Now that we were traversing along in the shadow of the mountains and not exposed on their uncomfortably hot crowns, we were actually beginning to enjoy ourselves. Just before the mouth of a long gaping tunnel, we hung a sharp left. The skinny road, narrower than the current highway along which we had been travelling, was a welcome break from the high speed traffic that was buzzing relentlessly alongside us for miles.

Though fast and sometimes closer than comfortable (without malice I might add), passes for the last few days had been generally safe, but after a while the frequency of those passes and the volume of cars on these bigger roads made me feel shell-shocked. Just as you start to feel less vulnerable, someone passes a little closer than you'd been passed for hours and your fragility is thrown right back into your face, clear and present.

I remember telling Scott after the tour was over that there were times I was so sensitive to the noise and smell and presence of passing cars, that I had the urge at times to get off my bike and curl up in the roadside drainage ditch just so I could make it all stop. The constant din of traffic became intense enough to drive me mad. Thankfully, I never did actually climb into the ditch but there were moments when I allowed myself to think that I could if I needed to, which somehow helped me cope.

But my newfound traffic coping mechanism would soon be put

to the ultimate test. We thought we were heading to the "quiet" mountain domain of Andorra. Then we passed the border crossing straight into vehicular hell. These roads were the exact opposite of quiet. It was like trying to ride through a go-kart track surrounded by a Superbike circuit surrounded by a NASCAR oval. But only if you ripped off all the participants tail pipes. And then blindfolded them. It was mayhem and we were unceremoniously funneled right into the heart of the chaos as we tried desperately to follow our neon arrows in a sea of belching catalytic converters and thumping basslines from rolled-down windows and laid-back seats. I've done my fair share of motorcycle track days but saw more knee-on-the-ground cornering (with high-heeled wearing passengers perched precariously on the tail section) than I thought physically possible.

After spending too long at the last rest stop and letting ourselves get too flustered by a tire change and tricky chamois cream re-application (no bathrooms at this stop, just the back end of the stifling box truck and believe it or not there was a line for that) we were feeling anxious about getting back on our bikes so we could get the stage completed before dark. The last stop of the day wasn't exactly restful. It was barely wider than the sidewalk we were perched on, squeezed between the vans and the concrete railing keeping us from tumbling into a fast flowing river. It was hot and bare and the pop up tent provided little shade. But Sarah had done the best she could in choosing this spot, as there was nothing else available in the bedlam of the area or she would have certainly found it. No matter. We needed to keep moving. Phil had warned us at breakfast that If we didn't keep up a steady pace, some of the group would likely not make the last climb in the daylight. We hadn't slouched out on the road, but may have lingered too long at a few stops along the way for one insignificant reason or another. Pause for shade here, take in the view there, nature break, tire change, etc. All those extra minutes really added up and by the end of a 100 plus mile stage with climbing, could add two hours to an already 8 hour day.

Just as soon as we left the sidewalk rest stop there was an arrow pointing right. We turned and the road immediately rose at an escalator-like angle, straight up the side of a leafy hill before disappearing into a tangle of trees and switchbacks. Our legs did not agree to the instant onset of output necessary to turn the pedals at so steep a grade. We both let out an audible groan as the fatigue began to build and burn relentlessly through our over-worked bodies. I remember hating this climb with all the passion I could muster, which believe it or not was still a lot. Scott had found some secret gear and was pedaling away as cool as a cucumber, leaving me a few bends below a whimpering mess. It was steep and not that far removed from the mayhem below and the noise of the traffic on those crowded streets were still haunting me. Plus, the silent war between me and my sit bones was reaching its zenith and I was feeling like the loser. The pain on this climb was excruciating. It was so steep, I had no choice but to push to the back of my saddle and right onto those throbbing little protrusions. I could stand, but only briefly before my legs screamed their own battle cry. Up and down and up and down, balanced between the dismay of sitting or standing as I wrenched out this dreadful ascent. It was short for all its steepness and Scott waited graciously at the top under the shade of a tree while I dragged my self-pitying bulk up over the final few meters.

We had a mile or two of reprieve across a flat spot at the foot of a second layer of mountains where the roads were less crowded and the heat less intense. Though it still wasn't the rustic country I had envisioned in my mind's eye, just a collection of modest suburban houses arranged tidily in neighborhoods in the shadow of a soaring mountain backdrop. I kept daydreaming that at every bend of the road we'd find arrows pointing the way to the end of the stage a quiet hotel, though I knew in the pit of my stomach there was more hell to come. And come it did, quickly and far steeper than the last of our tribulations.

Oddly, this climb bothered my throbbing derrière half as much as its predecessor but messed with my head two-fold. It was slow and deliberate and took incredible focus to turn the pedals over one at a time without fail. I could hear Scott several bike lengths ahead, his deep breathing interrupted by a half-chuckle at the ridiculousness of the grade. My brain was beginning to question my body's sanity, asking more than once why it shouldn't just send the signal to unclip and walk. My body, well trained to ignore such stirrings of dissent, kept pedaling and I was grateful for its loyalty. I stole a breath to yell out to Scott, how much farther? Seven hundred meters, he responded. Ok, I thought, I can do that. But it was a lie, albeit not an intentional one. Around the next corner was a marker declaring the summit at seven kilometers, ten times the distance he erroneously quoted. My eyes shot daggers at his backside. I thought it unlikely I'd ever forgive his fabrication. I remember telling him so in the most unbecoming string of expletives and then regretted the tirade for its waste of valuable oxygen.

At the summit was Ian and what a sight he was for sore eyes. His signature techno and caffeine aromas were echoing off the top of that mound like a beacon to weary pilgrims and come they did in spurts, inching their way over the top of the road with tongues wagging from slackened jaws, eyes glued on the façade of the van and the signature green arrows guiding us all to sustenance. We lingered to cheer others over the summit and didn't worry much about the waning daylight. We were spent entirely and the urge to go on was slowly extinguishing among the good company. Go on we did, though towards the hotel and not towards the glory of the last HC climb. We had no fire left to tame that dragon, no lights to show us the way or keep us from harm and no impulse to see the view from her heights. I think Scott was relived with our decision and still looks fit and proud in the photo I snapped of him in the setting sun on the way down to the hotel.

As either payback from a vengeful mountain or as proof that continuing up it would have been a bad choice, I was almost flattened on the way into town by a red sports car driven carelessly around a corner at high speed. His tail end had broken loose and was drifting across both lanes of the narrow road. When his rear wheels regained traction, it spit him across my bow. I had just enough brainpower left to steer left into the oncoming lane and we passed each other with inches to spare. Scott, who was several turns below, missed the whole incident but surely heard the last of my energy expended in a string of ugly words at high-volume. At the bottom of that near-death descent rested two arrows on a post. One left towards the comfort and safety of the hotel and one right towards the final climb of a departing day. Scott had taken a left and I without hesitation followed him.

I lamented the decision not to climb Arcalis almost immediately upon arriving at the hotel. Then spent the next few hours of cleaning bikes and washing kit feeling guilty about it. So much so that Scott got rather annoyed at me mentioning it every fifteen minutes and swore aloud if I said it again, he was going to look into getting a separate room. But this is what I do. I beat myself up about my perceived "failures" in a compulsive way. Of course, I'm over it now. Well, almost. I actually do care about seeing Andorra again because I won't be satisfied until I've actually finished stage 8, Arcalis and all. This was the first of several important lessons in "expectation management".

What exactly did I want out of this experience? Was it to ride every kilometer no matter what? To punish my mind and body and poor husband in the process? Or were we allowed to enjoy ourselves? Save our matches or burn them? Push on the pedals and take risks, sometimes beyond our capabilities and comfort zones? Or safely soft pedal just to make it to Paris in one piece?

This was a turning point and I struggled with such freedom of choice. Having a choice is hard. I wasn't a professional cyclist depending on results to pay my bills or expected carry the weight of sponsorship dollars on my shoulders. This wasn't a race. So what did I have to prove? To anyone else? Absolutely nothing. To myself? Well, that was a different story altogether. We had already covered 1,120 miles in 9 days. It was more than half of the total distance of the entire three week tour and if you've ever ridden a century, that's like riding nine in a row. We had so far climbed more than 77,000 feet, over half of the total ascent of the whole 21 stage route. I really needed a reset. Scott and I had made a pact in the days after committing to ride the Tour de France route that we would ride as far and as high as we could, as long as we were happy and healthy.

That agreement was repeated a few weeks before we even began when we knew Scott wasn't starting 100% sound. Now it resonated more clearly than ever. We couldn't choose for an easy experience or perfect weather or unfailing bodies, nor would we want to, but we could choose the how and what and why of it all and after a infuriating internal struggle, that's the approach we elected to take. The rest of the ride would be about choice not necessity and once I stopped self-deprecating, it was very liberating.

My warm and fuzzy feelings barely lasted through dinner. Scott made an announcement over a bottle of Spanish red that would test my new found resolve. I guess he took my little pep-talk to heart. He said he wouldn't be getting back on the bike after the rest day for an un-foreseeable number of stages. Before dinner he'd had a discussion about his injuries with Dr. Julian and they both agreed that he should stay off the bike or risk permanent damage to both Achilles as well as his knee. Without an ultrasound it was impossible to tell just how bad things were, but the swelling and weakness and pain said plenty. He could no longer tolerate stairs and even standing was becoming a chore. There was no room for me to object. Scott was limping along because he didn't want to let me down but it was time for a reality check. He needed me to be ok with him taking a few days off, if not quitting altogether. That was tough. There was a small, deep part of me that was feeling selfish and resentful and I really, really didn't want it to surface.

It had been a long, trying day. No one in the dining room seemed in the mood to celebrate. The landscape and weather had changed dramatically and the course was shifting towards unknown territory. Some of the staff we had grown to know and trust were leaving, to be replaced by fresh faces and new personalities. Familiar fellows were heading home and new riders, with their nervous, eager energy were joining on for the next week's stages. A few other participants were abandoning from injuries. It was a good thing tomorrow was a rest day. Twenty-four hours of down time was more than we'd had in days and every last one of us needed the chance to recharge our batteries. I've never appreciated a night's sleep more than this one. We drained the entire bottle of wine at dinner and Scott followed that with a few glasses of beer. Yes, we would probably regret it in the morning thanks in part to the altitude, so we swallowed a few aspirin before bed for good measure. Scott recalls being up half the night with various forms of limb pain. I remember absolutely nothing.

REST DAY; ANDORRA:

Independence Day

"July 4th, 2016 ~Escaldes-Engordany, Principality of Andorra. No rest for the weary they say. I was up with the chickens, which was entirely too early. Actually it was the noise of the traffic outside our window that did it. With no air-conditioning, it was too hot to close. We lingered over a great breakfast. Finally some eggs (other than hard-boiled or as a garnish on a salad). I can't get enough of the pan con tomate. Crushed tomatoes on toasted bread rubbed with garlic and olive oil. And Spanish sobrassada. It's nice to be able to enjoy the morning without the anxiety of a food shortage or forgetting to put a day-bag on the support van. We were free to be lazy and forgetful and what a feeling that was."

"Madria Valley is a UNESCO World Heritage Site with 65 summits higher than 2,500 meters! At least that's what the brochure on the bedside table said. I'm not interesting in climbing a single one of them on a bicycle, thank you very much. Andorra is an interesting place. By interesting , I mean dreadful. Crowded, close, claustrophobic. Tax-free, high-end retail boutiques and bad commercial strip-malls where the crowds go to blow their paychecks. It's a shame about all that because the landscape is striking. There are mountains stretching sharply towards the sky all around this clustered, busy metropolis. Think Machu Picchu, but the Las Vegas strip version. I'm also quite convinced that the country has zero emissions regulations, as every car and motorbike does nothing but spew noxious black gas with every piston stroke."

"We rested some then walked way too far to do our load of laundry at a coin-op. After walking way too far back, we had a pleasing lunch of tapas at a local cafeteria. Generous plates of squid, cuttlefish, pig's feet and blistered padrones. It was a memorable departure from the last nine days of cold pasta for lunch. Then we walked (well, Scott hobbled and limped) back to the hotel for a digestif and to sit in the sun on the front square."

"I was restless all day. As much as I found it difficult to accept, Scott's decision yesterday to take a break from the tour was absolutely the right one. He's been suffering for days. His ankles look terrible. Thick and swollen and he says they make a thick thumping noise when he walks. If he doesn't rest now, he'll be taking the broom wagon to Paris."

"I'm crushed and fighting the urge to stop riding myself until he can get back on the bike. I've got my own issues; like an electric pain shooting down my arms stemming from my neck. Not so bad until I have to get in the drops and descend down a mountain…which is every hour on the hour these last few stages. We're quite the infirm pair. Truth is, I'm dreading going it alone. So much distance in a strange land, without my reliable partner…my safety net. We came here together to ride this as a team and now I'm on my own for an untold number of days. I feel rudderless, with no wind in my sails. Tomorrow will come no matter how long I delay putting my head on the pillow. I still don't know if I'll ride without him. Hopefully sleep will bring clarity and courage."

↔

I woke up the morning of our rest day feeling like a sea cucumber. I was alarmingly puffy from my shoulders to my feet. I no longer had any discernable wrist bones or ankle joints. My limbs, while not painful, were warm and swollen. I felt heavy and groggy and slightly out of sorts. There was something wrong with me. Figuring it had more to do with the altitude and the red wine from dinner than anything terminal, my first priority was breakfast and copious amounts of coffee. Fortunately, Dr. Julian was breakfasting at the same time, giving me a chance to finally inquire about my rather significant case of body swelling.

He said not to worry too much about it and if I were uncomfortable, I could take a diuretic. Wanting to know more, I did what anyone these days would do and Googled it. According to the internet, I either drank too much water, not enough water, ate to much salt, not enough salt, didn't eat enough protein, ate too much protein, have an undiagnosed allergy, didn't warm-up well enough, didn't ride hard enough, didn't stretch enough, have a terrible pedal stroke, have a rare and debilitating disease, didn't take cold enough showers, or am making the entire thing up. As it turned out, exercise-induced edema was fairly common, particularly among women participating and training as endurance athletes. So there was no cause for alarm, unless I failed to shed the water weight in a few days' time. Until then, the only treatment was to lay off the alcohol and (gasp!) caffeine, elevate my limbs whenever possible and engage in some low-impact, low-stress exercise like walking or stretching. I'm no physician, so excuse the laywoman's diagnosis but in a nutshell I overworked my poor muscles (no kidding), which produced an excess of lymphatic fluid, which thanks to gravity settled primarily in my limbs. The situation was made worse by low resting-heart rate, the circulatory and hormonal complexities of being female and finally, the high altitude. Aside from my pants not fitting properly and my socks leaving an indentation around my ankles a half-an-inch deep, it seemed like an affliction that would go away in time. Compared to my recent sit bone trouble, which was finally improving, it would do no more than make me sluggish on the bike. As long as it went away by Stage 12, Ventoux day, I had no qualms with feeling like an over-ripe tomato. A nice stroll around Andorra would be just the thing to cure my ills. Scott shouldn't exactly have been walking…not far anyway…but being the agreeable husband that he is, surrendered himself to amble with me (albeit slowly) to find a laundromat and some lunch.

The Andorra of my imagination looked a lot different. I envisioned this peaceful, mountain-top municipality perched above verdant pastures filled with herds of sheep and rustic stone cottages. My mind's eye never could have pictured the thumping, beeping, fuming, whizzing, chaotic tangle that it was; crowded streets and tall, tightly packed buildings draped in a

156

confetti of "sale, sale, sale!" signs. It wasn't the most relaxing spot for a "rest" day and I thought with empathy how the professionals would feel about their surroundings the following week. Then I thought that they probably didn't have to walk ten blocks to wash their own laundry and stopped feeling so bad for them after all.

Given the choice to attempt Arcalis on our rest day (as some of the group did) or eat tapas at El Cachirulo, I'd pick the latter again and again. The mountain wasn't going anywhere anytime soon but great restaurants have a way of falling off the map if you put them off until "next time". Besides, Scott deserved a decent lunch for all I had put him through by accompanying me on my walkabout. He had been looking forward to this place since we started the tour. In fact, it was the first time all day I had actually felt relaxed. Sometimes a good meal has greater value than just a source of nourishment. For two hours we shared that small, quiet space and thought nothing about our aches and pains, pedaling a bike, close passes, bumps in the road, the wind rain or sun. We exhaled, indulged in the flavors of an unfamiliar culture and enjoyed the repose of well-known company.

When I laid my head down to sleep in the final moments of our day of rest, there was no doubt I was depressed and frustrated about the next few solo days. Nevertheless I was resolved to ride. This would be a litmus test of how much cycling was truly mine. In other words, was this a sport, a hobby, or a pastime that I loved of its own accord or did I partake because it was "our" thing, something I had only ever known in the company of a man who introduced the whole two-wheeled world to me and loved it far longer than I had. I ultimately decided to ride alone because I needed to know if I could legitimately claim cycling as my own heart's desire. I could think of no better opportunity to prove my independence, if only to myself.

Tomorrow I would have to claw my way out of this valley, across the highest paved road in the Pyrenees. The next day was a rolling stage through the sunbaked vineyards of southern France then finally, up the very mountain that intimidated me most from the start, the beast of Provence. Ventoux. I felt like I had barely learned how to swim and now I wasn't just letting go of the edge, but diving right into the deep end of the pool.

STAGE 10:

Sans Chaperone

July 5th, 2016 ~ Escaldes-Engordany, Principality of Andorra to Revel, France. "You've lost your chaperone" said Phil upon seeing my solo morning departure.

"123.6 miles and 7,343 feet climbed. It was a relief knowing we were heading back to France. That and the fact that I would get to see Scott at the hotel, hopefully waiting with a cold glass of wine, lit a fire in my belly that hasn't been there the whole tour. I was one of the first riders to arrive at each rest stop the whole day. I put my head down, hands in the drops and pushed hard on the pedals for over 120 miles. It was a satisfying day indeed. I guess the rest day paid off. Although the swelling in my arms and legs and around my joints is still present. I feel like a bloated frog, but even they have a stupendous leap when they put their minds to it."

"The 27 kilometer climb from Andorra went on for an eternity. It started right from the hotel and was an upward, fume-filled slog through morning rush-hour. Busses and cars belching nauseating exhaust in our faces as the weather turned cloudy and wet. There were times when I held my breath. The sky tried hard to not drench us, but it got colder and colder towards the top and I had to stop to put on a rain jacket as the faint drizzle turned to tiny drops of sleet."

"It ended with a post-card panorama of an incredible range of snow-capped peaks that looked more movie set backdrop than reality. Here I am at the top of the world. The weather's almost fine. Wish you were here."

"I tried in vain to keep one eye on the landscape and one on the roads, but the volume of traffic coming off the pass was dizzying. Drivers were on a mad dash for the French border and were wasting no space or time in passing us. Construction didn't help the matter, only narrowed the lanes and increased the anxiety of the congestion. Barely paused at the border, before flying through the remnants of the midi-Pyrenees. This is the place of caves and rivers and felt like very old France. Still, the traffic was distracting from the view. The cars just kept coming. Fast and close."

"Beautiful rolling hills interlaced with bright green fields and soft blue sky. The plowed fields smell earthy and metallic. Even the streams have a fragrance. I can tell when one is close. The road into Ravel was lined with aged plane trees, their shade welcome since I forgot my sunscreen and the mid-day sun was strong in the sky. I had the descent to myself and let the road set the pace, not really pushing anymore, finally remembering to take in the view before the end of the stage. The hotel, a converted monk's quarters, was as beautiful as it was comfortable. Sarah outdid herself. I also think we got the best of the rooms. It is grand. Tall ceilings, a fireplace, a wall of windows. This is the best place yet. Certainly the most French, which seems to irritate some in the bunch. I think it's divine."

"Easy stage tomorrow, Phil announced at dinner. Short and flat he says, through some cycle paths and vineyards. Scott doesn't feel up to riding yet, so I'm going solo again. I'm still

disappointed but far less worried about it than I was yesterday. Tom and Sylvain have offered their company and I'll gladly accept. They are both a pleasure to ride with though in different ways. I'm sad to not get to share the sights of the stage with Scott. I tried my best to explain them at the end of the day, but it isn't the same. His demeanor tonight said he's disappointed too."

↔

I may have lost my chaperone, but I gained some valuable perspective. Most poignantly, by the end of the day, I felt selfish for taking riding for granted. Scott got to see the stage through the window of a car. And that sucks. I got to see the stage from my bicycle and that doesn't suck, despite the fuss I made internally about having to ride it by myself. On one hand, I must have sounded like a total jerk to my husband. On the other hand, I think he knew it was a big step for me as a cyclist and he let me sort it out without rubbing it in that I should have been grateful that it wasn't me sitting it out. Tables turned, I would have felt sorry for myself (for entirely different reasons) but at least he'd be happy as a lark, pedaling down the road. Which reminded me to start feeling less sorry for myself and more sorry for him. I suppose anxiety clouds good judgement. Or lack of experience. Or both.

Either way, this stage was full of life's proverbial lessons. Like: don't forget your sunscreen even though it's cloudy outside, because the sun will come out eventually and you will get burned to a crisp. Or: figure out how to put on a coat while pedaling or don't complain when you have to pull over, in the rain, on the steepest part of climb. Or: if someone kindly hands you a peanut butter sandwich, even if you're feeling bloated and disagreeable, eat it or deserve to suffer from a grumbling stomach for the next 25 miles. Or: having a buddy on a busy road does not make the whizzing cars any less dangerous, they just keep you from focusing on the whizzing cars and their potential for catastrophe and that's something to be grateful for.

Speaking of cars, you might go faster downhill than vehicular traffic but that doesn't mean they entirely like you speeding past them, especially in a construction zone. That just makes them angry and then they honk when they catch you on the straight away. That's ok, because you get the last laugh when you're waved through the border crossing by a handsome patrolman and they're pulled over to have the trunk searched for contraband. See, the French really do love bikes more than cars and the road really is the best teacher. Lucky for me, I got over a hundred miles of private tutoring.

Like most days during the tour, there were many hours spent on the bike and the landscape changed so dramatically, one day felt like two or more. The morning was vastly different than the afternoon, with the cool temperatures and the cloudy skies and the congested terrain. The group was warned that the climb out of Andorra would start right from the hotel door, and it did.

There's nothing more arduous than grinding out a relentless climb in snarling morning traffic, exhaust filling your nose and throat with every inhale. You want to hold your breath but you can't, not for long anyway and when you gasp again for air, the smell and taste of all that pollution is right there on your tongue.

There was no chatting or laughing as we picked our way from block to block, the pack spread thinly in a line, one rider glued to the wheel of the next, hugging the sliver of real estate between the outside line of the lane and the thick walls holding back the mountainside from the roadway. Finally, the road escaped the grip of the city and we could see the tiny cars at the top of the Port d'Envalira. The category 1 climb, first featured in the 1964 Tour de France, featured the highest paved pass in the Pyrenees and offered a reality-defying view from its summit. The mountains in the distance seemed to bend with the curve of the earth and were surreal with their peaks permanently blanketed in winter snows.

The remoteness of the pass should have meant a quiet road but peace was scarce and the beauty of the descent was interrupted by the constant wave of vehicles barreling towards the French border, drivers choosing this route over the costly toll-tunnel directly through the rock. The situation was amplified by road construction, no doubt a last minute effort to improve the surface for the professional peloton's arrival in a week. The weather didn't seem to be helping their progress. Either that or the workers were on labor strike. There wasn't a single construction crew around, just lots and lots of orange barriers and broken pavement.

After barely pausing at the border, I was relieved to finally see the sun come out again. Despite the eventual sunburn it would cause, I was relieved to be back on French soil under a French sun. The road condition immediately improved, ruts and holes giving way to fresh, smooth tarmac and wide shoulders. The horizon was still falling gently away from the lofty heights of Andorra, so it was a fast, fun push past rivers and bridges and grey stone mills built right into the wall of the mountain.

I had been passed on the descent before the border by a dozen or so fast riders, including Sylvain, the soft-spoken powerhouse from Quebec. The rest of the bunch were new guys, no doubt Sylvain was there to leave an impression of his prowess…after all this was his fifth time in a row to ride the entire TDF route. If there was a blistering group on the road, Sylvain was likely to be in it. I hung on for a while, until the traffic and condition of the tarmac got the better of my nerves. I felt safer navigating the hairy hair-pins on my own but a few miles into France, I spotted a lone rider and pedaled hard to close the gap between us. It was Sylvain and after a quick look over his shoulder, he wasted no time in shifting into another gear.

The chase was on and down in the drops, we burned through the kilometers as the road wound down and around and over, following the path of the Ariège river as it tumbled towards lower ground. It was an exhilarating game of cat and mouse and while I was no match for his power, I somehow had the advantage downhill. He later admitted to feeling less confident going down than up. I nevertheless took the advantage when I could get it because as soon as the road flattened, I found myself the *poursuivant* once more. Those few miles were some of my favorite and I can still feel the pedals turning beneath my feet and remember the smell of the river as the road rushed by.

After that the day seemed to blend from one stretch of straight road to the next. I don't remember passing anyone else on a bike, except for the handful of cyclists heading in the other direction, all men, as I had come to accept as typical. In fact, along the more than 2,100 miles of tarmac upon which I travelled, I passed thousands of men on road bicycles. That wasn't the surprising part. It was the barely 20 or so women I saw on road bikes that surprised me. No wonder they gaped at me upon passing. Not the women I mean. They, like I, always smiled and gently waved, a genuine indication of our comradery. Gentlemen cyclists of a certain age generally just stared. The younger set would usually offer a nod. (It is considered good etiquette to at least acknowledge your fellow rider in some fashion. In that case, I suppose a good hard stare counts. It shouldn't matter what kind of bike they ride or whether or not they're as fast or cool as you.) Despite the continued inequality between the sexes in the American cycling industry, we have made some progress. That fact becomes clear when riding in a country where cycling roots run as deep as they are able, all the way down to the very core of the sport, yet only a fraction of those participating are female. Whatever the reason, whether by default or design, it makes me ever more grateful to have the freedom of choice and ability to be sitting astride a bicycle, built just for me, assembled in my own bicycle shop, pedaling down the road, alone, in relative comfort and safety and peace of mind. I seem to have taken a lot about cycling for granted. I had also ashamedly forgotten the appeal of cycling long distances alone.

The impetus of this stage changed completely. There was a surprising simplicity in thinking about nothing other than turning the pedals over and covering the kilometers. I could have used a little less headwind perhaps, but even that encouraged me to put my head down and get to work. I'd never time-trialed and never desired to; though I think I finally understand the appeal. A rider and their machine. The course and the clock. The power and the pain. The rush and the reward. Although there was no timer ticking away the seconds, I was nevertheless driven by an urge to outrun my bashful self. I wasted no time at rest stops, only pausing long enough to eat and refill my bidons. I had arrived so early at lunch, the staff was still setting up and at the final stop of the day, I managed to roll in right on the bumper of the support van. I was enjoying the novelty of being on my own schedule and amused with my new found efficiency. Though as the day wore on, I did begin to miss Scott's companionship and the comradery of the Lifers. As I suspected all along, unless you've specifically set out to ride with only yourself and your shadow as company, there's something unique about the kinship of a peloton. No matter how small or dynamic, their very presence in the same space, sharing the same headwind, sunburn and rain storm or the same stretch of silky new road can completely change the feel of a ride. Although I was genuinely enjoying the day, not having someone there with whom to share all the simple moments was the very thing I feared all along.

Into the rural landscape of the *département* of the Tarn with its rolling gilded hills, I gazed intently into the fields recently freed from their waving locks of wheat. Rolled bales of grain and chaff waited patiently on the horizon to be collected and ground into culinary gold. The space I presently occupied hardly looked real. A narrow road, barely two lanes wide, snaking around hillocks alternating between fallow soil and fertile crops in the bright summer sun. I could only see the horizon as far as the next rise of the road and behind me was more of the same. Aside from the birds swirling around in the atmosphere, I was the only one in view. It was such an agreeable place, it very likely could have been a painting or mistaken for a pleasing dream. I came to a stop and snapped a photograph, driven as I was to imprint it forever in my mind. There were many moments like this, the urge to capture the scene greater than the responsibility of moving onward. And often the view over our shoulders was just as impressive though necessity mostly dictated an eyes-ahead approach to sightseeing. I still wonder what the tour would have looked like if we rode the whole thing backwards. Slowly, my 100-plus mile individual time trial with its rolling course and stiff breeze was taking a toll on my legs, freshly rested or not. (Professionals ride on their day off. Amateurs eat tapas.) With roughly twenty miles left, I succumbed to my fatigue, sat up on the hoods and started to soft-pedal.

There was one last climb to go, one Phil warned might hurt a little. It did, but probably less than it would have had there been someone around to complain to. Short but stout, the category 3 Côte de Saint-Ferréol seemed to sneak up out of nowhere and felt out of place hidden just beyond the beautiful tree-lined boulevard in Revel. But it primed the line for an entertaining descent past the *pont* Crouzet and beyond. The official race route would continue back into picture pretty Revel, already bedecked in blue, white and red regalia. I peeled off the official course and pedaled on to our hotel, the incredible abbey of Sorèze, a thoughtfully restored collection of historic Benedictine quarters. The peaceful, manicured grounds were so inviting and the 200-year old oak shading the back terrace made the perfect place to put my feet up and rest while waiting for Scott to arrive. Pale plaster walls and a softly-gilded, soaring ceiling made the perfect canopy for the mound of white bedding atop the inviting bed. I felt like royalty on her highest horse. And not just because of the luxury of my linens or the breadth of my bedchamber but for the satisfaction of knocking out a good long day on my machine, at a respectable pace, all by my lonesome.

STAGE 11:

Fit Men on Fine Bicycles

July 6th, 2016 ~ Carcassonne to Montpellier. "There'll be a little bump here and there" as described by our ride leader about the next day's "flat" stage containing two category 2 climbs.

"104.6 miles and 4,364 feet climbed. Day number two of my Scott-less adventures. Today I rode with Tom, the metronome and Lionel, the most pleasant Parisian I've ever met. Sometimes we picked up a lone rider or two along the course and sometimes we sat in with a larger group. It was supposed to be a "slow" day for all of us but there's no actual calibration from one rider's slow to the next, so we went along at Tom's version of an easy pace which still turned out to be a workout for my tired legs. I thoroughly enjoyed the company (when I wasn't cursing them all for making me give chase half the day). I always felt a half pedal stroke off the pace."

"It was a rolling course, though described as flat. Funny how two cat 2's are now considered a flat stage by us all. One hundred miles under 5,000 feet is the second flattest day we've had. This morning was a mild start along a quiet canal. We were entertained during the early transfer by an animated, chain smoking bus driver, who despite the language barrier regaled us with a colorful running commentary of the rush-hour traffic. His hand-signals left little to the imagination."

"The day went by surprisingly quickly considering the two additional rest stops (in addition to the official three). One for a fortifying café au lait and nature break in a proper ladies room and one for a cold Perrier on a shaded terrace in the quiet square of a pleasant village. I had forgotten to bring any money when I left the hotel, so owe Tom for the coffee and Lionel for the water with bubbles."

"This was wine country. Hell, the whole country is practically wine country (when it isn't cider country) but this was the first time the land had the personality of wine country. Hot and dry with a unique yet prevalent odor of spent fire-works in the air. First the Auld then the Languedoc regions…vines, vines, a sea of noble vines. Lunch was in an empty, shaded lot surrounded by green leafy rows of ancient vines and we had a nice short break from the mid-day sun. We ride along a curious rolling road, flanked by chalky cliffs, pitted and carved by the slow-moving river now several dozen feet below. This place looks and feels very primitive and I am curiously drawn to it. While too damn hot for me to want to live here, I'm comforted by the sound of a thousand cicadas and the very powerful Frenchness of it all."

"Mon Dieu, the sea!" We saw it from the top of a wide plateau, glimmering, a world away below us. Just for a second and then the road bent sideways and it was gone. I looked more than once to make sure it wasn't a mirage but it was definitely the turquoise blue Mediterranean. I had little sense of my geographical bearings until today. What a feeling to finally be able to place myself on the map. Now I'll know to mark a big red X through Montpellier and its dizzying, rush hour traffic. We're all lucky to be alive. I had fallen from Tom's company just

after the final rest stop but picked up the tail of a group led by Kevin, another lifer. Having never said two words to me before, he added me to his brigade of exhausted riders and kept a keen eye out for my well-being as we navigated the head-windy, hot bike path towards the center of town. The real trouble started when the path ran out and we were pitched onto roads where we plainly didn't belong. A dozen roundabouts and far too many congested miles later, we arrived breathlessly at the hotel. Scott was there, waiting for me in the lounge with a perspiring glass of wine and a spot on the cool tile floor in front of a crowded television. The Tour was on and all eyes were glued to the screen. The stress of the day instantly forgotten among the clink of frosty glasses."

"Tomorrow we cycle across the top side of Provence and up a little bump in the landscape called Ventoux. Technically part of the Alps, though they seemed to have disowned it. Charmingly known as the bald mountain or the beast or the windy one. (Or the immortal, the notorious, the torturous?) Whatever. It's still just a mountain. We go up. All the way if we can. And we go down. Upright and on two wheels."

↔

Montpellier is the gateway to hell. At least during rush hour. I'd like to say that only the evening commuters wanted to see us cyclists flattened but our departure the next morning proved just has nerve-fraying as our arrival the day before. This was the first time on tour where I felt seriously exposed and in danger of being hit. Let's face it. Every time we swing a leg over our bikes and head out on a public byway, there is a chance of being struck by a car. Most of us try our darndest to mitigate such risk and refrain from dwelling on the obvious. Otherwise, none of us would ever desire to ride again.

I'd like to think that most drivers don't actually want to hurt a cyclist, especially in countries like this one where a bicycle is seen less as a road hazard and more as a national treasure. But these drivers were different. They were possessive of the entire road, seemed less concerned with our fragility and had no reservations about using their high-pitched French horns. It's difficult to place the blame entirely on the hoods of these hurried urban motorists, since we were clearly on roads where we had no business riding, especially during the snarl and congestion of the twice-daily commute. Plus, it isn't like those irritated drivers had one cyclist to pass, they had dozens, and we were strung out for many inconvenient miles.

To complicate the matter, it was a roundabout heavy stage (there were 28 total). We circumvented eleven in the stretch to our hotel. Usually benign, the swell of fuel-efficient automobiles turned a paved lazy Suzan into a tarmac death spiral. They presented a tricky choice of approaches. We could wait at the entrance because of traffic already in the circle and risk getting steam-rolled from behind while suffering temporary deafness from the anterior symphony of horns angry for us stopping. Then we'd have to pedal hard to come back up to a safe cruising

172

speed so that we wouldn't get steam-rolled while navigating our way out of the circle. Alternatively, we would start eyeballing the approach and adjust our speed accordingly then shoot the gap and thread the needle right between two cars less likely to steam-roll us while suffering temporary deafness by the surrounding symphony of horns angry at us trying to exit the circle. Oh, and we couldn't forget to keep an eye out for the arrows. Miss one and we'd end up on a concrete merry-go-round from hell.

There was no such thing as safety in numbers. I was better off alone. I tried following the wheel of a solid, trust-worthy rider but the traffic clearly made him nervous and he would hesitate when he should have punched the throttle. Second guessing is fine when it's only your backside on the line. Gaps could come and go and pinch off trailing riders in a blink. Even Kevin's iron-will was no match for the vehicular onslaught. I left him behind too, intent on finding the safest way through the gamut using the power of perception and a little dumb luck. It worked. Barely. Rattled to the very core, I followed the final arrows left into the hotel entrance.

Reminiscent of an American motel, it offered little reprieve from the bustle of the busy metropolis. It did however, have a well-stocked bar and sports lounge, complete with a big screen television tuned into the station broadcasting the Tour de France. All eyes of the riders finishing before me (there were already about dozen) were glued to the screen, limbs elevated on standard-issue furniture, cold beer in their hand and glazed look in their eye. Scott was there too, a smile on his weary face, holding out a glass of cold rosé. He saved me a spot on the tile floor in front of his own chair and I gladly took my place to cheer for our Tour heroes. Today would be the day they tackled Stage 5 and Puy Mary in the Massif Central. To my tired delight, it was a bright dry day and the screen was alive with images of wild green mountains and deep blue sky. Peter Sagan would wave cheerfully to the camera as he got dropped from the tail of the peloton. The Pas de Peyrol would also claim Nibali, Costa and Schleck. With less than 17km to go, a rider named Greg Van Avermaet would pedal away to a solo victory in fine, fine style.

The day wasn't all high risk and stress. Quite the contrary. I don't remember the whole stage, but what I can recall is how languorous I felt in the hot summer sun, riding along lazy rivers and passing mile after long dry mile of vineyards. My dallying mood not helped by the lingering effects of an lethargic lymphatic system, though the condition was quickly waning. Two relatively "gentle" stages, increased electrolytes, less altitude and the capitulation of my legs and body to their new routine were all helping. It was not the 2 or 3 days that Phil advised…more like ten or eleven before I began to ride into shape. Handy information to have for the next attempt at a 2,000 mile cycling holiday.

Here are snippets of the stage that I can clearly recall (the rest is just a blur of black roads and green vines):

In the Aude department there were snails. The first morning stop would have been forgettable but for the quality of the brioche. I had more than my fair share. Plus, I parked my bike against a pale stone wall which, upon closer inspection were affixed hundreds of armored bodies of little grey snails, slumbering away until the sun warmed them enough to ooze into life. Not the Burgundy varietal of culinary fame, but with the quality of butter in this country I could not help from being oddly interested in eating them anyway. Don't worry, I left them right there on that wall, dreaming whatever it is that little grey snails dream.

In the village of Azillanet there was pastis. Feed stop two took place in a pea gravel lot, shaded by young plane trees in a nameless provincial town. There wasn't much to look at but there was a bar and the bar had a rest room which we were permitted to use. I love French bars, especially in the mornings when they are filled with rosy-cheeked locals smoking and laughing and telling each other obviously hilarious tales. Each patron was nursing a delicate glass of cloudy yellow liquor. Some, with an accompanying shot of espresso. This is the classic pre-noon ritual of the South (other regions not necessarily excluded).

In the village of Agel there was the river La Cesse. A stretch of the river was actually a water bridge created for the Canal du

Midi around 1686. Back then, it helped ferry the rich products of the South to important inland port cities. Wheat and wine may have literally been worth their weight in gold. The small stretch that we paralleled was now afloat with small craft and tourist barges, its banks bloomed with shade trees and bright red begonias.

In the Hérault department there was wine. This was the vast and varied land of the Languedoc, an *appellation d'origine contrôlée* for some of France's most attractive wines. In fact, it's the biggest wine growing region in the world. Here, intensified by the summer sun, the air smells strongly of sulfur; not unpleasant but permeating. An aroma reminiscent of the aftermath of a backyard fireworks show just as the white smoke and tiny shards of paper are falling to the ground. Commonly called "Bordeaux mix", the odor originates from the copper sulphate and lime that is sprayed on vines to keep mildew at bay. It's powerful and unforgettable and while I found it strangely appealing and central to my memories of the region, I have no doubt it would singe some nose hairs after repeated exposure (though I grind, brew, drink and generally inhale coffee on a daily basis and haven't tired of it yet).

Bordeaux mix is widely used in the wine industry as a pesticide, and is even approved in the EU for use on vines destined to be labelled organic. There has been some heated debate about its use and long term safety for the very terroir on which it is being applied and the well-being of the very folks applying it.

Plus, it's highly detrimental to the health of fish, earthworms and snails, and you know by now how I feel about snails.

I will always remember this stage for its signature soundtrack, the deafening sound of cicadas. The noise from a million tiny rubbing wings permeated every thought in my head. Their relentless song is so strongly tied to Occitania. It's also linked to many youthful summers spent sweating in the Texas sun, so much that it is hard to separate the sound from the expectation of a painfully hot day to come. Not the case necessarily here, where they harmonized with gusto on a day that hovered in the mere mid-80's Fahrenheit and not the 100 plus of my childhood.

Then there were the dry-stone vineyard huts. With nothing better to do than pedal and scan the horizon, I found them aplenty. Somewhere along the way, deep into another fathomless hour of sun-drunk cycling, my mind and eyes began to wander over the landscape particular of Languedoc. Without a sure-footed donkey, plus the adoption of modern tractors, the flatter more fertile land is now easier to harvest. Rock strewn fields now barren of vines seem like a lonely place and only the small shelters remain as signs that the vintners of antiquity were ever there at all. What remain are small, cylindrical mounds made of mortar-less pale limestone. Some in a half-crumbled state, dotted the hillsides and small valleys on both sides of the road. In tourist literature they are named capitelles, but it would be safer to ask a local what he or she thinks they should be called. They were fascinating, with their pre-historic looks but their modern ingenuity. They looked like a smart place to get out of the mid-day sun after a long day of harvesting grapes or tending to flocks of sheep. Examples have been found elsewhere in France dating to 6,500 BC. The huts in this region were built by shepherds between the 12th and 18th centuries. Their parched white, cone-like silhouettes seemed to coyly foreshadow a grander, more famous pile of rocks a few *département* away. While these blended seamlessly into their landscape, tomorrow's mountain would not. Quite contrarily, as is her style, Mont Ventoux would soar obscenely into the upper atmosphere, visible in the distance for hours, her exposed summit starkly pale against the azure heavens.

STAGE 12:

Beast of Provence

July 7th, 2016 ~ Montpellier to Mont Ventoux. "It's just another pile of rocks." Author replies dryly when asked by another cyclist if she's nervous about tackling the giant climb at the end of the day's stage.

"135.3 miles and 9,272 feet climbed. The 'Beast of Provence' turned out to be quite a lovely climb, despite the nasty reputation. This was the single most dreaded stage for me, made especially so by my solo attempt at the most mythical of road cycling's mountains."

"The day started fine with a decent sleep and a good dinner, despite the rumors of horse meat in the buffet that set my stomach growling unnecessarily all night. The morning was cool and pleasant. I was anxious to get out of the Montpellier morning rush hour alive, so I jumped to the front of a small group of riders and got down to business. Then I sat in with slower groups most of the late morning, intent on saving as much energy as possible. Spent a pleasant 50 miles with Kevin and two or three other riders, each of us taking pulls at the front of our small pace line to stay fresh in the rising heat of the day. Nervous about standing in the sun at stop #2, I left the morning gang to finish second breakfast and headed out with a group of fresh legs…much faster guys than I'd been riding with earlier. Surprisingly, I found I easy to sit in and their unfamiliar wheels

were reliable. These were obviously accomplished cyclists and I appreciated a spot in the rotation. Far less surging and way better jokes."

"Lunch was oddly quiet. Everyone was gobbling food and vying for the shady seats. Nerves were high and patience thin. For good cause. Phil had terrified us all the night before with a bedtime story and accompanying chart depicting a stifling forest of death, 10% grades on switchbacks, on to the moonscape of despair, before finally clawing our way (if we made it thus far) to the bleak and lonely summit. He sold that impressionist painting of cycling hell for a hefty sum, as he had done his other works of art, donating the proceeds to the Wates Foundation. At least our mental suffering was for a good cause."

"After a second helping of watermelon I topped off my bottles and went forth to meet the mountain. She was just there on the horizon, though small and out of focus. I left the café parking lot and immediately caught the back of a group of cyclists, most of whom I hadn't ridden with before. I tried to sit on their tail but they were too slow up the mild climb and too disorganized to help each other stay out of the wind. One rider comes with me, also wishing to up the tempo. This is when I realized I'm turning into a cyclist who is entirely new to me. I'm beginning to get particular about who I ride with, how I ride each section, what I eat and drink, how I sleep, etc. Practically every pedal stroke is under my own scrutiny. This is it, isn't it? Where you truly start to know the bike as an extension of your own self...?

"Up into the heat of the day's first climb, a category 4. I went at it boldly, happy to have empty road ahead and closed down the distance between myself and the beautiful postcard

village of Gordes clinging to the white rock. Freshly blackened, crackling tarmac, laid recently for the upcoming Tour, radiated heat like a pizza stone. The smell of tar was nauseating. After passing through the village, I pulled into the only shade I had seen for miles. The friendly Irishman, in my rearview since lunch, did the same. We shared a few chatty moments before I headed off again. He stayed a bit longer to catch his breath. The road spikes, then bends then there's a quick descent but it doesn't provide much respite from the heat building up in my legs and core. It was difficult after to get my heartrate steady. The sun was starting to burn my skin."

"Vines in the small valley and more sulfurous smells and the incessant song of cicadas. I needed no reminder of the heat. A lovely category 3 climb began at the bottom of a narrow ravine. It felt a short way to the summit, followed by a sweeping decent through a wide dramatic gash in the canyon. It looked utterly Neolithic there, primitive and beautiful. Upon exiting the rock walls, I had my first clear view of the Beast. All day she'd been in our field of vision lurking, shadowy at best. She was really there no matter how many times I tried to blink her away."

"Then the heat became troubling, as did the surface of the road. It was rough and overly taxing on my legs. Knees and ankles were starting to ache. The Irishman caught up to me and we chatted while riding and his pleasant company kept my mind off my dry mouth and dull headache. He's a keen cyclist, so we weren't exactly soft pedaling. So much for conservation. I blew through my last bottle of water on the run into Bedouin. The last feed stop appeared like a mirage. We'd arrived early and descend like locusts on the snacks laid out for the group, including the pocket food meant for the final ascent. I was too

hot and too hungry not to eat everything in sight. I did eat everything, then smuggled a banana into my pocket just in case."

"Legs. In. Fountain. This is what I texted Scott and that's exactly where he found me when he arrived in Bedouin. I was sitting there in that amazing fountain with Sylvain, right under the spout. We'd both stuck our bare feet in the clear water, a magic tonic to cool down our overheated cores. Amazing. I could have stayed there all day. Sylvain decided to leave for the summit. It was only 4pm and the hottest part of the day. I was advised to wait until it got later to start the climb but I couldn't put it off anymore. Scott sat with me on the fountain ledge, his feet in the water too. He promised to be there when I return. He was the only thing on my mind as I pedaled away from the picture-book village."

"The whole scene made it hard to go. It would be a long several hours before I returned and could put my feet back in that magical fountain. Two hours up if all went well, a water stop part way, pictures at the top, then the final descent home…potentially slow if caravans were present. So I started out easy, trying not to dwell on the effort ahead."

"The sun was baking. There was no shade anywhere as I pedaled through the cherry orchards and vineyards growing grapes for the locally produced wines. I kept the tempo mild, breathing steady. A sharp switchback and a steep ramp. Then the forest came on heavy. Stifling heat, but at least the trees offered a small patch of shade, though frustratingly on the opposite side of the road. The road was quiet and I thought about risking a swerve across for some relief, but thought better of it for a while. Tempo was steady and legs felt fine, though my heart was racing and I was no longer able to catch my breath."

"It was worrisome so far from the summit and I was running out of water, so I stopped in the shade and focused on my heart beating normally again. I did this once more a little ways up after a wave of cold chills and goose bumps lingered."

"Then I found my rhythm again and all systems seemed content. I started daydreaming about a breeze and I swore I could feel an occasional tuft across my brow. A tiny gift from a generous mountain. It was tough but not terrible. The trees were a nice distraction from the climb, as were the cars passing downhill, the drivers all waving. They seemed to slow to get a better look at the idiot aboard the bike, wondering who might attempt such a thing in the heat of the day without a number pinned to their back or a contract paying them dividends. Then I spotted our water truck. I hesitated to stop again but my bidons were bone dry. That was the second time today. Plus, it was hard to ignore Ian's dutiful pleas for us all to pull over and refill, so I did. He's a kind soul and gave me a welcome shove back up to the waiting pavement. My legs were pissed by then but relented to their duty."

"The glorious next few kilometers felt flat at 6%. The forest was behind me and ahead was nothing but moonscape. The white rocks seemed to have a lavender tint but maybe that was my parched imagination. Not really a moonscape up close but unique and hauntingly pretty. A few scattered caravans were there, the drivers early to stake out their places for the Tour in a week's time. Some quietly nodded from their folding chairs as I labored by. Some offered a half-hearted "allez". I exchanged a bi-lingual quip with a rotund German man who raised his glass of beer and told me to hurry up. I told him I would if he gave me his beer. He shook his head no and chuckled. Not today, my

friend. Maybe next time. I think that was the gist anyway. Then I passed the two kilometer mark and started to tire. Back and up and forth and up. The ribbon of the road prolonged my effort. There was the 1 kilometer mark. The tower still seemed so far away and I fought the urge to panic. It was the longest kilometer of my life. I began to hear the cheers of known voices from up the road. I stood on the pedals and mustered as much poise as I could and mashed over the summit marker. Done. This mountain was not a beast at all and way more than a pile of rocks. I caught my breath, took in the view and posed for some photos. Thank goodness for Sam, one of the staff mechanics, offering to play photographer or I'd have no evidence of the accomplishment. Familiar faces were at the top and we congratulated each other on a job well done."

"I take in another few minutes of the marvelous view and then feel impatient to get back to the bottom. I remounted my steel hero and pointed her nose downhill and feathered the brakes to keep my speed low. I stopped to pay respect to Tom. A few solid tears and some sad-happy thoughts and many waves of conflicting emotion. Exhaustion does that to a person I suppose. Now my only thought was Scott in Bedouin and putting my tired feet back in that cool fountain. So I pulled back onto the road and descended like a bat out of hell down that bald mountain. A huge grin was on my face, the reverse of the grimace on the riders coming up. I yelled hello to each. Some smiled back, some barely nodded. I could hardly hold it against them. They'd have their own reward soon."

"Not my fastest downhill effort, but I wasn't entirely present mentally and I had reserved enough sense not to push it. Plus, my body aches in all the necessary places to stay properly mounted to *my bike. I reached the orchard flats and a switch in me flipped. I started to push harder and harder, time trialing my way back to my waiting husband. I had to see him. Right then, he was the only thing that mattered. Not the pain, not that mountain, not the rest of the tour."*

"I was flying, big ring, legs on absolute fire, knowing I'd regret it tomorrow. Then I saw him, just past the fountain on the shaded terrace of a café. He was there waiting, as he promised, with a huge smile. And then a comforting embrace. We sat down for a nice dinner in view of the magic fountain, just the two of us and I enjoyed some of the lovely local rosé. I think it was the most perfect French evening. This mountain has changed my life. There will always be a version of me "before Ventoux" and a version of me after. That's what makes this ionic mountain a legend…the power it has to change us."

↔

People often talk about defining moments in their lives; births, deaths, tragedies, windfalls, etc. I don't know anyone who hasn't experienced one or more of life's swings and I suspect that even the smallest of ripples have a hand in shaping who we are. I have been fortunate to live a full life. A life of my choosing, for the most part, a life that has felt balanced somewhere in the middle of all those ups and downs and sideways. On Ventoux, it was mostly up. There were some serious negotiations going on. With myself. Self, I said, sit pretty and keep pedaling. When you hit the 1 kilometer mark, you can stand and squirm and come unglued but until then just keep it together, ok?. This was the method I'd adopted back on Puy Mary, a technique designed to keep my mind focused and legs pedaling. So that me and my bicycle were always moving forward, no matter how slow. Sitting while climbing was usually the most efficient way to get to the top but sometimes the grade was so steep, the only way to turn the pedals over was to stand on them and let your weight help sink the cranks towards the tarmac and then rely gravity bring them back round again. But this was taxing in its own right, my wimpy core muscles working hard to hold the weight of my body upright. Then my arms began to weaken as I realized I had been leaning on them for support…and the more I depended on the bars, the heavier my bike began to feel and the more Sisyphean it became to push the both of us towards the summit.

Somewhere around the 2 kilometers to go mark my legs began to tire and my mind began to wander. All the discomforting thoughts I had locked out since the beginning of the climb from Bedouin started knocking and there was nothing left to do but let them in. I found it comforting to acknowledge the difficulty of the effort and the aching of wind and limb. It was important to allow myself to feel awful, at least for a moment before the summit came, bringing with it the reward of relief for my brain and body and ego. That is why I climb mountains. For the addicting wave of adrenaline and not as I am routinely sold by magazines and clothing manufacturers for the "suffering".

I have always found the notion of cycling as suffering ridiculous and overblown. Starving to death is suffering. Terminal illness is suffering. Abuse is suffering. If we want to romanticize cycling, we absolutely should. It can be beautiful, poetic and sometimes even tragic. Riding our bikes in this manner is elective. Yes, it may cause us discomfort but we're doing it of our own volition and despite how high, hot, cold, windy, tiring, steep or dangerous…riding a bicycle sometimes hurts but should never qualify as suffering.

With a kilometer to go, on the legendary Col des Tempêtes, I begin the sit-stand dance to the summit. Then I see my friends at the top and hear their shouts of encouragement and I muster all the composure I have left and try to look like it was no big deal. All smiles, I pedal hard across the official finish line. The day was hot and so was the hour. Despite the tendency for legendary winds to whip riders across and sometimes nearly off the temperamental lunar landscape, July 7th, 2016 was still and stifling. Just seven days later, on July 14th , was the national French holiday known as Bastille Day. The professional peloton would be barred from reaching the top of the bald peak by brutal winds, whipping upwards of 60 miles per hour. *Le Mistral* was hiding one last punch from his spring stirrings in the protected forests of birch and oak and would strike again. Lopping off the last six kilometers seemed like a good idea at the time, but the organizers had no idea it would cause the pandemonium that ensued. The hoard of fans, many of which had been camped out roadside since I rode by them a week before, were now uprooted and pushed further down the barricaded route to share valuable real estate with thousands of other territorial race watchers. Fans flooded the course, narrowing a usually two-vehicle-wide road to less than 5' across. A width hardly appropriate for the mass of team cars, officials, motorbikes and riders, it was chaos. If you didn't watch it unfold on television, I won't spoil it for you. It's a sight you must see for yourself and a spectacle that would have made Henri Desgrange roll over in his grave. Let's just say that grand old mountain got the last laugh.

I was gloriously spent. As such, the evening was all the more beautiful, the meal all the more delicious and my dinner date all the more treasured. I had survived the siren song of Mont Ventoux. For some it was a haunting sonnet drawing them to her barren heights but for me a toe-tapping victory tune, a theme song for my successful day. Something had changed in me on that climb, as a cyclist for sure but even my personhood felt different, as if my entire existence had shifted course ever so slightly.

It's difficult to explain it or pinpoint the exact moment but I have a feeling the same phenomenon has happened again and again to countless athletes. I hope I get the chance to ask Phil about it, though I don't think I'll be surprised if I hear an affirmative answer. Here was a man who had climbed thousands of mountains and was well aware of their power. It might not have been Ventoux but some other deity of granite or basalt, limestone or schist that modified his life in the most permanent way. I think I finally understood his quest to keep climbing just as I understand the sacrifices others make too, sometimes giving their very lives in an attempt to reach the summit.

Perhaps the most famous of those sacrifices was that of Tom Simpson. He is known to fans of cycling worldwide, but to others, his is just the name etched into a roadside memorial a mere one kilometer from the summit of Mont Ventoux. To some he was a cheat, a doper, a villain of the sport who somehow influenced the culture of performance enhancing drugs that still permeate the sport of cycling to this day. To others, he was a well-documented victim of the times, an innocent pawn who finally folded to the pressures of his life, his sponsors and his own popularity. Though for many more, he was and still is a hero. For me, he has always been something of a sad curiosity, an important figure in the history of cycling. I love to read about such history in books, when I'm not watching the drama of modern racing unfold on television or trying to ride in the footsteps (or fore steps) of famous riders.

Standing on the stone steps of Tom's memorial, he suddenly became more than any of those things. He was a young man with a big smile, adored by his fans and most poignantly, he was a father who was loved by his daughters. I found the inscription written by them deeply affecting and in no time, my eyes filled

189

to the lashes with tears. I, along with thousands before and after me, had closed that gap to the top, the one he never would. It was so close, yet he perished just a handful of pedal strokes from his desire, a victim of his own self-destruction. It's easy to take that last kilometer for granted but for Tom it was worth turning himself inside out, filling his body with a potent brew, casting aside his better judgement and throwing himself at the mercy of the mountain and her elements. The few moments I spent at his memorial was a reminder to take little for granted, to find balance between blind drive and blissful folly and not forget that the most important things in life may not be at the summit at all, but waiting for you patiently at the bottom.

↔

Like clockwork our fellow riders whizzed by the café's patio. We clapped and hollered for them all as they passed, exhausted smiles alighted on their sun-burned faces. We cheered the loudest for Indy, for his accomplishment was probably the greatest, having only begun riding a few months prior to signing up for the tour. He was already a changed cyclist from stage 1 to now. The pride shone on his face and we were so happy for him. It was apparent from the strength of his smile that he had finished a good ride.

With the sun setting behind the shops and houses of the village, we settled the tab and made our way back to the bus. I let Scott ride my bike the half-mile, to keep him from angering his tender ankles and I walked barefoot with my cycling shoes in hand, happy to use my legs in a manner other than pedaling. The clouds were thin in the darkening sky and a deep orange hue was spreading across the horizon. Stars had begun to shine delicately around a sliver of moon and I could just make out the flitting of tiny bats around rows of gnarled vines along the road out of town.

The bus was idling in the parking lot, its driver eager to get on the road. Its contents were eager for a warm shower and soft pillow. We had a long drive to Montélimar and it was already nearing ten pm. Half-asleep and heavy lidded when we started nearing the outskirts of the city, our driver began a rapid-fire conversation with Dr. Julien, himself dreary-eyed in the jump seat. It appeared that Germany had been beaten by France in the European soccer championships and was advancing to the final. While the match had been held in Marseille, the elation of a French victory was still being felt full-strength and late into the evening across much of the country.

It seemed everyone under the age of 50 had poured from the cafes and bars into the streets, clapping, laughing, singing. With revelers filling the narrow boulevards, we had no choice but to stop and wait for the crowds to disperse. Then suddenly, their attention turned to our bus and we were swarmed. It was an intense few moments. Unsure of their intentions, we all sat on the edges of our seats as the crowd of hundreds pounded the flanks of the bus, chanting and shouting. It was a mob, but thankfully a happy one and we relaxed as the driver began to chuckle at his fellow countrymen and their antics. If he wasn't worried, then we wouldn't worry. Eventually, the reveling masses tired of us and moved aside to let the bus pass. We drove the few final blocks to our hotel and were unceremoniously dumped at the back door. It was locked, so we dragged our heavy bags and tired bodies around to the front entrance. The experience was a bizarre way to end an already surreal day. Montélimar was the nougat capital of the world as explained by the chipper concierge and evidenced by the small piece of nougat resting on our pillows. A small, glorious sweet-ending was a fitting way to put an extraordinary day to bed.

STAGE 13:

Belle Ardèche

July 8th, 2016 ~ Bourg-Saint-Andéol to La Caverne du Pont-d'Arc. "I really missed my bike." Proclaims Scott as he pedals into the morning sun after a three day hiatus from the tour due to injuries.

"23 miles and 1,991 feet climbed. Quite possibly the most beautiful 'time trial' we'd ever ride. Lavender fields of purple flowers knee deep as far as we can see! Deep canyon of limestone. Blue-green sparkling river. Dramatic arc of rock spanned the gap in the ravine. Such an ancient landscape oozing with history…plus we ended at the famous caves of Chauvet. Sadly, there was no time for a visit."

"After the lovely short stage, which we used as a recovery ride, we headed back to Montélimar for half a rest day. We stayed off our feet, except for a quick stroll to town for lunch then back to the hotel to wash some kit in the sink. Dinner was at a 1950's replica 'American Diner' and we were served what I thought was supposed to be a burger and fries and a slice of 'apple pie'. Nice people, terrible food, embarrassing attempt at authenticity. I now have a sense of what it might be like for the French to dine at an 'authentic bistro' in the US. Sorry about that."

"Scott felt strong on the bike today. The rest did him some good. Sometimes I think he missed his bike more than me. Well, I

for one am happy to have my partner back. It's been a valuable experience riding without him. I've had room to grow as a cyclist but I missed him sharing all those miles with me. I am looking forward to the stages again, not dreading them. There are times when you might struggle less to ride alone and times when you might struggle more without the support of someone who loves you and knows your struggle well."

↔

It was an incredibly lovely day for a bike ride. No heat to sear our faces, no rain to soak our chamois, no wind to batter our sails. We boarded the bus for a quick trip to Bourg-Saint-Andéol, where we filled our tires and mounted our bikes in a large, open square to start the stage. It would be a 37 kilometer time trial for the professionals in a week's time but for us it would just be a nice ride through the Ardèche. Some among the group wanted to race, perhaps to compare theirs against their Tour heroes, but I had no intention of pushing any harder than it took to turn the pedals around and keep from having to walk up hills. Despite the short course we had two climbs of note, a 7 kilometer slog right from the parking lot and a roughly 5 kilometer bump to the Pont d'Arc caves.

Bourg-Saint-Andéol is the traditional base for exploring the wines of the Ardèche. Home to the *Côtes du Rhône and Côtes du Rhône Villages*, both AOC varieties, these are some of France's most expensive wines. The whole region had a softness to it, perhaps stemming from the airy sand and pebbly soil which left a mark on everything from the grapes to the flowers to the plaster on the walls of village houses. But that softness gave way to bold blues and greens of the rivers, as the Ardèche and the Rhône joined forces to take on the Mediterranean Sea.

Perhaps their boldness came from their source waters, rain trickling down from the ancient lava-spewing giants of the Massif Central, spellbound in their current slumber. The rest of the course led us through tiny Saint-Remèze, whose inhabitants were far outnumbered by heads of deep purple blooms and whose claim to touristic fame is a splendid lavender museum. We stopped several times to take photographs against the stunning and almost surreal backdrop of millions of aromatic plants, tiny industrious bees buzzing from flower to flower, collecting the ingredients to make what must have been the most mouth-watering of honeys.

From Saint-Remèze, we traversed the high plateau of Laoul through miles of scrub oaks and brittle looking shrubs. The road here was rough. It seemed to match the scratchy landscape perfectly. Not pot-holed or pitted or in poor condition, just an unusually knobbly surface that sent micro-vibrations through our legs that made waves all the way to our fingertips. It was also confoundingly slick for all its coarseness and in places the loose limestone of the fields had washed onto the surface and collected in gravelly pools. It would make for an interesting time trial, with the professional racers astride their stiff carbon aero steeds. Riding our handmade steel frames smoothed out the surface as steel is want to do, but still the reverberations of the road were notable and would be a considerable factor in the hunt for the fastest time of the stage. The beautiful route was going to prove tricky for the riders of the Tour and I doubted they had dared a glimpse at their surroundings, afraid to lose a fraction of a second by taking their eyes off the road. In fact on the day of their TT, the wind was howling madly, blowing a rider named Edward Theuns off into a tree, fracturing a vertebrae and ending his race.

Next we entered the Gorges de l'Ardèche where the steep rock faces along the road were streaked with the colors of pre-history; ochres and rich brown veins softened by pale yellows and bright whites. The environs here reeked of history, older than we could even fathom, and something inside us stirred unknowingly as if reminded of the beginning of our very being. We pulled off the road at an overlook, among the dozens of cars who had done the same. All of us eager to take in the enormity of the canyon and river below, resplendent in the gold rays of the French sun. Canyons have that mythical property of at once staggering you with awe and simultaneously if not unnervingly, drawing you closer and closer to their edge.

From these heights you could see the shimmer of moving water and hordes of tiny dots swirling about and clumping together in the whirls of the river. It was a popular spot for renting a raft and floating care-free in the gentle ripples. The road looped down and along the steep walls of the canyon, leading us closer to the Ardèche with every bend. The sound of river over rocks and laughing and splashing echoed off the stone protecting the narrow valley. The bright primary colors of the rafts popped against the blue water canvas. The heat was now rising, not uncomfortably, but enough to make me wish I could park the bike for a spell and submerse myself up to the chin and just exist for a while in this appealing scene of summer.

I found it frustrating at times to have to keep moving, ever onward, from one kilometer to the next instead of pausing for a few hours or days in a place I felt most drawn to explore. Though I forget that was the very point of the Tour in the first place…a quick spin around a vast and varying country so full of life and culture it would be impossible to experience it all in three weeks if you lingered. It was teaser if you will, to inspire you to return and get to know more about a village or a region so different than your own.

Then all too quickly the stage was complete. It was so dynamic, so visually stimulating, I had the urge to do it again. I couldn't imagine the peloton having to race through those miles of road, head down and pushing to the limit, seeing nothing but the sweat dripping down their nose and the clicking by of the minutes on your computer with the race radio screaming in their ear to go even faster. Hopefully, those men had the chance to pre-ride the route slowly and deliberately and were able to look around at the wonder surrounding them before returning to blur all those colors and sounds and smells through a tunnel of pain. Time-trialing is fiendish, if done properly and if that doesn't sound pleasant then you'd be right. Fortunately, I would never have to find out the strength of my own will in inflicting the self-punishment that time trials require. Climbing does that well enough on its own.

As we lingered in the shade of a grove of scrubby oaks, eating baguette sandwiches and waiting on the remaining riders to finish the stage, I regretted not being able to visit the museum and cave whose parking lot we were borrowing for our impromptu picnic. *La Caverne du Pont-d'Arc* is actually a replica of the Chauvet caves, a 36,000 year old masterpiece of Paleolithic human artistic expression, specifically of the beasts with which they shared their natural world. The rocky canvas is overflowing with mammals. Fifteen different species are represented, including those not commonly (if ever) found in other cave paintings. Along with herds of horses and deer, bison and aurochs, there are also predator hyenas, bears, lions and panthers. Incredibly, there is also a rare scene of a volcano erupting…almost certainly the oldest portrayal of its kind. Perhaps my favorite individual piece is the charcoal bust of a rhinoceros, dual horns arcing gracefully over its withers, mouth agape in a call to arms or from drawing a galloping breath.

The short stage meant a free afternoon with plenty of time before dinner to wash laundry and venture into town in search of second lunch. A small table in the shade, in front of a quiet café, is where we spent the remainder of the day while we watched the locals stroll by. It was nice to be back in a routine where both Scott and I were riding. The tone of our relationship seemed realigned, familiar. We were back to being birds of a feather, responsible again for ourselves instead of each other. With the distraction of his own day in the saddle, he worried less about me, no longer fretting about my bike or whether I was drinking enough water or getting enough sleep. I worried about him either way. If he wasn't riding, I grieved over his disappointment. On the bike, there were all his aches and pains and I feared he was being overwhelmed by them. Though not at this moment, when there was peace to be found under the shade of an attractive old plane tree.

Tomorrow our ride could be run off the rails again, spoiled by any number of elemental or corporal setbacks but today would go down as a triumphant day of encouraging miles and lasting memories.

STAGE 14:

Le Merde d'Oiseaux

July 9th, 2016 ~ Montélimar to Villars-les-Dombes Parc des Oiseaux. "Merde!" Exclaims the author, using the only poorly pronounced French swearword she knows.

"135.9 miles and 6,119 feet climbed. A shit stage. Too bad after such a beautiful beginning. Superb morning light shone in our faces and we pedaled easily past endless rows of herbs; purple blooming lavender, bright yellow dill and white flowered savory. The plant's deep green leaves gave way to golden fields of wheat being harvested and the stalks being rolled into round bales."

"Down narrow farm roads we cycled, dodging the most direct of the sprinklers' aim but enjoying the finer mist. Scenes of a glorious French summer. Then came the winds. Early and strong and they would last all day. It felt like 135 miles of riding on a trainer with an industrial fan blowing hot air in our face. Today's "flat" stage included 6'000 feet of climbing and three category 4 climbs. The 35 degree Celsius heat made everyone grumpy. So did the driving. Terrible. Near misses and intentionally close passes. Stupid decisions, inattention, angry honking, fist pumping, the works. Fifteen of us were nearly flattened today by one of those stupid decisions."

"This is a beautiful but dangerous part of the country for cycling. Young, arrogant, disrespectful drivers are playing a careless game of auto roulette with our lives."

"There were rolling hills in the distance, spanning much of the horizon as we rode along the perimeter of an arching plateau with almost 360 degree views of the rural valley below. The churches here are lovely in pale stone. Their clean lines more refined than in the north. Noon bells loudly chimed a dozen rings. Smaller villages here, their central squares busy with cafes and commerce. Far less tourists. I enjoy riding through the narrow lanes and over road pillows, weaving around manhole covers and avoiding drains. Speaking of drains, Scott and I started to tire with 30 miles to go. Thankfully, Andy and Gary were there to save our hides and give us a generous tow. Scott awarded them the chapeau this evening. They deserved it."

"Finally, we finished with a pleasing last section through the curious bird sanctuary. We didn't see any birds, but mile after mile of marshy wetlands and ponds. The wind finally disappeared and the evening sun softened. There were no cars on these roads and we pulled into the driveway of one of the park's lonely hotels. Our group of cyclists were the only guests. Probably for the best after the day we all had. The food was decent and the rosé was notable. The bar tender refused to sell us sparkling water no matter how many different ways we asked. He kept telling us they were out. With three varieties displayed behind the bar, I had trouble believing him. At least the two-man kitchen didn't overcook the chicken and I got a rather large helping of perfectly creamy gratin dauphinoise. Impressive with 50 mouths to feed at once."

"Tomorrow we climb. A lot. I just hope there's cheese."

↔

It was towards the end of this day that Scott and I both really started to tire. It was also the first time where I began to feel like the whole point of the tour had shifted. I was happy to get up in the morning and start pedaling, because if I didn't I'd clearly never get to Paris. But it wasn't with the same kind of wonderment of the last two weeks. Ventoux felt like the last song at a great concert and every successive stage now seemed like a drawn-out encore. Maybe this was the true test, fighting the attrition of all these miles.

In fact, the Tour de France has long been ominously nicknamed the Tour of Attrition for its ability to drive even the best of athletes to the brink of their personal limits and back onto the team bus for a disappointing journey home. Riders are exposed to the elements of wind and sun and rain. They are at the mercy of the road and motorists, bad driving, close passes, noise and fumes. They ride roads going up and down and rolling and steep, loose, bumpy, sometimes smooth, sometimes sticky like glue. They have sore bits and stinging legs, throbbing in their chest and head, skin burned and eyes watering. Tired. Nervous. Then scared. Then amazed. Then half asleep and wide awake. Then back to tired. Their mind full. Their mind empty. They try to stay focused, try to enjoy the ride, try to remember why they did this to themselves in the first place. We ultimately did it for some good people and their great cause. We did it for the memories. For the adventure. For the chance to ride our bikes for a long, long way.

I can't speak for Scott's state of mind, other than to say he was tired of being injured. Aside from that I think he was feeling more undermined than depleted, especially since he had an unplanned three days off the bike. He was like a laid-up race horse...fit as a fiddle and pacing his stall...wanting to stretch his restless legs but not without the risk of never being able to run again. That was the element I think affected him the most. Not knowing if his condition would worsen to the point where he'd never ride the same way again. It was bothering him to his very core and he wasn't good at talking openly about those feelings. So instead of expressing his worry, he'd externalize the physical aches often and to everyone close to him, as if their empathy would help heal his internal wounds too.

As for me, I was beginning to feel burned-out and un-focused. His injuries were wearing on me as well. It was hard to see him in pain and know that he was trying to tough it out so we could finish this thing. I felt responsible for his worsening condition. I felt guilty every morning he got out of bed and limped to breakfast. I felt guiltier every time I had a good push up a hill, while he winced his way to the top and worse yet when it was his turn to take a pull in the wind, when I got to sit in his draft and soft pedal. It was an uncomfortable burden for both of us.

The tow from Andy and Gary was a selfless act. Both accomplished cyclists and quick on the pedals, they could not have been more different. Andy, tall and lithe, had the traditional look of a two-wheeled athlete. He was friendly and approachable and we enjoyed his company often on the road and many mornings over breakfast. Gary, compact and powerful, had the build of cycling heroes from a century ago and the look of eagles to match. Quiet and unobtrusive, he was also warm and generous. Off the bike they seemed like an unlikely pair but on the road, they made a compatible team and sitting on their wheel for the final stretch of the day was a real pleasure. Both Scott and I tried, in vain, to go around and take our turns out front, but neither would allow it for long. It was an unspoken gift of compassion, a token of goodwill that revealed the depths of their character. That night, Scott had no trouble passing along the chapeau award to them both. He had received it from Indy for his sideline support on stage 12. We could think of no two Lifers more deserving of the award today. A well-worn cap seems hardly a fair trade, so if either of you are reading this…thank you.

I've forgotten who won the elephant award that evening for the most foolish act on the road, so I'd like to award it postscriptum to the idiot who nearly killed more than a dozen cyclists around the half-way point of the stage. Had he not jerked the steering wheel when he did or had been traveling any faster than he was, he would have plowed us plumb over with his SUV. It would have been messy. He made an eleventh-hour decision to pass a limousine on a narrow, two-lane stretch of road leaving a nameless village on the D538. Apparently, the limo was keeping him urgently detained and he couldn't wait the few moments for the road to be clear. He also presumably didn't see the 15-deep peloton cruising his direction on the slight down-grade towards the village. We were riding two abreast, with our lane clear fore and aft of any traffic. He accelerated at the exit of the roundabout and passed the limo by swerving over the dividing line and into our lane. He kept accelerating, rather than hitting the brakes and returning to his own lane of travel. I suspect he didn't consider that bicycles could be carrying any significant speed and therefore, he figured there was time to make the pass. He made a calculated error and it nearly cost us all our limbs, if not our lives. There was a sickening sound of squealing tires and rubber skating across the pavement as most of the group instinctively went for the brakes. We split several directions, each rider left with only a grain of a second to find a path away from the oncoming car. In order to not slam into the rapidly decelerating riders at the front, those of us at the back of the group avoided our brakes and made the desperate choice to swerve around our skidding aggregation. With a curb on the right and the offending car now in our path, the only viable exit was on our left, into the opposite lane. It all happened in a heartbeat.

In the time it took for my brain to tell my body it might be the last breath if we didn't move, I was so convinced that evasion was futile that I actually closed my eyes for the impact. In a blink, I was leaning hard to move the bike back to the proper lane. In less than a nanosecond, the driver had over-corrected his way back to his side of the road. There were squealing tires, two and four alike and lots of shouts. Fear and anger and relief came flooding out of our throats as loud as we could project them and the conductor of all this chaos sped away without a rearward glance in the mirror. The incident was the worst that we would experience in over 2,000 miles of riding among motorists on French roads. I can only speak for myself and Scott, because who really knows what trouble the other participants faced on a daily basis. They likely had their own close calls.

Just after the next rest stop there would be second episode that raised our anxiety to an almost unmanageable level. Especially when combined with the hours of deafening hot headwind into which we pedaled for much of the day. We were alone on a busy stretch of byway, hugging the far right strip of concrete, when a woman in a compact drifted so close to Scott he put his elbow on her passenger door and pounded to remind her that they presently occupied the same narrow space. He also bellowed at her at a volume that made me jump. She either didn't hear him over the road noise or refused to acknowledge his presence but the risky move paid off and she instantly moved a reasonable distance away. I was a few bicycle lengths back watching this all unfold, my blood pressure spiking as I wondered whether my husband was about to be bumped off his bike into a ditch. Intentional or not, the situation was not amusing.

That made two close-calls and we were in no mood for a third. It was high time to get off these roads. What a stark contrast this was from our morning jaunt through uninterrupted swaths of furrowed fields, wheat stock and irrigated flutes of delicate herbs. Their aromatic notes filled our lungs with each draw of cool, dewy breath. But therein lies the story of so many stages; memorable not for their consistency but for their capricious nature and their tendency to shift from one incongruous scene to the next. A single day could feel like two or three or a whole week and the feeling of being lost in the planes of time and space was only getting worse.

We were becoming more dutiful in our approach to riding. Our job was to get to the final arrow, refuel and rest before doing it all again the next day. I was struggling to look up and around, to drink in the sights and sounds and serenity of the landscape. I was losing the desire to be present in my surroundings. I just wanted to pedal and keep pedaling until it was time to stop. I was getting testy with traffic and allowing their slightest transgressions to rub me raw. I was irritated with the elements and the terrain and the food at the rest stops. I was even beginning to let some of the new staff grate on my weathered nerves. This day was a hard one for me. I was feeling beaten and vulnerable and lost. I couldn't tell you where I was on the map. The landscape didn't stand out above the general attractiveness of most of the French countryside. It was a relief to get back to the hotel, to spend some time washing my bike before taking a quick shower and sitting down on the front patio to enjoy a cold drink. Our simple but well-prepared supper was a comforting way to end a trying day. As food often does, the communal meal provided more than just sustenance but a means for the group to unburden themselves of the stresses of the stage and find empathy in their fellow cyclists. We were beginning to rely on the bonds we had built with the other Lifers. We supported each other, out on the road and here in the quiet moments of our down time. Our brains and bodies were taxed to their fullest so there was no room for extra stress. We all required the basic creature comforts like a filling meal and a fulfilling sleep, but also a familiar smile and a supportive word from someone who shared the same experiences on the road.

The group as a whole seemed to be growing intolerant of any extraneous source of negativity, anything that would upset our sensitive state. It was nuanced, but it was there. The strongest riders were often riding and dining and resting together. They were growing protective of one another. I was becoming increasingly protective of Scott's legs. They were failing him a little bit more each day and supportive therapies didn't seem to be helping. He was now covered in so much blue physio tape he looked like a house being re-painted and was downing so many anti-inflammatories I was sure he'd succumb to liver failure before we even reached the Alps. There was a lot of climbing left on the calendar and we still had the Jura mountains to traverse before we even saw our first alpine switchback.

The first two weeks of the route had been designed to warm us up then wear us down, testing our resolve for the biggest challenges yet. The official TDF organizers knew exactly what they were doing designing what had been described as one of

208

the toughest Tours in modern history. They were trying to unseat the royalty and dominance of Team Sky, a well-oiled and highly successful professional cycling team from Great Britain, including the 2-time Tour de France winner Chris Froome. Despite their best attempts, they would fail to keep Chris from winning his third title on July 24th, 2016. In the meantime their tricky climb-heavy course might be more than two amateur cyclists from Virginia could master. There would be no podium for us in Paris, so we held on to the hope that we could at least feel the time-worn cobbles beneath our wheels for one lap along the Champs-Elysees.

STAGE 15:

The Jura Giant

July 10th, 2016 ~ Bourg-en-Bresse to Culoz. "Whoa! Are those THE Alps?" Author exclaims. Scott in half-amusement, half-dread asks 'We aren't climbing those are we?' "Yes dear." Author smirks. "I'm afraid we are."

"88.7 miles and 10,879 feet of climbing. What a glorious day on the bike. It started with overwhelming happiness as we climbed into the morning sun, cool temperatures and light wind. The first descent poured us into a deep green valley filled with postcard pastoral images of rural France. I couldn't tamp the welling of emotion and tears just started rolling down my face. The moment was too perfect and I dared to even breath in case it all disappeared in a flash. Perfect light, perfect road, perfect temperature and right on the wheel of the man I love in a country I adore. These are the moments life's purest memories are made of and I hope this one never, ever fades away."

"This was a day of perfect serenity, no road too taxing. Each village with tree-lined boulevards, narrow and virtually car-free, providing shade and respite from the growing heat of the afternoon. The road started to roll gently, then pitch and finally dropped us a long way down with stunning views of endless green canvas. No wonder so many people hate the French…it's nothing more than jealousy of their perfect terrestrial landscape."

"Fields of straw and wheat, pine and oak forests and infinite blue sky. Fragrant and fresh. Today's ride was damn well near the best one of our lives. Even the infamous Jura Giant couldn't dampen our mood. Hailed as being brooding and difficult, we found solace in her dense forests and windswept flanks."

"This giant turned out to be a friendly one, at least from the side we climbed. (There are reportedly four ways to the top.) Our route was the longest with some of the steepest sections averaging 10% with a 15% max and the remainder roughly 6-7%. The road through the woods seemed endless. More shade followed by more views, rivulets of water running down over the road and single-track trails branching off of every bend. It's the kind of mountain you want to revisit, to explore each of those hidden paths and discover all of her hidden secrets."

"Near the summit, the forests thinned to fields, the fields thinned to low-shrubs and strewn rocks. We crossed cattle guards into muddy pastures smelling of mineral earth. The wind was starting to really blow but at our backs as if the very mountain wanted to lend a hand. We were glad to have it. The last ramp to the summit was a long one and looked so steep from the bottom, with tiny riders marching their way up like dutiful ants. At the top you could see forever. Behind us, from where we climbed, you could see the Ain. To the side, the Rhone."

"We tackled seven climbs today though true to form only five were categorized. Grand Colombier was a queenly Hors Catégorie. Everyone seemed to hate this climb but us. Except for nearly getting run over by a vintage Porsche, the drivers were great."

"The descent off the GC was very rough with the asphalt cracking and popping and moving under our wheels. The heat was so intense on this side of the mountain, the road was literally melting. Saw the shimmering lakes in the distance which made the heat feel all the more intense. As we picked our way down past the potholes and rough pavement, a plane flew below my right shoulder. We were still so high."

"Ahead, was the saw-tooth outline of the imposing Alps. Foreboding and unreal, so many jagged peaks still capped with snow. Hard to believe in a few days' time we'll be lost somewhere in those steep folds."

↔

The day started fine though I can't for the life of me remember breakfast. Then we must have boarded a bus that morning to ferry us to the start, because I recall passing billboards advertising *Bleu de Bresse*, a local and notable blue cheese and the AOC awarded *Beurre de Bresse*. Bourg-en-Bresse, if you aren't aware, is also the home of the famous *poulet de Bresse*. A sumptuous black legged variety, the Bresse chicken is known in the most exacting of culinary circles (ok, maybe just in France) as being the queen of all hens and the most delicious of all poultry. It is so revered for its taste, the breed gained an *appellation d'origine contrôlée* designation in 1957. This is the only bird in France with an AOC label. You can be certain

you've purchased an official Bresse *poulet* at the market because
the famous blue-black legs will almost always remain attached
to the carcass as proof of its rock star status. I remember riding
excitedly through the outskirts of town, if not only because of
my atypical affinity for French fowl, but also because Phil and I
had quite a lovely chat about chickens.

The category 1 designated Col du Berthiand came up fast on
cold legs. We were warned it would be a tough way to start the
day, a 6 kilometer no-nonsense ascent with an average of 7.6%
and short sections at 15% but I didn't mind it so much. I fell
into a rhythm and Scott sat on my wheel, happy to let me set
the pace. The group thinned out early, stretched by the climb
and we would practically have the rest of the route to ourselves,
rarely passing another group of riders except around the feed
stops. The official climb started just after crossing the Pont de
Serrières-sur-Ain, a beautiful 20th century concrete bridge,
spanning the Ain river. What an impressive sight it must have
made with the entire professional peloton racing in a long line
across its single arch.

After cresting the summit, there were several cherished
textbook perfect miles which I can do no better describing than
my journal entry already did. I can still feel the warmth from
the late morning sun on my face, the smell of the air change
ever so slightly as the road dipped down into a voluptuous
valley of farms and fields. I can easily recall the lump in my
throat as I realized I was being driven to tears of happiness and

the taste of those tears as they trickled down my cheeks and into my mouth as I drew breath after breath, pedaling hard to stay on Scott's wheel. I remember him looking so fit and healthy and fluid on his bike, as if (at least for the moment) there were no aches and pains affecting his tanned, lean figure.

Basking in the glow of pure cycling bliss, the miles ticked by in a blur. We missed an arrow and nearly blew off the rest of the tour. We laughed and joked about finding our own roundabout way back to Paris, skipping the Alps altogether. Or maybe getting there by way of the cycle path the gentleman in Brittany had teased us about. While enjoying a monumental tower of shellfish and oysters in Cancale, a kindly couple had inquired innocently about our business in France. When Scott explained to them we'd be riding up and over many mountains on our way to the heart of the Alps before cycling back to Paris, the gentleman teased good-naturedly by asking why on earth we would do such a ridiculous thing. He said he had himself ridden a bicycle in the Alps and gave us some pointers. Why not ride the perfectly good (and flat) cycle path to Lake Annecy then hop a train to Gare du Nord? Then we could spend more time eating and less time hurling ourselves over the mountains. He had a good point.

Back on track and convinced we'd better get to the Alps by following the arrows, our brief detour meant we arrived at the morning feed station next to last. That meant there were a few crumbs of brioche and a sad banana to tide us over until the next stop. You snooze, you lose especially when dozens of hungry cyclists have passed over breakfast like a hoard of starving locusts. There were also no bathrooms and barely any cover, so I hoofed it over to a notch in the rocky wall of the shallow canyon where we had stopped and hid behind a screen of slate. From the detritus beneath my cleated feet, I wasn't the only one who used this crevice for a nature break. Undeterred by our slim pickings, we pedaled gleefully along the road, a shallow river gurgling away to our right.

There was a small uncategorized climb to Peyriat, a tidy but plain village before descending down a rough and pitted road to the village of Cerdon. We rode around a sign declaring the road surface unfit for travel and the gradient substantially steep. It was both, so we gingerly picked our line to the bottom of the petite valley and tried to avoid enormous pot holes and rippled asphalt. I miraculously managed to do so while simultaneously and repeatedly stealing glances at the picturesque views of the rows of vines clinging steeply to the mountainside. The smell of copper was heavy in the air. Not from the now shuttered copper mine (the only one of its kind in all of France) but from the application of fungicide on the delicate Gamay grapes, used to make the commune's pink sparkling wine.

It took no time to leave the picturesque Bugey region behind us and as the road tilted towards the high noon sun, we came face to granite face with an awe-inspiring monument to the area's significant past.

215

She was splendid in her starkness, the hard set of her jaw and her hair drawn softly towards the cloudless sky. This was France, often depicted as a woman and she was honoring the *Maquis de l'Ain* and *la Résistance Cerdon.* The long, grueling, inhumane and complicated years of the second world war, are difficult to truncate, so I'll do my best to briefly describe the deep message of this memorial. Not everyone in this country took kindly to occupation. Especially those who might have otherwise found themselves submitting to forced labor. Those who resisted, who revolted, who ultimately would give their land, their liberty and oftentimes their lives for freedom, were known as *la Résistance* or *Maquisards,* or simply the *Maquis.* They were guerilla fighters, bonded deeply to their livelihoods and the country they loved since time immemorial. Often they were farmers, sometimes they were farmer's wives and occasionally they were immigrants who had decided to embrace the idea of *fraternité* and call France home. If you loved this land and wanted to fight for it, you were accepted as a Maquis.

Over 700 Maquis gave their lives in this region, as tens of thousands of other resistance fighters did all over France. This terrain was defensible because of the intimate knowledge of the land by its tenants and the dramatic hillsides funneling all those who traversed them into a rather distilled locale. The efforts of the guerilla fighters of the Bugey, including their bold actions of flying the forbidden French flag and singing the outlawed national anthem *La Marseillaise,* may have inevitably been the beginning of their untimely end. It also showed such bold, unwavering loyalty to their country and their cause that the British and American governments decided to assist the French resistance by supplying guns and ammunition to help them continue to thwart the actions and advancement of their occupiers.

The monument was installed at the base of the Col du Sappel, a debutant climb for the Tour. Also known as Sappel pass, the Frenchman Thomas Voeckler would be the first to the top during the chaos of the race. Seems fitting. Today though, all was quiet on the winding switchbacks of the category 2 climb and we nearly had the place to ourselves. On occasion and especially on weekends, we'd pass other recreational cyclists out for a ride. Sometimes they were singles, or small groups of friends, other times whole clubs or regional teams would be out on the roads.

About halfway up the Sappel, we passed a man riding several paces behind his wife, the pair pedaling slowly but confidently towards the summit. Both were riding high quality equipment, decked out in matching kit in the latest styles, looking accomplished; they could have been an older version of Scott and I. We both smiled and spoke our *bonjours* as we passed them, our pace being a gear or two the faster. I remarked to Scott that it was sweet to see them out riding together. Well, *Monsieur* would have none of it. Even before reaching the next hairpin, I heard the telltale sound of labored breath and a hardworking chain closing in fast on my wheel. I looked back then said to Scott, we've got company. Scott chuckled and mentioned, so much for his wife. He blasted past us both, looking very determined and stood on the pedals just as he reached the next hairpin then disappeared around the bend. I looked down the road to check on his better half and she was steadily making her way up, a look of resignation on her face. I waved and she smiled at me. Up a ways was the worst of the climb, a stretch of narrow road at 13%. We put our heads down and dug in to the grade, riding side by side. It made me grateful and the climb felt less steep somehow.

Next up was the Col de Pisseloup, which Phil jokingly referred to as "wolf's piss pass". Curiously, the nickname never popped up on official TDF course descriptions. "Pisse" does in fact mean what you think it does and "loup" does mean wolf. But it translates literally as wolf piss only when presented as two separate words, not as a compound. Serious delving down an internet rabbit hole produced some interesting insight; Pisseloup is a common last name in the northeast of France, specifically the Haute-Marne, where there is a village with the same title. The name is the result of the joining of two words from old French, you guessed it: pisse and loup. The word meant "the place where wolves piss" or more to the point, a place of danger. Wolves were serious business in the middle ages. They ate livestock and children. Entire forests were demolished just to rid villages of the devilish beasts. In the Ain, the name refers to places instead of persons and means "thin streams of water". No, not that kind of water but you can begin to see where the slang may have originated from. As the road leading over the pass of Pisseloup was indeed a narrow stream of a road, jutting a path right through the dense forest, the name seemed fitting.

Unfortunately, standing next to the sign at the top of the Col de Pisseloup was the last thing I could recall until we started the long slow climb to the summit of Grand Colombier. The Col de la Rochette and the unmarked but supposedly tricky little climb called Côte d'Hotonnes have just vanished no matter how hard I try to remember them. Thank goodness I took pictures.

For the purpose of writing this book, I relied on a few methods by which to revive my thoughts. With a little help, they usually came flooding back. I would start a chapter by reading my journal. Those hurriedly scratched notes took me right back to the road and the sights and sounds and smells of the day. If that didn't help, I'd pull up the official Tour de France website. It was a valuable resource for detail of the route, the climbs and the start and finish locations plus all the regions through which we passed. Then I'd usually go back to my own Strava account and look more closely at the map. Zooming in on it could often show exactly where we pulled into a feed stop or a café or where we missed an arrow. By then, most of the gaps in my memory had sufficiently filled back in. Sometimes they didn't and this was the disappointing fate of a few of the "lesser" climbs of an eight climb day. We were expected to tackle 6 categorized and 2 uncategorized mountains. Pictures which show myself or Scott, grinning widely next to a sign indicating the summit do nothing but frustrate me. If they were as much of a pleasure to ride as our faces portray, then why couldn't I remember them? I guess there was just so much data for my brain to process, that it simply ran out of storage. In my attempt to observe every last detail of a more than 2,000 mile ride in the French countryside, I inadvertently let some of the experience escape down the drain hole. This had happened before. I tended to focus on the myriad detail of things versus the big picture and have struggled to remember small chunks of my past. Moments that Scott, who misses the obvious when it's right in front of his nose, can remember with startling clarity. I guess he's the forest and I'm the trees.

The woods surrounding the D120 road helped to insulate us from the heat punishing the rest of the region. We felt a breeze now and then rattle softly through the beech and spruce and the faint trickle sound of water somewhere in their depths. We had just started the 18km climb after warming up on the narrow rolling road through the village of Lochieu. The construction of the traditional houses belied the current temperature. Their ground floors were packed to the rafters with cut wood.

We rolled slowly past *le lavoir*, an aged communal fountain. More of a stone trough used for watering animals or people or the weekly wash, it was now providing a cool respite for some fellow cyclists. It was an immensely peaceful place with only the sound of an occasional songbird and the distinct low hum of our tires rolling over the imperfect pavement. I fell in love with this mountain, as I seem to do with them all and could picture Scott and I tucked away in a small stone house in the glade of an ancient hamlet. Here, we'd enjoy the kind of life that ticked by slowly while my two handsome horses grazed idly away on a sloping field, hock-deep in herby grass.

Phil mentioned at dinner the evening before that many a climber found this mountain pass unpleasant. He said it was the lack of rhythm found on her flanks, going from the steep early switchbacks to the slight descent midway to the long, straight slog to the summit. Indeed my legs found complaint when I put them back to work after a short downhill around kilometer 7 or 8. The next two kilometers after averaged between 8% and 9% but the woods there were so appealing and the bend of the road so welcoming, I was easily distracted from the effort. Then around kilometer 11 there was a punishing stretch hovering at 12%. With the inevitable resolve that came with already having climbed over 115,000 feet in two weeks' time, we stood on the pedals and began to push to the top.

I remember passing a tree of some notoriety on the right side of the road. There was a sign, but not speaking any useable French (and Scott in no mood to play translator) all I could do is stare longingly at the sign affixed to its gigantic trunk, wondering what story it was trying to tell. The climb here was so steep, the horizon disappeared from view and all we could see was more road meeting sky. Then we followed a left bend towards the shoulder of the mountain and another steep stretch of road rose back towards the forest. This steep pitch gave way to a more humane few kilometers, feeling flat at only a few percent grade. Then, we left the solitude of the woods in our wake and began to reel ourselves towards the stark meadows of the subalpine zone. In the shadow of the summit we were protected from the worst of the sun's rays but now had to contend with the capricious wind, blowing generously at our backs until we crossed the second cattle guard and veered right for the long march up the western face.

The final ramp to the top averaged 8% but it was the promise of what we'd find there that defied the strain of the effort and filled our sails for the last few pedal strokes. The view from those heights is still burned into my memory. It's dizzying and I felt both elated and strangely out of place, like an ant standing on top of its mound, dwarfed by the enormity of the lawn. It was only the Alps in the distance and not the edge of the earth, yet I still felt the power projecting from their shadowy silhouettes. It was a holy-shit moment and despite the vastness of the panorama, I did not feel insignificant but empowered. I was ready to take on the whole wide world. With the wind swirling strongly, I laid my bike on the ground and readied the camera to capture Scott cresting the summit of the Grand Colombier. Someone had spray-painted a message across the width of the road in large bold letters. "For those about to rock, we salute you." The image of him pedaling across those words, with a proud smile on his face is still my favorite of the whole tour.

Then, like a skipping record on an old stereo, my memory of this day jumps forward to the pleasures off the bike; feet resting lazily on a plastic chair, tepid glass of wine in my hand, the country's most watched bicycle race unfolding on a small television screen behind the bar of an open-walled cabana. The summery sounds of children laughing and splashing dives and belly flops into the cold water of the small lake, whose sandy shores are blanketed with colorful beach towels and lazing families. Scott and I would later soak our tired legs in that petite lagoon, guarded by the lower rungs of the many tiers of sheer rock and hefty base of the Grand Colombier.

This side near the finish town of Culoz boasted the infamous *lacets*, the narrow hairpin "shoelaces" and one of four ways to the summit. We opted out of the last climb of the day, Scott with an obvious excuse but for me it was for less obvious reasons. Maybe it was the waning hours of a hot day. The stiff headwind we had already labored against getting to the finish would have to be faced again after making the second albeit shorter loop of the mountain. Plus, the lure of taking a well-earned respite in the shade of a park with friends was just too tempting. Seeing Scott, a few beers later, rocking gently on a spring coiled hobbyhorse meant for toddlers told me it was the right call. Seeing Dr. Julian rocking cheerfully beside him on his own mount, confirmed the theory that sometimes rest and good company is the best medicine. Besides, I was suffering from my own aches and pains. The road that brought us off the summit was a rough one. Hunks of tarmac were missing from the best lines of descent. Washboard ruts multiplied at breaking points the further down we went, making carrying any amount of speed a risk and finding a sense of rhythm difficult. There was a steady stream of traffic trying to make their way around us, closing the gap along the straight-aways and losing ground around the turns. Descending was becoming a literal pain in the neck. Over the last few stages a nerve in my neck had started acting up, spreading shooting pain followed by numbness down to my fingertips when I spent too long in the drops.

In hindsight, what I needed was a longer stem and more drop to the bars. I simply didn't have enough room to get low and flat and was jamming myself up in the cockpit, my upper spine bearing the brunt of it. I was having to sit up and put my hands on the hoods for as long as it took to get the feeling to come creeping back in my fingers and stop the lightning bolts shooting though my vertebrae. Descending this way, however briefly, was incredibly unsafe but it was a decision I was forced to make. Not sitting up meant I could no longer keep a reliable hold on the drops, so the risk seemed the lesser of the evils.

About halfway down, I hugged the shoulder to allow a van to pass and in the shadow of the trees lining the road, failed to see a pothole. I saw it too late to move and lacking the skills to safely bunny hop the thing, braced for the impact. My front wheel dove in and bounced out and my sweaty hands simultaneously slipped off the hoods. The effect was terrifying and the whole of time and space slowed to snail-speed so that I actually watched my hands levitate and could see the gap of daylight between them and the bars. They continued their sickly arc towards the ground before miraculously sticking their landing; one hand back on the tip of the hood near the lever, the other on the precarious edge of the drop. They were as far off the bars as possible while still maintaining a qualifying grip. That made two near-death experiences on the same mountain, the first being nearly flattened on the way up by a vintage '60's era Porsche out with its auto club for a nice tour of the Jura. Despite driving on the wrong side of the road, it was a beautiful machine and I'm sure worth a mint. No doubt the driver would have provided a nice sum to my family as reparations for my demise and my father would have at least been happy I wasn't taken out by a car of lesser collectable value.

Using up two of my nine lives in the same stage made me less inclined to continue on. Tempting fate a third time seemed like pushing my luck, so I declined the request to join Phil up the Lacets. I regret it now, as I write this from the safety of my arm chair. I really regret it. It was the last Tour de Force Phil would lead, though it didn't occur to me then that I might not get another chance to share some one-on-one pedaling time with him, hearing entertaining narratives about his beloved France. Forget a conversational pace. The more likely scenario would have me hanging on his wheel for dear life before watching him disappear around the next hairpin, leaving me with only my heavy breathing for company and an amazing view of the Rhône valley for solace. I think I would have been fine with either.

STAGE 16:

Swallowed By A Whale

July 11th, 2016 ~ Moirans-en-Montagne to Berne. "It feels like we've been swallowed by Moby Dick." Author screams over the ear-splitting din of the Swiss tunnel.

"131.5 miles and 5,728 feet of climbing. The day started out just fine. In fact, more than fine. My legs felt surprisingly fresh and my mind clear despite our tiny, dirty lodgings. Last night's buffet dinner was decent and the view soothing on the eyes. Had a restful night's sleep with cool mountain air creeping in through our open window."

"Phil ~~instructed~~ *forced us to ride in groups today. We fell in, luckily, with a good group of men save one, whose wheel had grown weary and un-steady over the last few challenging stages. The morning roads were gentle and winding and gratefully for us all, pointed generally downward. Lush, wide pastureland – more wheat and barley – straw bales sitting fine in the fields in the gentle morning sun. But these were the calm moments before the proverbial storm."*

"We were warned that it would rain late in the day but as the noon bells chimed, the rain began to fall. I was totally and unforgivably underprepared. No rain jacket in the day bag and not worried about keeping warm because the expected high was to be in the 80's. My weather expectations were wrong. It turns out that hypothermia can strike even when the temperatures are mild…any time your core temperature falls…you are done for.

Teeth chattering, limbs numb and inoperable. Brain ceased to think lucid thoughts, operating in safe-mode only. Very, very unpleasant. Though that didn't seem stop it from sending the signal to my poor body that it was experiencing a terrifying, and potentially life-threatening event and it should start to panic. Oh, it's nothing, just a never-ending concrete shaft to hell. The concrete whale. A huge tunnel bored into ground, pitched steadily downward, deafening noise radiating from every direction. The fans churning stale air and exhaust fumes into our faces. No light. Sensory depriving as much as overloading. It was the last place on earth I'd ever want to find myself on a bicycle. Lorries and cars speeding past, as startled to see us there. A recipe for disaster."

"I'm still not sure how no one was obliterated into a thousand pieces by a speeding truck. Scott had the gumption to usher us both onto the tiny pedestrian platform, a sliver of an elevated sidewalk barely out of harm's way. When a lorry passed in the right lane, we both had to lean against the tunnel wall to stay away from their side mirrors."

"By that point I was a frozen bag of limbs and was now panicked and agitated. I thought the terror of that concrete tube would never end. With the roaring noise and wetness, I had a sense of what poor plankton must experience as they slip down the gullet of the great ocean's whales (if they are capable of such dire thoughts)."

"As soon as I saw the light at the end of the tunnel – no pun intended – I was ready to quit only there was nowhere to go. We immediately began a lengthy descent into the village below…a huge canyon to our right visible through the rain and the trees. Lunch did nothing to warm me. Sarah managed to find us

emergency shelter, a gymnasium opened just for our benefit, but it was hard to generate any heat sitting in an un-heated space in wet clothes."

"When we departed the lunch stop, my teeth were still chattering, limbs still numb and by the bottom of the first small descent, I couldn't feel the controls or manage to shift or brake or even muster the strength to unclip. I was in real trouble today. I've never experienced an almost total physical failure due to the elements and my own stupidity. Fortunately Scott was there to hug some heat into me, enough to keep pedaling. A few miles up the road, the rain came down heavier and we had to stop. He bought me two espressos from a gas station."

"The rain finally sputtered out and while not exactly sunshine, we felt a little warmth through the grey sky. The next section of road was somewhat kinder and we stopped for the best gelati ever made by a local Swiss farmer and his smiling wife. I tried the rosemary and Scott tried the orange and basil special. The celery flavor was awesome but I was too chilled to eat more than a bite or two of each flavor despite the now 80-degree temperatures and stifling humidity. The ice cream vendor Muck had opened his shop just for us on a day he would otherwise have been closed. It was kind of him and I felt bad for being grumpy."

"The last 35 kilometers brought a mysterious and sudden knee pain. A pain so sharp, I could hardly pedal, never mind stand to relieve the pressure of my tender soft bits. I complained a lot. Then I remembered that Scott had his own share of hurts and I complained a little less. Though I'm convinced the less I complained, the more it hurt. Just as mysteriously, as soon as we hit the jarring cobbles of old town Bern, the pain disappeared. Goodbye kneeache, hello headache. Seemed like a fair trade."

*"Bern is a beautiful city. Spectacular postcard "old town",
its traditional Swiss architecture splendid in the protective bend
of the impossibly blue water of the Aare river. The river
downright marches through the heart of the city, ferrying brave
floaters and rafters downstream. It moves frighteningly fast,
how do they get out? I'm looking forward to a good night's sleep
and then exploring tomorrow if Scott is feeling up to it. That,
and a good cup of coffee and a proper breakfast. We're both
getting weary of day old croissants (not a decent one since
Normandy) and tasteless yogurt."*

*"Despite today's ills, I can safely say I no longer fear
distance or climbing. I only fear the weather and my own
stupidity. Next time it rains dummy, better pack a rain jacket."*

↔

I have trouble even writing about this stage much less wanting
to remember it in any great detail. But the frightening part is
that I can, every miserable mile of it. Maybe I haven't had
sufficient time to recover from both the physical and mental
trauma. I wish I were kidding. This is the one stage I would
never, ever repeat for all the money or bicycles or cheese in the
world. We should have gone around. I wouldn't give a pigeon
fart if the official Tour de France route sent me to hell and back.
I'd go, but not through that godforsaken tunnel or any others
like it. Forget about pushing a rock up a mountain for all
eternity, hell would be an endless loop of riding through Swiss

tunnels on a bicycle. The noise alone is enough to drive you senseless, from the reverberating baffle of industrial fans churning through the petrol-thick air to engines of all taxonomic ranks and the cacophony of a hundred sets of tires barreling across granulated tarmac. Add to that the closeness of it all, passing relentlessly fast and close and without even a hint of knowledge of you, in all your vulnerability, standing only inches away. From the interior of one of those vehicles, the tunnel must seem like a temporary womb, dark and quiet and fascinating. When viewed through the eyes of a hypothermic brain, it really is as bad as being swallowed alive and not knowing if you'll make it through, undigested by any number of hungry machines.

Hypothermia is the pits. Especially when you don't know it's happening. It's like pulling a prank on yourself. There's cold. Then there's this kind of cold. And it can happen frustratingly when the temperatures would be considered "mild" to a person warm and dry and wearing appropriate clothing and not participating in strenuous, prolonged exercise. Pedaling for hours through the driving rain, in the mountains, temperatures in the low-50's with only a croissant in your belly for breakfast makes you the perfect candidate. First you feel a chill or perhaps goosebumps. That's your body politely mentioning that its feeling cold. Ignore it and you start to shiver, on and off. Ignore that and the shivering becomes uncontrollable, sometimes causing your jaw to clench and your teeth to chatter. Now your core temperature has begun to drop below the 98.6-ish that we all require for copasetic internal functionality. Disregard those warning signs and your body cleverly keeps heated blood around your heart instead of sending it to your limbs, which start to tingle and eventually go numb. That makes it particularly tricky to hold on to the levers.

Let's say you do. Hold on to the levers that is. Then keep pedaling foolishly along because you think you're just being wimpy and no one else seems to be bothered by the rain or cold. I mean look at them, they're not complaining so suck it up and move it along. And just like that, your brain goes all foggy and you start having irrational thoughts. And getting emotional and you finally break down and start sobbing on the side of the road because you can't feel your fingers or toes or arms or legs for that matter and you just want to lay down right here and take a nap. But you also know that's the stupidest thing you've thought all day because it's wet and cold out and your husband is staring at you like you've lost your mind and is holding on to you like a fragile bird. And the last synapse fires straight and true before everything goes blurry. You better fix this and fast you sopping wet idiot.

Unfortunately we didn't have many options at our disposal. There were no additional dry layers stashed away in our day bags. Cafés were absent along this stretch of soggy road. We deviated from the route and took shelter beneath a diminutive overhang belonging to a sparsely stocked petrol station. At least they had a Nespresso machine and we put that overworked contraption through her paces with two café crèmes and two espressos each. What I didn't know then that I know now, though only half-heartedly believe, is that caffeine worsens the effects of exposure. That may be so, but those tiny porcelain vessels were my lifeline. I drank them as if my life depended on each drop, slowly and deliberately. We sat outside at a temporary table intended for employee smoke breaks, beneath a dripping awning on the right side of the building. We didn't have the heart to stay indoors, leaving a wide puddle on their spotless tile floor.

Spirits lifted, if only temporarily and rather falsely by the injection of caffeine, it was time to hit the road. The rain seemed to have lessened ever so slightly and we weren't getting any warmer or any drier lingering there. The first few miles were misery. I braced myself as best I could for the cold pelt of rain and the spray of road and pouted my most determined pout, as if the universe would somehow grant my silent wish for sunshine. Perhaps it was not my wish but the power of a million wishes that caused the rain to end and the sun to finally break through the density of the grey Swiss sky. And just in the nick of time too before I drifted away again towards hysteria.

↔

I was nonplussed to be sitting in front of an ice cream shop. Seriously, I just had spent hours sopping wet. My jaw hurt from all the teeth-clenching and I was in no mood to shovel tiny spoonsful of ice-cold handmade anything down my gullet. But the place, named Muck's, won me over in spite of my delicate condition and I reluctantly helped myself to a few kindly offered samples. If ice cream can be perfect, this was.

The flavors were unusually appealing and seasonally appropriate and the ingredients were nurtured lovingly from the soil by the proprietor and partner, his wife. They were farmers that had a fondness for turning their crops into creamy bounty and had unselfishly offered to open their tiny, rustic retail shop for the sole benefit of the riders of the Tour de Force. Thanks in no small part to the magic that Sarah continuously worked on our behalf, we'd otherwise have passed the lovely place by, never having tasted such treats from the very soil of Switzerland and the bounty of both farmer and the farmed. Bolstered by sugar and the contagious good nature of the ice cream shop owner, Muck, we set out for the final run into Bern. We passed through a few small clusters of commerce on the outskirts of the city, rows of traditional chalets standing proudly above narrow streets, their intricately carved railings and eaves stained the rich dark brown of generations.

This wasn't the land of the big mountains yet, so the road rolled gently across fields of corn and wheat and past stable yards housing stout, fine horses. The sun had finally warmed the air to the forecast 80 or so degrees and steam was drifting off puddles lingering on the blacktop. We rode through mobile curtains of buzzing blackflies, attracted by the livestock and energized by the heat. One ill-timed inhale of and I swallowed a mouthful of the tiny buggers. They had no flavor to speak of but stuck uncomfortably at the back of my throat.

What I had hoped would be an easy lope along the last stretch of the stage before our second and final rest day, was anything but. I developed a painful hitch in my giddy-up. My own knee, perhaps through some strange sympathetic connection to Scott's injured appendage, decided now was a good time to start throbbing. This was particularly flustering since I had never had knee issues, not in the slightest, even after years of riding and racing a single speed cyclo-cross bike. Anyone who love ridings with one gear (always the wrong one, eh?) understands that such feats of strength and single-cog-shenanigans are not always easy on the knees. Mine, up to this very point, worked just fine. This sudden onset of pain was inexplicable and I was beyond perturbed. I had been drenched, flash frozen, spatially tortured and now taunted with unnecessary tendon pain. So I fought back against my unseen enemy the only way I knew how and complained about it repeatedly. Scott says he can't remember me making a fuss but I'm certain I aired my grievances indiscreetly. Or maybe I only thought them. Either way, it was another low moment during an already trying day.

The route map claims there was a climb at the end of the stage, but I only vaguely recall it. I can picture myself sitting on the bike, wincing with every left down stroke. Sometimes whimpering. Sometimes uttering nothing at all. That's when it got really bad. Amusingly, I have a photo of Scott on that climb, his outline striking against the blanket of green wheat to his right and the blank blue canvas of sky above him. Seeing that, it's hard to feel sorry for myself, since I had enough gumption to ride one handed and snap a picture. After weeks of whole body discomfort, such acute pain was an entirely new sensation.

We closed the distance to the center of the city and I was immediately distracted by the surroundings. Bern looked like a pop-up book with its myriad layers of colors and shapes and lines on the horizon. At Scott's behest, we stopped for a photo against the oddly blue river. I hobbled my bike across the tram-track lined cobbles to lean against the railing, the river coursing behind my back. We remounted, with only a mile or two remaining to the hotel. The last stretch, a cobbled kicker, rattled some sense back into my cantankerous joint. Freed from any further pains, I was able to put some power into the pedals and float along the well-worn stones of the *Klösterlistutz* before turning towards home for the next two nights.

I was spent. I felt like the tube of toothpaste flattened repeatedly and then rolled in order to get every drop of content to come out. And I was testy and intolerant of any more input, good, bad or benign. I was impatient with a former lifer who tried to introduce herself and make polite conversation at the front doors of the hotel. I was still holding on to my bike like a crutch and felt in no mood to be social. I should have tried harder to at least be kind.

The evening's routine dictated that we ferry our bikes to the second floor ballroom and hand them over to the staff for storage. I snapped at one of the new mechanics for wanting to pile my bicycle up with the rest. At that very moment, that bike felt both like a temple and my trusted friend and I somewhat insanely only cared about cleaning it and checking it over before I even got out of my dirty kit. I reacted rather brusquely, when his singular crime was suggesting I come back to it tomorrow if it had no pressing issues. The poor guy just needed the space to work and here I was, growling like a territorial dog over a bit of chew toy. In my defense, I had grown accustomed to a particular routine. Even in a bleary-eyed state, my routine was my lifeline. So ingrained by now, even the tedious act of degreasing and lubing my chain felt cathartic and I would not be derailed. I was no longer the fresh-faced greenhorn, malleable to anyone with an authoritative air. I only abided the rules of the road, the desires of my corporeal machine and those goddamned arrows.

Aware now that I wasn't fit for appearing in public, I made my way up to our room for a shower and a change of clothes before dinner. Scott brought up a round of drinks to help us unwind and I sat next to the open window to write in my journal. We were more than a dozen floors above a posh equestrian campus, riders working young animals in the outdoor arena, the aroma of straw and horseflesh pungent in the evening air. It was a scene familiar to me and equally torturous as it was soothing. I missed my own herd, now one member smaller and wanted so badly to bury my head against their warm coats and breathe deeply the earthy musk of them. During times of duress, I yearned for those creatures, as I did now and the clip and clop of well-shod hooves on hard surfaces had a calming effect on my demeanor. Regardless of the incessant rain, I left the window open for two nights, so the smell of the neighboring stable could waft in.

REST DAY; BERN

Bear Market

July 12th , 2016 ~Berne, Switzerland. "Zero sleep last night. There was a staff party outside until midnight. Heard their laughter all the way up on the 11th floor. Tried closing the window but nearly smothered without air conditioning. Then the upstairs occupant came home from her evening out and brought the party home with her. Until at least 2am. So much for rest. I guess it was Karma for not being nicer yesterday."

"We bypassed the sorry looking breakfast buffet for an early walk to the laundromat (with a stop for a pastry and a tiny coffee). There was a coin-op laundry was at a funky bar – coffee house – commune – music venue – laundromat named Café Kairo. They had a simple shrine to a recently departed feline. His picture and a lit candle made a touching display. I miss my own cat, gone last fall. He would have been mad at me staying away so long."

"The cappuccinos there were really good. I had two of them while waiting for our clothes to dry. It was a pleasant and comfortable place and a nice reprieve from the dreary weather. It was dumping dogs outside. The café began to fill with other Lifers, looking for coffee and an empty washing machine, so we gathered up our still damp clothes (ran out of Swiss franc coins)

and made the long walk back to the hotel. We took a roundabout way to swing by a bike shop. We bought a set of emergency long fingered gloves for yours truly and headed off in search of 1st lunch. Walked into a nice looking Indian buffet, but left after finding out we were limited to one plate each. It was the size of a salad plate and the thought of so little food terrified me, so we left without sitting down."

"Next stop was a bright and lovely gourmet grocery chain with a satisfying collection of small sandwiches and canapés of smoked salmon and tuna. I adore fish spreads and appreciate a country that loves them as much as I do. Plus they had these Pringle-like chips in a tube that were hot pepper flavored. All of that and two bottles of the finest sparkling water and we were set until second lunch. We walked back to the room, laid out our damp clothes to dry in the open window and set off again for old town, this time taking the tram."

"One short ride the wrong direction (both trains said number 9!) then another short ride downhill then across the river into the center of Bern, a UNESCO heritage site (all of Old Town actually plus a quirky astrological clock from the 13th century). It is now a busy tourist shopping district, lined with quaint shops vastly different in character from the gaudy stores of Andorra. Chocolate and coffee, cheese, flowers, busy cafés, clothiers, toys, plenty of pharmacies, jewelry shops and of course the famous Swiss timepieces. We popped into a tidy sliver of a shop to look at all kinds of delicious running cheeses and left with a small taste of something gooey, a homemade roll, a slender local saucisson and a tiny bottle of kirsch, a local cherry brandy."

"Sitting on the steps beneath a covered sidewalk, we were lucky to witness the old clock strike the hour over the heads of hundreds of tourists strolling the cobbled streets."

"Though the rest day is greatly needed, sitting idle is making me restless and pessimistic and I can't shake this depressed mood. I'm ready to get back on my bike and pedal. Today, while enjoyable, felt like delaying the inevitable. The mountains will still come. I'm eager to face them and return to rhythms of French roads and the country that has begun to feel like home."

↔

I liked Bern. It had some spunk to it, often lacking in Swiss cities. It still ranks as one of top ten places in the world to reside for the highest quality of life. Not surprisingly, that kind of accolade comes at a price and being a tourist there even for a day is not easy on the wallet. I am just half-heartedly complaining since we only had to support ourselves during our rest days, of which there were only two, and the occasional café stop or ice cream break or pre-dinner dinner or second lunch (thrice so far) plus any alcohol that didn't already appear on the communal table at our hotels during dinner.

I didn't wake happy however about the lack of decent sleep on a rest day, thanks partly to the late night revelry of the staff outside our open window until after midnight. That said, I can't entirely blame them. It was their rest day too and there would be further turn-over, with some members leaving and new ones appearing and they deserved to celebrate. It was just unfortunate that our rooms had no air conditioning, so closing the window meant suffocating in the small humid space and the thin glass provided little defense against the howls of laughter a score of floors below. Just as we thought we'd finally catch some shut-eye, the ceiling above us began to pound with the heavy (drunken) footsteps and boisterous (angry) shouting of another hotel guest (not unknown to us). Thin walls and the late hour meant we had little in the way of rest and woke early, ravenous and grumpy.

Sitting around a quiet table at Café Kairo, soothed by my second cappuccino and the quiet hum of half-a-dozen tumbling dryers, Scott and I chatted some with the jovial proprietor before being joined by Tom for a spell. One of our most frequent breakfast companions, I always enjoyed conversations with Tom. His easy demeanor and consistently positive stance on the state of things had a settling effect on my own tumultuous outlook. I was feeling more like the laundry inside those machines, being tossed about and shriveled, my enthusiasm for this adventure drying up by the minute. Rather symbolically (I hoped), no matter how many coins we fed into the slot, our clothes never did dry completely and we left…over- caffeinated and out of coins.

It was time to get some air, take in the sights and find a fresh distraction from the events of the last few days and the foul weather. Donned in layers and a rain coat, we hopped aboard the city tram and headed to the center of town. Bern was a visually stimulating place, full of colors and layers. It looked very much like the center of a children's pop-up book with a make-believe city leaping from the pages, medieval and modern mixed in perfect portions by an illustrator's pen.

There is still some debate as to the origin of the name Bern (*Berne* in French, *Berna* in Italian; also languages spoken in this multi-lingual Capital) and despite the keeping of bears in the *Bärengraben*, it is unclear if the name actually means "bear". It wasn't until the year 1220 or so that the animal first appeared in the heraldic coat of arms and the city isn't likely to adopt a new symbol after an almost eight-hundred year relationship.

Another of the of the city's 800 year-old icons is the *Zytglogge*. A medieval gate tower protecting Bern's once western gate, it is now topped with the more recent addition (a mere 600 years-old) of an astrological clock. The tower and the clock, collectively called the *Zeitglockenturm* is a UNESCO treasure. First constructed between 1218 and 1220, the tower served as a defense post, keeping roving wanderers from liberally entering the village. In the 1270's it was heightened by 7 meters to keep up with rapidly expanding fortifications of an increasingly populous city. During the mid-1300's, the tower changed roles from a defensive structure to a prison specifically housing women. These inmates were *Pfaffendirnen.* Translated to "priest's whores" these women were accused of having unholy relations with the clergy, who were undamnable to be sure. Perhaps to cleanse the structure of its sinful contents, it was completely destroyed in a catastrophic fire of 1405, and the prison was never re-instated. Instead, a clock and bell were installed to provide sound timekeeping to the bustling town's residents. The current clock-workings, constructed in 1530 by the self-taught clock maker Kaspar Brunner, whose handiwork still ticks reliably to this day.

Bern is also home to eleven 16th century water fountains, each topped with a detailed allegorical figure. Allegory was much used during the middle ages and the renaissance to depict a moral story, a history lesson or a dire warning. Since they had a dual function as public sources of water, visitors to these fountains found themselves captive audiences to the bold and sometimes fiendish characters and the poignant, if not dark tales they told. Perhaps the most startling (and Scott's favorite) was the *Kindlifresserbrunnen,* or fountain of the children eater.

Having no children ourselves, Scott harbored no guilt in his amusement of the portrayal of a portly ogre, caught eternally in the act of devouring a screeching infant while a writhing bag of toddlers hangs from his belt. There are many theories attempting to decode the message as well as the messenger. Some say it depicts Krampus, of Alpine folklore fame and Santa's alter-ego. Clad in the traditional colors of Christmas, perhaps the figure kept naughty children scared straight year-round or else they faced being served up as a holiday snack. Speaking of snacks, Old Town had no shortage of delicious offerings from high alpine cheeses to the famous Swiss chocolate and plenty of opportunities to sample local cuisine. Sitting in a comfortably cramped and canvas covered patio in view of a pedestrian-only zone bustling with vendors and market-goers, we dried off from the drizzle striking gently against the worn cobbles outside.

A bowl of homemade beef stew in a silky broth chased away any lingering chill and we dove in greedily to a huge helping of *rösti*, a specialty of the canton of Bern. A simple dish, typically eaten by farmers at breakfast time, consisted of grated potatoes, generous salt and pepper, served in the shape of the pan used to fry it. Ours was adorned with diced onion sautéed in butter. Between mouthfuls of tuber, we made quick work of the ham steak drenched in richly golden egg's yolk oozing though a mound of unadorned elbow macaroni. There wasn't a leafy green in sight.

We had stuffed ourselves so thoroughly, it was hard to imagine eating dinner in just a few hours. Though after resting a spell at the hotel and spending some time washing the bikes, I had miraculously re-developed an appetite, as evidenced by the rumbling in my stomach. I felt less put off by the thought of another meal by the time we had ridden the elevator to the dining hall. Besides, there was grilled salmon and fresh salad on the buffet line which seemed like a fair way to balance out our starch-heavy second lunch. I was trying to conveniently forget about all the oil and butter which made that entire meal possible.

Really, I didn't spend much time fretting over portion sizes or the richness of ingredients these days. For the first time in my adult life, I didn't have any calorie-guilt. It was awesome. Not that I wanted to eat irresponsibly. I still wanted to fuel my body properly and with healthy ingredients but I didn't give pause to dessert after dinner or a second (or third) helping of cheese. It was fun while it lasted and the habit took some effort to undo once we returned to our "normal" lives. For a few weeks after the tour, I was hungry all the time but without burning upwards of 8,000 calories a day, I could no longer give in to food-related whims.

At dinner I had the chance to sit across from Kevin, another lifer and finally get to know a little more about the eccentric fellow. For the first two weeks, I only knew him by the wrinkle of his furrowed brow and downturned mouth and the bellowing of orders to fellow cyclists. He hardly gave me the time of day. I didn't mind so much, as we were about as far away on the spectrum of similarities as two people could get. But there had been stages leading up to the second rest day where he had begun to take me under his protective, albeit assertive wing. He was gruff, painfully direct, loud and sometimes off-color but I had begun to see in him a softer, generous, more delicate side.

I liked him and was amused though not surprised to hear more about his personal life and to understand that we shared a common outlook on life, how to live it and the general state of civilization. It would feel like a betrayal of his confidence to share too much about the things we discussed over our meal but I hold that conversation dear. It took trust to share the details of his existence with someone so seemingly different than himself and it turned out we weren't so different after all.

By nightfall my mood had improved, my outlook repaired and I felt closer to another Lifer sharing the same journey but experiencing it in a unique way. Like most of us, Kevin had something to prove. Not to anyone else in the world, but to himself. He was a long-time smoker, but chose to quit for the duration of the tour (and not one minute longer). He had dropped weight dramatically from the first stage to now, more so it seemed than any other rider. He wanted to ride with Tour de Force to raise money for the foundation and do something good for the less fortunate, even though he had lost his life savings during the downturn of the economy not so many years back. One might never have assumed from first glance that this unlikely individual was undeniably capable of both a colossal physical challenge and selfless generous acts. I went to bed that evening feeling different about the day and myself. I felt less on-the-outs with the group and less interested in remaining in a funk knowing there were still surprises left in the waning days of this adventure.

STAGE 17:

The Mont Blanc Express

July 13th, 2016 ~ Moirans-en-Montagne to Megève . "These tickets are only for your vélos." The train conductor informs. "Our bikes need train tickets?" Author inquires. "Oui, as do you." He answers dryly.

"50.2 miles and 3,497 feet of climbing. The day started cool and lovely. We had gentle traffic leaving Bern, an easy pedal through the city and out into the countryside. There we passed more postcard chalets with their intricately carved eaves. Our first morning stop was at a beautiful traditional Swiss mountain house, built in 1618. The date was carved above the door. It amazingly looked brand new. We filled our bottles from a cattle trough, the water crystal clear and spring fed."

"Back on the road, we began a gradual climb. Then, not surprisingly, the rain started to fall. We had out-pedaled the darkening clouds as best we could but to no avail. It came gently down at first, then a deluge. The route took us up a small incline and over a double set of train tracks, where a few riders had trouble. Most slipped across, rear tires breaking loose and stepping out sideways. Two went down hard and the rest of us began to pile up behind them. One was out with an injured wrist. His spirits were worse off than that I'm afraid."

"*The first climb was a piece of cake. I was cold but not uncomfortably so. I found a great rhythm and stuck with it before I looked back and saw no sign of Scott. I wasn't going to leave him today, just as he didn't leave me the other day when I was out of sorts. I pulled into a driveway to wait. He was having knee trouble again. Poor thing. He couldn't catch a break. At least the rain had stopped and I was asked for an autograph, so the morning wasn't all bad.*"

"*Up the road it began to rain again. Many had disrobed for the climb and were all caught out in the downpour. There were dozens of us on the shoulder, madly donning layers. There was another climb ahead to warm our bodies, if not our legs. We pulled into stop 2 feeling optimistic about the stage. Phil said there'd be rain early but clearing skies, so hopes were high for a dry afternoon. We seemed comfortable enough initially, but no more than five minutes later standing around in the wind and rain blowing through the tent, a chill set in. Then one of the staff relayed a message that the temperatures at the top of the next category 3 climb had dropped to an unexpected 1 degree Celsius. That's 33.8 degrees Fahrenheit and very, very cold in wet lycra. And that was followed by a 20km decent in the driving rain. I was growing increasingly anxious.*"

"*Scott was already wincing and mentioned taking the van to the next feed stop. He didn't know if he could manage the following climb. He was cold and tense and that was affecting his pedal stroke. My own chills were increasing in intensity and my teeth had begun to chatter again just as Scott mentioned my bluing lips. Maybe getting a lift to feed stop 3 wasn't such a bad idea. We had no spare layers in the van and while dressed for the rain, weren't dressed for the cold rain.*"

"Bad news from the staff. Both vans were full of abandoned riders from the train track incident and the weather. There was room for Scott but not for me. I told him to get in, I would go on but he wouldn't have it. It was time for an emergency back-up. It was time to get creative."

"In a soggy bit of serendipity, Scott needed to use the loo and as it turned out, the toilets were located behind a small train station across the parking lot from the rest stop. After hearing our limited options (keep riding in the cold rain or wait indefinitely in the cold rain for a lift), we made the hasty decision to buy tickets and take the train wherever it was headed then sort it out from there. Thanks to Scott's French and our emergency credit card stashed in his jersey pocket, and in no small part to the efficiency and reliability of Europe's mass transportation systems, we bought tickets at a self-serve kiosk for a line that we were pretty sure went the right direction. As luck would have it, this tiny platform supplied a stop for a train (three trains, actually and a bus) that would take us all the way to the Finhaut dam…precisely where we needed to go. All for the sum of $160 Swiss Francs each…about the same in US dollars. When the universe offers you a train, you get on board."

↔

The entry for Stage 17 ends there…rather abruptly, which I suspect was due to the lateness of the hour when I wrote it and the effects of the unusual day. There are notes scribbled in the margins which I believe I wrote in the days following so as not to forget some of the most interesting details. So let's start with that serendipitous train ride, and the 2nd class car into which we climbed, a captivating panoramic tube with windows reaching all the way to the roofline so as not to deny its occupants a fine view of the Alps. Suitably named the Mont Blanc Express, I would later come to realize this was the very train I had casually daydreamed of riding someday.

For years I owned a copy of a vintage travel poster by the French illustrator, Roger Broders. It depicted the Trient gorge between Chamonix and Martigny. It was a romantic, softly verdant scene and I had spent many moments staring into its layers wondering if such a place and a train could exist. That was years ago and the poster is long gone, ruined beyond repair in a cross-country move. Yet here I was, sitting in a modern relative of that very train on those very rails about to traverse that very gorge and what a strange and wonderful feeling did dawn on me then.

The train was not much warmer than the outside. Drier, yes, but not warmer. That's what you get when you're sitting for hours in wet cycling clothes, thin as they are, in a train with no heat. It was July after all and supposed to be summer, so the heating system had long been disabled in favor of the air-conditioning, which blew relentlessly across our dimpled skin like tiny blasts of arctic breeze. How weird it felt sitting there, rain leaching from our bibs making puddles on the train floor and leaving a damp ring on the polyester seats.

There was a heavy anxiety weighing on my chest, that feeling of being somewhere you shouldn't be…like playing hooky at school and going to the movie theater instead. You made a clean break but your guilty conscience won't let you enjoy the show. It took a few minutes to put those thoughts aside and as the alpine landscape began scrolling by, I wondered how it was that we ended up here.

↔

The streets of Bern were quiet for a workday morning. Not too many cars on the wide boulevards but row after parallel row of tracks to ferry students and tourists and the employed to their destinations. The air was crisp and clean but not cold and although rain was forecast for late afternoon, we enjoyed a dry sky and a touch of sunshine. There was no transfer today, so our rollout from the hotel parking lot felt almost leisurely, as did most stages when we didn't have to budget our time for an early morning and a lengthy trip on the bus. Honestly, I never minded those rides. I enjoyed seeing the sights from the large picture windows and it was a varied view from the one I had from the saddle. Plus, it gave me time to reflect without needing to use valuable brain power to turn the pedals, hold a straight line, keep an eye out for traffic and the like. It was bonus down time for some and extra sleep time for most others. We were all getting tired. The Lifers especially.

Bern, like most intelligently and sustainably developed cities, gave way hastily to surrounding countryside, wrapping itself protectively in rivers and farms and forests that keep urban growth in check. The road began to roll and the houses turned from tidy and efficient to more traditional, engineered to keep out centuries of harsh mountain weather while designed to age with measured grace.

The sky was bulging with plump, darkening clouds. This had an effect on the filtered sunlight, somehow magnifying it and the mountainscape was awash with bold color. It was mesmerizing in the same way you fight to peel your eyes from the twisting of a tornado on the horizon or lightening electrifying the night sky. Like a beautiful warning sign of the building storm. And then it began to rain.

Somewhere along the road to the first feed stop I managed to lose Scott. It was just as the pavement began to steepen again and he was in no mood for heroics. I bridged my way up to the back wheel of another cyclist in our tour, not a Lifer, but a rider joining us for the Alps stages. He was a jovial fellow and we were cycling merrily along when a car came speeding past, only to brake hard as it pulled onto the shoulder in front of us.

We slowed, then stopped, expecting to be confronted for some perceived car vs bike transgression though before we could even raise our hackles, a cheery man sporting a huge grin bounded from the car like an excited Labrador. He positively loped towards us with a pen and postcard outstretched in his hand.

252

To my pleasant surprise, it was none other than Muck, the owner of Bern's most delicious gelato shop. How on earth he recognized us from any other cyclists on the road, I still wonder. He pulled over to wish us happy travels (in broken English) and to ask me for my autograph. Yep. My autograph. I've never been so honored or humbled or prideful on my bike than that moment and it's as close as I'll probably ever come to feeling like a cycling superstar. If I wasn't in such a state of giddy shock, I could have kissed that jovial man for making my day, my year, my entire attempt at this whole rolling parade worth it. My riding companion guffawed as we were setting off again and asked if there was something I wasn't telling him about my fame. No, I giggled. It's just plain old me.

By the time I rolled into the feed stop, my cheeks were hurting from excessive smiling and I couldn't wait to share the news with Scott. He was feeling cheery himself, despite his aches. The rain had subsided to a light drizzle, even clearing briefly for a spell. We ate the most delicious caramel brioche, local of course, so good I helped myself to about three or four hefty slices. We were also treated to a functioning flush toilet, a rarity on most days so spirits were high among the whole group. In front of the chalet was the most picturesque fountain, an antique trough actually, spewing forth clear cold water which we used to replenish our bottles. The photo I snapped of my husband there is one of my favorites, him looking the picture of health and happiness. His grin may not have told the whole story, but his recent days off the bike and our change of approach from "must ride every mile" to "ride one mile at a time" for the remainder of the stages had lifted a certain weight from his shoulders. It was nice to see him smile without a hint of grimace behind his eyes and I desperately hoped he was enjoying himself despite the setbacks.

We barely pedaled a mile up the road before the sky heaved and leaked its heavy burden of thick, liquid cargo on our heads. It was an unpleasant rain, cold but not cold enough, wet but in inconsistent spurts. So there we were, stuck between wearing our rain capes and sweating with the effort of the climb or disrobing but getting drenched in the meantime. The air temperature would eventually drop but not until we had worked up a good, old-fashioned lather in our layers. Any cyclists knows that it's the transitional seasons that are the hardest to dress for. This day couldn't decide if it was winter giving way to spring or fall giving way to winter.

Technical cycling jackets, even the best of them, can't always keep up with the whims of mother nature and accumulated sweat against your skin doesn't act as a good insulator. You're fine as long as you keep riding and thereby producing warmth but no sooner than you stop and start to cool down, that heat turns to chill. That's precisely what happened at stop 2. No one could have foretold that the expected low temperature for the stage would be off by almost 20 degrees. But such is the nature of the mountains and we should have known better by now to be prepared for the worst even when given a best case scenario.

What started out as a mild but humid morning with threatening skies turned to rain and wind and temperatures plummeting by the moment. Events happened rapidly from there. One fluid moment I find myself listening to the warning of the forecast at the summit of the Forclaz, the next I'm hearing Scott remark about my lips turning a troubling shade of blue, then the sound of my own sure voice suggesting we take the train. No, it was more deliberate than that. I rather insisted that we take the train, before even knowing to where it would ferry us. I only cared that it would.

Sheltered from the wind on the tiny, unheated platform of *Saanenmöser's* station, we clutched our tickets in frozen palms. We had barely decoded in time that the one upcoming train would deliver us from this Alpine pass to somewhere in France. Only we weren't exactly certain where. The electronic ticket kiosk was in Swiss German but the word Finhaut appeared on one of the lines, so it seemed like a safe bet. The machine spat out our tickets with only minutes to spare before the arrival of the train and we hastily boarded one of the cars bearing a bicycle symbol. As expected, this car accepted bikes and there were hooks on which to hang our drenched machines. The conductor came by momentarily to check tickets. He was mildly perturbed at our misinterpretation of what he felt was an abundantly clear procedure for booking passage for both our bicycles and ourselves, yet he would prove to be both lenient and helpful. Neither did he fine us for our accidental stowaway nor did he boot us off the train at the next station and both were legitimately within his power. He demystified our itinerary then went on to run our credit card through his nifty hand-held ticketing machine. We would not be traveling by just one train but three to reach our desired destination. Until then, we were welcome aboard this locomotive gem named the Mont Blanc Express.

Had we not been sitting in damp layers, racked by waves of uncontrollable shivering, it would have been a perfect voyage. Undeniably and overwhelmingly beautiful terrain was scrolling by and we were in a suspended state between thermal shock and aesthetic awe. Our spirits were periodically lifted by the passing of the beverage cart, though there were only so many six-euro espressos we could stomach. Scott, once he turned to six-euro beers, seemed to warm up exponentially more quickly. I on the other hand, seemed plagued by a chill that I couldn't shake for the duration of the journey. I tried to take in all the views but some of the soaring peaks were too tall for even the panoramic windows to reveal and the rest were slowly being engulfed by the thickening clouds. It appeared we wouldn't outrun the bad weather even by train and despite the soggy state of our attire, we were glad of our new, dry mode of transportation.

We disembarked at the first transfer nearly two hours later. My clothes had dried but I was still bone cold and now desperately hungry. Our well-schooled routine, had we been cycling instead of train hopping, would have supplied us with a food stop. Without it my stomach was in knots. There was a half hour wait until the second train would arrive and Scott managed to find us a sandwich and some paprika Pringles while I huddled in an enclosed pavilion, out of the wind barreling through the double platform of Montreux.

Too cold to care then, I would learn that the station at Montreux is the only one of its kind in Switzerland. What makes it unique, among other tidbits of architectural novelties, is that it houses three types of rail gauges: standard, meter and narrow. We would hop aboard the latter for a breathtaking half-hour ride along Lake Geneva. We clattered through various tunnels and along precipitously placed switchbacks carving between the dense forest and clinging to dramatic drops on our way down to Martigny just skirting the Gorge du Trient.

In Martigny, we muddled through another half-hour delay before boarding our third and final train. This time, there was no shelter from the wind that had begun to blow again in earnest, bringing with it occasional flakes of snow and wisps of freezing mist. Travel weary and hungry to the point of delirium, we nearly missed the train as I stood there holding both our bikes scanning the empty platform for any sign of Scott.

All the other passengers had boarded and he was nowhere to be found as the station clock displayed the very minute of our departure. We all know the efficiency of the trains in this part of the world, so my pulse was quickening with his absence. Just as I was about to resign myself to missing our only hope at deliverance, Scott comes penguin-trotting across the platform, half-skidding with the lack of traction provided by his slick road cleats. He shoved a crumpled white paper bag my direction, grabbed the bikes and made for the door of the nearest car. Hearing his foot make contact with the metal steps meant we wouldn't miss the train. The smell of a recently warmed pastry wafting from the sack meant we wouldn't starve.

Now's a good time to mention that when we made the decision to alight off that pass by train, we had no solid plan for how we would make contact with the group again. We knew the stage terminated at the Emosson dam, but that was the extent of it. A massive feat of hydro-engineering nestled in the decoupage of the Valais should have been fairly recognizable, so we banked on picking up the familiar neon arrows after leaving the Finhaut station. Fingers crossed. There was plenty of daylight left on the clock, despite the greyness of the skies, so we knew we still had time to get there before we'd be missed.

The compact, red train we boarded would bear us the rest of our journey. Only a half hour more on the rail but that leg would turn out to be the most captivating of the three. The Martigny-Châtelard railway would slowly but deliberately claw its way up and across the sublime gorge of Trient, with a rack and pinion system that helped it navigate up to 20% inclines and at times it certainly felt that steep. A deep and dramatic crevasse cut a thick gash in the mountain's flanks and the train crept defiantly close to the edge. I only wish the sky would have cooperated more fully, but there were enough bursts of late day light to reveal the unfeasible scenery but also a full-spectrum double rainbow, one end arching high above the tree-line and the tail disappearing down into the depths. It was a memorable ride and whatever chill that lingered in my limbs couldn't stop me from warming to the experience. I was finally letting go of the anxiety that had been clinging to my insides all day. So what if we'd had to abandon. Who cares if we let the weather win. I had grown tired of the guilt I carried in the center of my chest for not sticking it out and braving the elements. Chapeau to the riders who felt no fear of the cold or the rain or who were sufficiently motivated by whatever drove them to pedal forth in those trying conditions.

That was their story, their ride, their adventure and I don't begrudge them the accomplishment. But, this was ours and I wouldn't have traded it for sunny skies and temperate weather or checking off one more imposing climb. Rough seas make good sailors true enough but today's serendipitous two-railed voyage made for more valuable memories than a two-wheeled one would have done.

↔

Génépi is the nectar of Alpine gods. It must be since it took that celestial liqueur roughly half a second post-swallow to warm me from fingertip to toes. Thanks to fellow Lifer and all-around decent guy Steve, who upon hearing about our alternate ascent to the dam, suggested we celebrate with a stiff aperitif. (Steve, you are a gentleman of refined tastes, even if you refuse to adopt the cyclists' tradition of shaving your legs.) I have him to thank for my new found and difficult-to-satisfy craving for this cousin of Absinthe. Made from the family of high meadow herbs from the genus *Artemisia*, the stiffly alcoholic and somewhat medicinal tasting tonic is beloved across several countries spanned by the towering Alps. Originating in the Savoy region of France and naturally pale yellow to light olive in color, neon green versions should be avoided unless you like the taste of cough syrup and lawn clippings.

Sufficiently imbibed, we sat comfortably in the warmth of the restaurant as the last few riders found their way through the thickening soup of mist and low slung clouds to the top of the dam. The weather was changing again and fast and those still out on the climb would be chilled to the bone by the summit. Before the rain came again and the clouds closed ranks, there was a commanding vista across the Lac d'Émosson with Le Cheval Blanc peak on the horizon, snow blowing fetchingly from her brow. We settled into a decent dinner of perfectly roasted chicken and fries as the sun set below the picture windows of our dining room perched perfectly above the dam. Whether you took the two-wheeled option to the end of the stage or the two-tracked, it was a long day made longer by a white-knuckled 90-minute bus ride to Megève, where we'd be staying put for three whole glorious nights.

Our bus driver was well-versed in navigating those mountain hairpins, nosing the bus to the very edge of the anemic road. Our front row seats caused us to feel like we were angling suspended above the abyss. Even in the waning daylight, she managed to ferry us safely and expertly down the treacherous road without so much as a wayward blink. And with the last remnants of light, before the moon took hold and the army of evening clouds made their advance, she drove slowly past the oracle of the Alps, Mont Blanc herself. Bathed in a lunar glow, we looked on in hushed awe as night's curtain drew slowly across her profile.

STAGE 18:

Horsepower

July 14th, 2016 ~ Megève. "It's raining? Then turn off the alarm. I don't feel like riding today." Mumbles author groggily the morning of the time trial stage from Sallanches to Megève.

"Today was supposed to be a 17km uphill time trial. But it's raining outside, again, and cold. Speaking of colds, I appear to be have come down with one of my own, so I claimed this as a bonus rest day. Scott has no qualms with another day off the bike and we enjoyed lingering for once over our coffees. Our hotel, the "Old Sheep" is quaint and comfortable and breakfast was a thoughtful array of homemade fruit bread and creamy local yogurt from Alpine cows."

"Not much to report since our main priority was to rest. I bundled up in my one sweater and a jacket and we strolled slowly through the picturesque ski resort. We purchased a few small souvenirs for family and sat down for lunch at a narrow, bustling café specializing in thin crust pizza. Scott's had duck breast and arugula. Mine had incredible anchovies."

"As luck would have it, Megève is a popular international venue for equestrian sports and there was a show jumping competition going on today in the center of town. Brings back lots of memories of nearly three decades of my own time in the show ring. Can't help but provide commentary about each horse and rider as they navigate the sea of brightly colored rails. I spot *a few lovely mares I'd love to own if they weren't wildly out of my price range. I could buy a lot of bikes instead. "*

"*Feeling chilled again after sitting in the damp bleachers, we came back to the hotel for tea time and a hot bath. I was really craving a salad. Growing tired of meat and heavy carbs for dinner but have the distinct feeling the hotels' menus are manipulated to serve us exactly that. So much protein is getting hard to swallow (no pun intended). No dessert after tonight's dinner. That's just as well since we hit the patisserie this afternoon. Scott spotted in the window a confection he hadn't eaten since he was a kid, visiting in-laws in Albi and I think the taste of it brought back fond memories.*"

"*We're both worn out and distracted. The wind has rather left our sails. Neither of us are feeling 100% and since we've both now missed stages, are feeling restless and disappointed in ourselves. It's hard not to feel like a quitter. We aren't being paid to destroy ourselves out there. This isn't a race. There's no sense in being miserable, right? I hear myself repeating those rational sentiments, but there's another voice too. The self-deprecating one that makes me feel like a failure. I think I understand what the professionals feel like when they crash or get sick and have to abandon. They must be incredibly hard on themselves. They have whatever pity I can spare. The rest I'm reserving for myself.*"

"*There have been some staff changes and I'm sorry to say that we've had some unpleasant experiences with one or two and more than a few feathers have been ruffled. Plus, yesterday was a debacle beyond just the weather. Scott and I spoke candidly about it to those in the position to listen and now feel like we've created waves. It's no fun feeling like an outsider when before you felt like family. Though it's even worse not to be honest and forthright. Well my attempt at diplomacy may have backfired but I feel like a weight has been lifted from my chest though it wasn't my intention to place it upon another's. We will see what tomorrow brings."*

↔

It was on the evening of July 14th, 2016 known as Bastille Day that we would learn of the terrible events in the city of Nice which took innocent lives in the most horrific manner. A man, whose name doesn't deserve repeating, drove a cargo truck through a dense crowd of revelers in a pedestrian zone gathering there for a fireworks display on a widely celebrated French holiday. As you might imagine, the carnage was horrific and 86 people were killed painfully and heartlessly. Four hundred and thirty-four more were injured. I did not mean to be insensitive when I named the chapter "horsepower" and considered altering the title. However, the name speaks more to the grace and beauty and innocent strength of the horses who helped shape humanity than to describe the destructive capacity of the motor of a metal beast that was used to wreak havoc over fellow men, and women and children.

During times of both peace and war, humans have used the horse for eons to assert domination over each other and in equal parts build and destroy civilizations. We used them greedily until their potential was superseded by the combustion engine, then we used that in their stead. Once utilized only for transportation of goods and people, an engine now represents the new age warhorse and can be wielded as a weapon to harm one another, even unintentionally. Distracted driving continues to claim the lives of pedestrians and cyclists daily.

The symbolism is thought provoking at the very least, so shall it remain, lest I forget that beyond the confines of my relatively safe and secure bubble, riding joyfully around the country of France, does the real world exist in earnest. Cycling is often described as an escape; from our worries and stresses, fears, anxieties, daily routines, etc. and it is easy to put our heads down and simply watch the road whiz by under the span of our two wheels. This day and its tragedies were a reminder that we can't turn our backs on the reality of our times if we hope to find peace, tolerance or understanding among each other in a changing world.

The morning broke with the sound of rain tapping gently on the window pane. The window was opened slightly to let in the cool night air and we had both slept the sleep of the chronically weary, no dreams to speak of, just rejuvenating blankness. In the seconds after Scott forecast the weather, I made an instant assessment of my physical state and found it lacking. My throat was tender, my chest heavy and my whole body aching. Not the same ache I'd felt in the first days of the tour, but the ache one feels when a bug is taking hold. The thought of climbing on my bike for a soggy uphill "time trial" was not an appealing one and even though I could have made the eleven miles at a snail's pace, even in my tenuous condition, I knew better than to temp mother nature and the impressive power of germs. I was hereby invoking my rights as an adult participant in an elective activity. I was going to sit this one out so I didn't end up missing the remainder of the stages because of a stupid cold.

Breakfast was relaxing for once. Our late arrival meant we had little left from which to choose, though plenty of time to enjoy several cups of coffee. It also meant that I didn't feel a bit guilty about eating not one, but several delectable pastries from the nearest patisserie. After that, Scott and I spent the rest of the late morning strolling the streets of Megève,. We amused ourselves with people watching and window gazing before digging in to our lunch of gourmet pizza on the promenade.

It was a busy place, popular no doubt because of the fairly priced menu, high quality ingredients and clockwork management of the hard-working staff. Alpine ski resort towns such as this one, were not easy on the wallet and from the prices affixed to the sidewalk menus around the square, cheap meals were not the norm. Sufficiently energized by fat and sugar and a bottle of rosé, we strolled to the center square to spectate at the horse show grounds.

The smell of such events, the same around the world, brought back memories of the hundreds of shows I had competed in myself. How many times had I stayed late at the barn, deep into the hours of the night? Or arrived before the rising of the sun, when the nightingale was still shrilling away in a quest for a mate to plait the manes of sleepy-eyed horses? How many thousands of practice jumps had I soared across, before I felt prepared to face the judges or the clock? How many butterflies had flitted between my ribs as my mount and I adjusted our eyes to the landscape of the ring, her heart and mine thumping with excited energy.

I was lucky to have an incredible stable of horses in my time as an equestrian, each one unique, but all of them giving the most of themselves during training and at events. Although I enjoyed competing and still have boxes of satin rosettes stashed away in storage, it was the relationship with these incredible animals that I missed the most. It was hard to forget their willingness to allow me to teach them, their gentleness in teaching me lessons of their own, their trust and in some cases, their love. When I close my eyes, I can still see each of their gazes, from the playful to the reserved. One or two had the steely look of eagles. Every horse I loved had one thing in common; they knew how to look me square in the eyes, as if they could see right into my very soul. They have all left their mark there and I thank them for who they've helped me become. Having had my fill of fine horses, we headed back to the hotel before the cold, damp bleachers could worsen my sore throat. The show had been a good distraction from the depression I felt at missing the stage, though in hind-sight the extra rest day had done us both some good. While my physical ills would begin to recover, my emotions were taking blows left and right.

Earlier in the day, during a casual conversation with one of the staff, Scott and I felt compelled to address a respectful difference of opinion. We naively thought our comments would be taken as constructive feedback. Unfortunately that wasn't the case and were given quite the obvious cold shoulder for the next few stages. That left us feeling unwelcome and disliked and was an uncomfortable situation where the only solution was to let the dust settle. I couldn't help but feel like the whole mess was my fault, as I'm sometimes compelled to speak candidly. After, I felt motivated to fix it, to mend any hurt feelings and right any misunderstandings. I realized however, that some people aren't prepared to forgive when it's convenient for you and it's best to abide by their choice. I needed to get better at letting those relationships go and putting my energy into the ones that could withstand the occasional turmoil of a disagreement. But for the moment, the rub was really bothering me.

Sheepishly, we thought that maybe what everyone needed was a little space, which our traveling circus rarely offered. We skipped the evening's communal meal for a quiet dinner for two at the restaurant next door. We were desperately craving something other than the normal protein heavy prix fixe menu. We weren't as ravenous as we'd been over the last few weeks anyway (two pastries and a pizza lunch might have been the culprit) and the cold lingering in my chest put a further damper on my appetite.

Situated at a small table on a private patio next to a tiny stream trickling soothingly past, we mended our wounded pride with several small courses of local specialties; *escargot* in thyme cream and white wine under a pastry shell, *cuisses de grenouille* in alpine butter and vegetable terrine. Then we capped it off with a round of *génépi* instead of dessert. Satiated and feeling sunnier about the state of things, we strolled back to hotel, hand in hand for an early night. Of course, this meant that we had missed Phil's overview of tomorrow's route as well as the nightly awards ceremony, but we figured whatever the mountains had in store for us tomorrow, we'd deal with it, one kilometer at a time.

STAGE 19:

Moto Vélo

July 15th, 2016 ~ Albertville to Saint-Gervais Mont Blanc. "Le vélo a-t-il un moteur?" Asks the shepherd. "Non, author laughs." "Bon, très bon", he repeats with a smile.

"82.9 miles and 11,214 feet of climbing. Exactly who gets to decide that certain climbs on a stage just don't get categorized from one year to the next? Today's stage was miraculously dry and started out beautifully, with the sky partly cloudy and cool. Perfect climbing weather. Up we went. Straight out of the coach. And up. And up. The first climb of the day was a steep one and it wasn't even mentioned on the official stage profile. Someone mentioned this morning that the last time it was climbed on Tour it was ranked as a category 2. Figures. Nevertheless, it was a good way to jumpstart legs that have had far too much time off and were about to start spinning circles on their own. A scalding hot bath, two mugs of green tea and a handful of vitamins plus a day and a half off the bike seemed to pay off because I felt fit to ride and eager to put down some miles."

"There wasn't much flat road before the second climb, a category 1 beast called Col de la Forclaz. A bit of high-Alps altitude and tender lungs and I was feeling this one though it didn't keep me from mashing hard on the pedals. It felt satisfying to push, to assure myself that despite a brief setback, fitness had not abandoned me."

"We climbed around and away from the impossibly blue and beautiful Lake Annecy, after negotiating a rather hairy stretch of road. So many angry honks and voices, not so discreetly yelling at us to get on the cycle path. That slow moving path, with its joggers and walkers and slowly cruising cyclists were no place for our hard-charging peloton so drivers would just have to be patient. I was shaken though, after an earlier close call with an idiot van driver.

"The effort to the top of the Forclaz was worth it just for the views of the valley and lake below. The Alps have such incredible scale and a sort of intentional presence. Not the wild, untamed impression made by the Pyrenees. After the summit, a narrow and rough, twisting descent on broken pavement led us through a deeply shadowed forest on lovely quiet roads to lunch. We crossed small but hard-working stream siphoning all that alpine snow away from multiple summits. Then we started the slow, false flat towards the HC giant of the day. A 13km climb and many fretted about the length but I found it to be an elegant, generous pass and the road behaved more like an eager dance partner than a detriment to our forward momentum. It spun us back and forth, around and up with postcard views over both shoulders. Lovelier than I ever imagined. Towering peaks, perpetually snowcapped, deep green and grey. Like a movie set from a vintage Alpine romance."

"Scott was never far behind, but far enough so that we both got to enjoy a few private moments with the mountain. That's the best way to climb; knowing you aren't entirely alone but are alone enough with nothing but your thoughts, pains, triumphs, failures. These are the best moments to seek the truth about who you are. When you can ask yourself almost any question and

expect an honest answer in return. The winding, well-traveled road then led us through the busy ski resorts of the Col des Saisies. Obviously a very popular destination among the outdoorsy, especially the downhill mountain biking set. Every parking lot and restaurant and hotel was packed. Incredibly, I saw lots of women pedaling by, looking all business in their full-faced helmets on high-end machines. We ducked under a ski-lift passing over the road and then made a slight right before slipping down an exhilaratingly fast descent on the back side of Montée de Bisanne. Shadowed from the late afternoon sun, the temperature dropped dramatically and we went from a pleasant-cool to near-freezing in half a minute. Part way down we made a false alarm turn at an imposter yellow arrow, that one belonging to another event but looking very much like ours, especially when whizzing past with heavily watering eyes. Fortified by Ian's espresso and some local cheese, the freshest Tomme de Savoie I've ever tasted, we made the slow march back towards Megève."

"The itinerary called for us to cruise past our hotel (ugh) before we advanced up the last hill of the day, a category 1 called Le Bettex that Phil called a "proper" climb. It was either the subconscious lure of a cold bottle of cider in the mini-fridge or the fact that just 24 hours ago I was nearly levelled by a common cold, but we decided to follow the neon arrows to the center of town instead of around it. What we found there was the warm and bright patio of our lovely hotel. All's well that ends well as the wind had just started to blow in our faces and Scott was beginning to limp, again. My raw lungs had enough puffing for one day. Instead we lingered in the evening sun, wiped down our bikes and chatted with friends until an early turn-in. Tomorrow is l'etape du Tour. Très bon."

This was an important stage in that we were joined by a another of the teen benefactors of the funds raised through the Tour de Force. As I would later discover, a previous Lifer, an alumni of the 2013 edition, would personally fund the travel expenses of a select few "Charity Visitors" each year. First was Johnny and his father who you met in an earlier stage. Now, we met 15-year old Tyrese and his mentor Thandi, both guests from an organization called the Westminster House Youth Club, one of the charities directly supported by our fundraising. Tyrese, who had never before left the United Kingdom, was going to attempt to ride as much of this steeply pitched stage with us as he could manage. Not being a cyclists but rather involved in the classical sport of fencing, his sincere enthusiasm and unflappable courage to tackle such a colossal stage was ambitious. In flat pedals, no less! I had the chance to ride with him for a stretch up the Forclaz and his pragmatic determination was motivating. To him, it was simply a road over a mountain. It needed to be climbed to reach the other side, no more, no less. An pleasant and genuine young man, I sincerely hope he approaches all of life's future challenges that way and wish him all the success in the world.

As I slowly pedaled away from both Tyrese and Scott, I found enough open road to sink onto the saddle and pedal into the grade. I was finally blooming in my independence and found climbing easier alone. Not that I didn't enjoy Scott's company, but on a day when I didn't feel exactly tip top, having no one from which to seek sympathy meant I put all that energy into the climb. And a beautiful climb it was. It was growing ever more difficult to pay attention to the road ahead when the views asunder were staggering. Lake Annecy, which was now behind us and sometimes off our right shoulder, the kind of sparkling blue only found in expensive paint chips.

The cleanest body of water in Europe was its claim, and perialpine was its adjective. Meaning "incomparable", the description was difficult to argue. A natural lake, nestled delicately between several matronly peaks had been made naturally by retreating glaciers nearly 18,000 years before I had the good fortune to cycle along its shores. Fed by crystalline mountain streams and a powerful spring called the Bouboiz, this prized body of water has seen a steadily rising number of tourists each year since the 1960's when environmental protectionist actions were taken to reduce the level of pollution and subsequent loss of fish and wildlife of the lake and surrounding habitat.

The traffic on this Friday afternoon in July spoke to its popularity and the reprieve we took on the cycle path mirroring the lake's shore provided a few miles of quietude in an otherwise perilous journey to the start of the Col de la Forclaz de Montmin. This wasn't the only cycle path we would traverse along today's stage. Not part of the official Tour de France route, there was a lovely stretch from Albertville to the southern tip of the lake. It paralleled the busy multi-lane highway which we were forced to cross to reach the protection of the path and was buzzing with microcars and small delivery vans. One of those vans nearly sideswiped me as I signaled with a left hand my intention to cross behind him. It was a close call and adrenaline began to surge through my limbs. I kept pedaling and once safely installed on the narrow strip of car-free concrete, the trembling of my near-miss diminished in time and we hummed along happily with a dramatic mountain backdrop to keep our minds pleasantly occupied. I thought briefly back to conversation with the Monsieur in Brittany and his suggestion. Turns out he was right and there really was a flat path through the Alps…for a short while anyway.

↔

Standing with my face towards the soft golden light atop the Forclaz, shielding my eyes with my hand across my brow from the glistening blue-green brilliance of the lake below, it was hard to focus on anything more stressful than drawing breath. I was beginning to understand why we placed ourselves in such perilous conditions, be it bad weather or bad driving. It was all for this; to stand triumphantly on the sun drenched summit of a glorious mountain in a land not ours but propelled there by the will of our own mind and the strength in our two legs. They were conquests fought hard, harder for others, and won using vulnerable bodies affixed upon a simple motor-less machine.

On fine days like this, the task felt easy and the road whizzed by lickety-split. Before long we were speeding away from our prize-heights and plunging down the other side. No spoils gained in this battle, only memories remained. An occasional picture was our only evidence of ever being at the top at all. Well, there was also the digital record but looking back at the effort on a computer and seeing nothing but a squiggly line and some timed segments, and that hardy seemed comparable.

That said, I don't remember much else from that category 1 climb. I rode away from my small group somewhere near the bottom of the almost 10-kilometer mountain and just got down to business. The first gentle stretch of the road up Forclaz set a false tone. There were a few taxing switchbacks early in the climb and those were followed by several steep ramps near the top, averaging 9% and 10% respectively though sneaking in a kilometer at 12% and another at 11%. I remember increasing the tempo when I saw daylight at the top of the road near the end of the climb and my lungs felt sufficiently ready to work so I put them through their paces until the summit sign rolled by. Then I dismounted and shouldered my bike to the viewing platform next to a densely cluttered souvenir shop and soaked in the view, blowing hard until I caught my breath.

My legs were grateful for a snack before the descent, even if my stomach was disinterested. I had finally learned to eat like an athlete, overcoming the urge to carry-on without food simply because I didn't feel hungry. That was a poor if not dangerous mistake that had cost me plenty of pleasant rides early in my cycling career. Now, hungry or not, I understood to fill the tank routinely and sufficiently. This has got to be one of the hardest lessons new cyclists have to learn. It seems especially difficult for women who are more likely to fret over calories. Paul De Vivie , the Father of French bicycle touring, would dictate in his commandments of cycling: eat before you are hungry and drink before you are thirsty. Fine advice even today. He also wrote this inspiring piece, which is painted permanently on a wall in our bicycle shop:

"After a long day on my bicycle, I feel refreshed, cleansed, purified. I feel that I have established contact with my environment and that I am at peace. On days like that I am permeated with a profound gratitude for my bicycle. Even if I did not enjoy riding, I would still do it for my peace of mind."

"What a wonderful tonic to be exposed to bright sunshine, drenching rain, choking dust, dripping fog, rigid air, punishing winds!"

De Vivie, better known as his penname Vélocio, was also an early champion of a multiple-gear and derailleur drivetrain. He believed in their power to help riders ascend mountains more quickly and certainly with more ease than the single chain ring, single cog setup that was fashionable and preferred in professional pelotons. So much so, that he devised a challenge to prove critics of his mechanical advancement wrong. His

277

staunchest critic was none other than the imminent Father of
the Tour de France himself, Henri Desgrange who called gears
only fit for "invalids and women." Words that would
undoubtedly raise hackles in today's times, were a common
sentiment in 1902. If you care to read more about it in detail, an
account of this bold moment in the history of cycling appears in
the modern magazine called Bicycle Quarterly (among others
I'm sure). The challenge Vélocio proposed was this; one woman
named Martha Hesse would ride 150 miles in the mountains,
climbing 12,000 feet astride a three-speed bicycle of de Vivie's
design. She would be pitted against a professional cyclist named
Edouard Fischer riding a single-speed race bike over the same
course. The first over the finish line would be declared the
winner.

I'll give you one guess who won that challenge and it didn't go
over well with the editor of L'Auto. He patronizingly responded
in an article in his own publication that *"I applaud this test, but
I still feel that variable gears are only for people over 45. Isn't it
better to triumph by the strength of your muscles than by the
artifice of a derailleur? We are getting soft. Come on fellows.
Let's say that the test was a fine demonstration - for our
grandparents! As for me, give me a fixed gear!"*

Not only did Martha Hess win that day, but so did Paul de
Vivie and his derailleur. The cycling world would slowly start
to come around to the idea of gears and by 1937, a rather

staggering 35 years after proving their worth, derailleurs would make their peloton-wide debut in the Tour de France. It was Jacques Goddet who would be the director of the Tour that year. The dominant Henri Desgrange had finally handed over the title the year prior, in 1936.

As a lover and rider of single speed bicycles, this story amuses me. I applaud Madame Hess for kicking the snot out of Fischer with her three gears (not twenty-two like we so luxuriously enjoy now) and I appreciate Vélocio's contribution to making climbing both efficient and enjoyable. But reading Desgrange's words about "triump{hing} by the strength of your muscles", stirs up some romantic feelings about the early history of our sport and the euphoric simplicity of riding a bicycle with one gear. I think Desgrange was a headstrong, brutish man with some very unkind ideas about women (as well as the infirm). Though I wonder if he didn't see, in the advent of gears, his own beloved history with bicycles slipping slowly from his grasp. The world he knew and loved, the world of one cog and all its tiny tines being used heroically to propel ordinary men up extraordinary mountains. Then I remember his remark about 45 year-olds being geriatric and whatever empathy I may have felt for him begins to fade. As I write this, I have logged nearly 40 years on the clock but that doesn't stop me from wondering when I'm going to plan my next outlandish cycling adventure. I've been toying with the idea of riding the 684 kilometer *Route des Grandes Alpes* from Geneva to Nice...on my single speed.

↔

The second Forclaz of the stage, this time named after a neighboring village of Queige, was a pleasant category 2 climb spanning only 5.6 kilometers and averaging just under 8%. By the bye, the name Forclaz meant "narrow gap" and was a popular way to describe several cols in this part of the Alps. Climbs like these were starting to become routine, dare I say even "easy". Scott seemed to think I had a knack for the 8 percenters, something having to do with my particular power to weight ratio. It was a compliment at the time, in top shape and rare form but now it feels like he was talking about someone else, myself having lost that level of fitness long ago. These days I have a little more weight and a little less power and 8% sounds like a lot of work.

Big climbs don't intimidate me anymore but I'm not so naïve to think that I could still hammer them out without being fit. The secret to successful climbing, enjoying them even, is being prepared for them. Body as well as mind. On today's stage, I felt alright. Not 100% but plenty happy to be pedaling uphill in a marvelous landscape with my health and sanity pretty much intact.

We rode down through Queige along the D925 toward Villard-sur-Doron. What waited for us there were traditional wooden ski chalets with their picture-perfect balconies overflowing with bright red geraniums. What waited for us beyond that was the

Montée de Bisanne and the long climb across the Col des Saisies. The name *"Les Saisies"* may have once meant "country of the rocks" in a patois not heard for eons. The name now translates literally to "seizures" though not the infliction, rather the forceful taking of property. The area was widely used from the 13th century onwards as pastureland for surrounding herdsman and in the 16th century a chapel was erected there, drawing local pilgrims. In the shadow of the Signal de Bisanne, the rustic path connecting the valleys of Beaufortain and Val d'Arly drew traders and merchants to exchange their wares at annual fairs. Legend goes that in early days, it was prime ground for smugglers and in later times it became a clever place to catch tax evaders. Now home to a dizzying assortment of ski resorts to whet every type of touristic appetite, this high mountain pass has obviously had a long and prosperous history and has been trodden across by humans for centuries.

Now here we were, cycling the same pass on our own form of pilgrimage. Whatever motivation sent myself (for cheese) and my fellow cyclists (who knows) up and over such a majestic stretch of mountain road, we would be followed in a week's time by the thundering professional peloton, coming to claim the final few victories in this year's Tour. Only a handful more climbs stood between them and Paris and by the time they rolled over any evidence of our own tracks, the action would surely be heating up and boiling over. In fact, this year would differ in the way the pass had been used during its previous 11 inclusions in the race. In an attempt to add flair to an already climb-laden event, the organizers decided to utilize the narrow D123 road from Villard-Sur-Doron. This alternative way up to the category 1 Col des Saisies, instead of the traditional D218B road, passed under the shadow of the Montée de Bisanne and was thereby granted the penultimate honor of Hors Catégorie.

The most remarkable part of this climb, besides the dramatic backdrop, were the age-old pastoral scenes unfolding before us. The traditional way to make hay on these steep alpine meadows was to hand scythe the native grasses and wildflowers, spreading then turning the cuttings by hand to dry in the summer sun. Before the rains can come to spoil the crop, the hay was windrowed and baled as winter roughage for livestock. The herbaceous aroma of the drying plants was intoxicating and must have melted in the mouths of those animals lucky enough to consume them. No wonder this was cheese country, varieties whose flavors were so tied to their terroir.

As I passed by one such scene, there were three generations of men laboring in their small *alpage*. The first two younger men nodded quickly and they returned to their laborious tasks. I passed them and returned the salutation with a wave of my hand. The elder also nodded as he raked hay into a narrow row. I smiled, then waved and that's when he paused to shout to me in French if my bike had a motor. Hearing him but not sure I heard him correctly, I cupped my hand to my ear in a universal symbol for "what was that you said?". He repeated himself, bluntly but tinged with humor. Does your bike have a motor?

That time my rudimentary French filter caught the key words it needed and the sentence revealed itself. I laughed and emphatically responded no. He smiled broadly. Good, he bellowed. Chapeau, he followed up gently, turning his attention back to his work. If I needed a proverbial pat on the back, this was it. And it couldn't have come at a more perfect moment.

Up the road, Les Saisies was a circus. Jam packed with alpine thrill-seekers, the traffic along the pass was dense and the sheer number of visitors bedecked in the uniforms of their respective extreme sports was head-spinning. Plus photo-takers, hikers, day-trippers, holiday-makers and caravans made the scene look like a well-choreographed movie set. The atmosphere was party-like and somewhere there was techno rhythmically thumping on the breeze. It was hard not to slow pedal to take it all in. The air at the top of the mountain was much colder than at the foot, so we couldn't linger long but to speed by such a scene without pause was to miss the world that was happening while we were busy pedaling away the days. A long, frigid decent away from the revelry caused goose-bumps and frozen fingers. We were grateful to see Ian's coffee stop set up at the bottom of the road. He was blaring his own flavor of dance beats in the slanted rays of the late afternoon sun.

Just as I had hoped, there was cheese. Sarah had delivered on her promise to source the local varieties of Tomme and Beaufort for our late-day snack. Beaufort, an AOC cheese made from unpasteurized cow's milk since the Roman times was made in the Savoie valley just below the mountain we had just climbed. So I helped myself to a lion's share. When in Rome...

Towards the end of the day my energy was waning. The two espressos I had at the last stop helped some, but the climbing and the chilly air on all the descents were taking their toll on my lungs and throat. Besides, both the wind and the volume of traffic were starting to pick up and the road heading back to Megève was getting increasingly busy. After the third irresponsibly close pass by a motorist, my mind was made up. Instead of bypassing town to head towards the final climb of the stage, I'd follow the arrows back to the hotel. That meant missing Le Bettex. It was only a handful more kilometers, but tough ones coming at the tail end of a climb-heavy day with a lingering illness in my chest. That was my excuse. Scott didn't need one, though I asked him whether he felt like continuing on without me. He didn't, choosing instead to save his legs for tomorrow's final day of towering mountains. Both ankles were still sickly thickened and his knee in steady pain. Miraculously he was maintaining a level of discomfort he could tolerate and the half-roll of supportive tape he flaunted on both legs seemed to be holding him together.

We arrived at the hotel to find several other riders already attending to their bikes and gear and resting on the front patio. Seems we weren't the only ones who took the fast track option home. I had stopped feeling quite as guilty about such decisions, viewing them instead as a necessary sloughing of parts for the

284

health of the whole organism. Though I would still like to see the views from the top of that last category 1 climb, as I hear they were stunning. In fact, there are a lot of things I'd like another crack at, given the chance. Not because I feel I have something to prove to anyone but because I still feel the sense of loss over what might have been. Those bypassed miles, those missing mountains felt like lost memories. That is was what I lamented the most. So I found consolation in a bottle of local cider and the calming act of cleaning my bike and let the lively bubbles tickle my raw throat and soothe my wounded spirits.

STAGE 20:

L'Etape du Tour

July 16th, 2016 ~ Megève to Morzine. "I want to remember this always" proclaims author dreamily at the café atop the Col de Joux Plane. "I want another beer" says Scott matter of factly.

"77.9 miles and 9,232 feet of climbing. Holy Alps! Phil said the views we had were rare for this time of year. The clarity of the air was something to be expected in the fall, not the height of the summer. But the cool temperatures kept the haze off the mountain, thus unspoiling the view. Alas, the view! No postcard or photograph or poet's waxing could capture the vista on this day. I couldn't recall what the road was like as I never stopped staring aloft. All day we rode in the presence of the mighty Mont Blanc. We saw her from every side, each more stately and superlative than the next, especially the scene of freshly laid snow billowing softly from her summit."

"The sun shone brightly yet the air was temperate. The drawing of breath was difficult for me today. Partly because of the altitude and partly because of this annoying cold. Not nearly enough oxygen was making it to my legs and they felt sluggish. I knew we were in for a long day in the saddle and at a deliberately slow pace, as if to linger on the last miles of mountain road. Scott didn't mind and we both wanted to make the most of the panoramic views and savor the final climbs of our tour."

"The short steep climb into the Forêt de Bisanne was not too taxing other than the cold morning air stinging tender lungs. My legs came around but quickly waned as they needed the fuel that my lack of appetite wouldn't allow. We hair-pinned into a steep, narrow valley to find an attractive village called Flumet clinging to the granite above a small but deeply cut gorge. Over an ancient stone bridge built on tall arches like stilts over the river Arly. Then up again towards the category 2 Col des Aravis. Steep yes, but also thankfully short and the views were worth every labored breath. Scott had been gaining in fitness and while still riding cautiously, was clearly feeling improved. I was hurting today, so keeping on his wheel was a struggle. We couldn't seem to catch a simultaneous break."

"Next up was the category 1 Col de la Colombière. The Colombière was a seriously gratifying mountain. A world class climb. Impossible views. I would ascend again and again just to see the world from the top. What a spectacular alpine experience and one we were grateful to have had. Staggeringly scenic, this climb should be on every cyclist's to-do list."

"Feed stop 2 offered us the option to delete a category 1 climb, a particularly troubling one that had recently been omitted from the official l'Étape du Tour because of landslides. The mountain road was recently re-opened but reportedly still littered with small debris and the passage was supposedly narrowed to one lane. A few riders chose to go around, us included and go directly to the final H.C. category climb. Towards the end, it had become clear that for us to finish comfortably (in our current state), some exceptions must be made. It was a good choice because being fresh for the Col de Joux Plane was worth the sacrifice of an unfamiliar category 1."

"STEEP! Average gradient 7.5% my ass. Did that include the "short-cut" through the village that I'm certain averaged more like 15-17%? What about the stretches of 12% around every switchback? If you looked closely, you could see the real gradients spray painted like graffiti on the tarmac, right under the official signs. The two never seemed to coincide. My legs wanted to believe the graffiti artists and my brain was hoping the signs were true. Oh well, burn every last match. Hell, burn the matchbook too. Last day in the mountains, last climb of the tour. Save nothing for Paris but a smile."

"Although over-dressed and sweating and a rather bland start, the mountain opened up before us as we ascended and gave us bigger and bigger views. Good thing, as they cleverly distracted us from the constant flow of annoying traffic, which was frustrating. According to the barrier at the foot of the climb, we should have expected a road closed to motorists. I had one rather close call by a tourist in a Europcar rental that looked startled when I yelled hey! into his partially opened window."

"2 km's to go and I became all business. Scott had been following steadily a few bike lengths back. He had paused earlier in the climb, rather romantically, to present me with a small yellow bouquet of alpine wildflowers that now rested limply on my bars. 1 km to go and all we could do was gape. So many peaks. Seven in all, stretched out before us like conical giants. Some grey, some snowy, some sharp...some softly eroded by time. This was it. We had climbed the last kilometer of our grand tour and come rolling in, grinning across the finish. We careened haplessly into a busy summit-side café to enjoy a victory beer and a house made dessert with summer strawberries and Chantilly crème."

"*The rest is a blur. A unmistakably closed road. Defiantly going around the barriers. Slow, deliberate descent on a sketchy surface. Two glasses of wine made it all ok. Stopped for a photo with a lazy herd of Savoie cows before advancing into the town of Morzine. I vaguely remember a sign for a UNESCO site. Must look that one up later. This was a lovely resort town full of mountain bikers, party-goers and lots of tourists. In our post-stage glow, we went strolling through the village before dinner and did some window shopping. I finally found some new earrings I've been craving for months. A tiny pair of silver poissons, inlaid with mother of pearl (nacre in French). They were handmade in Paris. Perfect.*"

"*Then we sat in the warm sun on the patio with other Lifers, uploading photos to share with friends back home. The six bells tolled the hour from the small neighboring chapel and I began to get teary. I knew it wouldn't be the last of our adventures in these Alps but I lamented our absence from them already, before we'd even gone. I was so sentimental these days.*"

"*Tonight, we enjoyed a dinner of traditional tartiflette. Two helpings if you must know. We drank expensive wine and didn't feel guilty about it. Everyone was more relaxed but not very talkative. I think everyone was sad that the tour was coming to an end. And what a grand tour it had been. The two of us turned in for an early wake-up call. As he closed his lids to sleep, Scott said: You're a cyclist now. I fell asleep smiling. That meant the whole world to me.*"

↔

The Queen stage was everything we'd hoped it would be. Clear skies with no rain to ruin our mood, zero haze to spoil the majestic views and enough energy left in our legs to make a valiant effort up the final climb. It felt surreal to be standing arm in arm with Scott on the top of the Col de Joux Plane, surveying the cirque of jagged peaks in the distance, feeling elated but painfully aware that these were our last views from a lofty summit on this tour.

We fought hard the urge to feel deflated, to let the cool mountain air leave our lungs too quickly lest we forget the taste of it. I fought hard the urge to shed tears of happiness and sadness combined. After sweeping my eyes across the horizon to try to capture the scene again and again, Scott wrapped an empathetic arm around me and kept me anchored to his side. When we first decided to ride the tour, I couldn't have possibly envisioned all the events that would lead us here but I had been able to imagine this moment or at least a moment just like it...standing together on the shoulders of the world.

It was the most tranquil setting for a victory dessert. Le Relais Des Vallées, the popular family-run establishment had perhaps the most spectacular view of Mont Blanc a café could ever hope to offer its patrons. Scott's face was nearly invisible behind an amusingly symbolic mound of bright red berries, capped with house-made Chantilly cream, white as the pure snow draped over the peaks in the distance. I'm not sure what was the bigger challenge, getting to the top of the HC categorized climb or getting to the bottom of that huge serving of summer fruit and liquefied sugar. So immersed in the moment, the elation of having ascended so many of France's most iconic climbs, it was almost easy to forget that this grande dame had really put us through our paces to reach her summit. She had made her presence felt with every hairpin bend and turn of the pedals as she had done since the first time the Tour had set their eyes on her sun-drenched summit in 1978.

Perhaps to let the dramatic dust settle after the last stage had crossed the summit sign here in 2006, the official Tour de France had not used the Joux Plane on course for a decade. Yet ten years had failed to see the prevalent habit of high-stakes doping disappear from professional road racing. In fact, doping had just gotten more refined and dopers more adept at avoiding positive test results. Even in this modern age of "clean" athletes campaigning for fair play, even after all the hype and shame and finger wagging at those convicted riders condemned forever for their chemical sins, stripped of their titles, their victories marred by asterisks…performance enhancements to body and bike were still prevalent.

Maybe now, after so much time had passed, the Joux Plane would have forgotten how to punish cheaters. Though once upon a time, she was a cruel disciplinarian. In 2006 Floyd Landis, in the leader's yellow jersey by the time the race reached this summit, would be stripped of the honor after testing positive for synthetic testosterone. In 2000, the

291

Frenchman Richard Virenque would claim victory over the Col, beating out a struggling Lance Armstrong on the climb. His relationship with doping is so well-known it hardly bears repeating. Virenque himself was no stranger to performance-enhancements. He was caught up in a drug scandal in 1998 noteworthy enough to be labeled the "Festina affair" (named after the team with which he was a member) and was ruthlessly mocked as "an unrepentant doper" for his remaining years as a professional cyclist.

In 1997, the mountain would turn the other cheek as the superhero Italian climber by the name of Marco Pantani passed her summit sign in a blistering 33 minutes. To put his effort into perspective, most professional riders and a select few uber-fit amateurs can make it to the top of the official 11.6 kilometer, 8% average gradient climb in 45 minutes. An accomplished enthusiast should expect the same effort to take over an hour. Consider that this climb is infamous for its lack of consistency and the tendency for some stretches to exceed 12% and you get the picture of how unbelievable Pantani's effort really was. It's legitimately difficult and not well-liked by the professional peloton even in modern times. Pantani didn't just make a molehill of the mountainous Joux Plane. He also set the record for the fastest ascent up Alp d'Huez just two days prior and finished the Tour in 3rd position overall. While never convicted of any chemical crimes in 1997 (the first year blood tests became mandatory for "health reasons") perhaps he only dodged punishment, penalty or banishment because his results mysteriously disappeared. He would not escape future convictions and would lead a tumultuous life thereafter, manically internalizing all the accusations against him. Pantani's lonely and terribly heart-breaking passing would come on Valentine's Day in 2004. He died of a drug overdose. Perhaps finally, Il Pirata as he was lovingly known to fans, would find the peace in death he had not found in life.

If the climb up the Joux Plane from the village of Samoëns was best known as punishing, then the descent down to Morzine was best known for being dangerous. Rough pavement battered by winter snow and ice and the occasional landslide plus blind corners and inconsistent bends in the road, the steepness of the ramps leading off the summit exponentially increased the trickiness of the narrow road. We were warned by Phil not to over-estimate our abilities to navigate this particular decline and after a glass (or two) of celebratory rosé, I decided to take my sweet time getting to the bottom. I even stopped to converse with a friendly herd of Savoyarde cows and to feel the setting sun on my blushed face.

It had been a safe and trouble-free experience for us but the naughty backside of the mountain had a dark past of catching unsuspecting riders out and a few professional cyclists over the years paid dearly for their lapse in judgement. During the 1984 Tour, a rider named Pedro Delgado would crash and break his collarbone. Perhaps with his painful crash still burned into the recesses of his mind, Delgado would give up the race lead on the final descent off the Joux Plane into Morzine. A lightning fast Irishman named Stephen Roche, would take home the maillot jaune and become the first and only Tour de France winner from the Emerald Isle. His success came in equal parts from skill, luck and determination.

Not so lucky was the Italian rider Carlo Tonon, who crashed in horrific style during the same '84 Tour. Speeding down the dangerous descent, he would crest a blind corner and collide with a spectator cycling uphill towards the race action. Reports mention the spectator may have been simply trying to cross the road. Nevertheless, the impact was sudden and powerful. Both riders were whisked away, unconscious. Tonon with a fractured skull, would linger in a coma for months. Upon awakening, he would discover that the crash and subsequent coma had left him with permanent and debilitating mental disabilities. He would sadly end his own life, in 1996, at the age of 41.

While researching to discover the condition of the spectator in the unfortunate collision with Tonon, I stumbled upon an account of the accident in the July 19th, 1984 edition of the Washington Post. It didn't mention the poor fellow but did mention something fascinating. It gave a brief but intriguing account of the inaugural Women's Tour: Dutch rider Helene Hage takes the 15th stage, while the American Mary Nanne-Martin retains the overall lead. Another American, Debra Schunway remains in third and "local" rider Patty Peoples, from Gaithersburg Maryland finishes in 10th. The coverage flummoxed me. Who were these American women and why had I never before heard their names? I had known only the most basic details about this race but never the racers. Astounded, I did a search for more information. I would begin to learn the incredible story of these women thanks to another Washington Post article by Ruth Marshall, published on July 22, 1984.

Reading aloud to Scott, I would have to pause several times as I fought hard to swallow the growing lump in my throat. Lots of feelings were flooding in. I felt prideful for the amateur riders of that historic 1984 Tour, yet I was troubled by the lack of respect they received from fellow male cyclists. It left me frustrated at the lack of progress women's cycling had experienced in the decades since. What finally made the tears fall was when I recognized the distinct and familiar happiness in the words those women spoke as they described the joy of riding their bicycles in such an iconic event and the honor they felt at representing their country through their trials. That was the bright spot in a rather gloomy reality. I am ever thankful that the author of this piece wanted to share these women's unique stories with the world. She cleverly included the statements from the official tour physician who also believed that they were physically capable of tackling France's greatest race course, albeit a shortened version as required by the stringent rules of the times. Still, they raced.

For 46 miles a day, for a total of 991 kilometers over 18 stages, being granted five rest days instead of the men's customary two, they would tackle many of the same monstrous climbs as their male counterparts but without the fanfare and hoopla or even decent news coverage of their event. They would also do it for pennies to the men's dollar, but prize money didn't seem to be the driving factor behind their performance. They did it because they loved their bikes, their country and the sport of cycling and they wanted to prove to the world as much as to themselves that they were capable. Sadly, the Grande Boucle Féminine Internationale would not last, due in part to a lack of interest and funding from sponsors. In 2009, the event would pass into the history books, a shell of its original self after shrinking in stages and sponsor interest.

The heyday of American women competing in the Tour would be brief. After the inaugural event, where the first and third place finishers belonged to the USA, only Inga Thompson would make a podium appearance in 1986 and 1989. No other American women would finish on the podium for the remainder of the races. It makes one think about the importance and support given to women's racing in this country during those decades. Their struggle continues well into the present.

Jacques Antquetil, the five times winner of the Tour de France turned commentator for the daily sports journal *L'Equipe* said of women's bicycle racing, *"I have absolutely nothing against women's sports, but cycling is much too difficult for a woman. They are not made for the sport. I prefer to see a woman in a short white skirt, not racing shorts "*.

It was ugly but was sadly the language of the times, though that doesn't do much to absolve him. I try hard not to think about who else among the ranks of my cycling heroes may have felt the same about women racing bikes. The language may have changed and the idea of a cyclist being cut from any cloth is more accepted in our day and for that I am grateful but this sport of ours is far from equal and change seems glacial in the speed of its progression. Technologically yes, socially no. We can stop on a dime and shift without wires but women still can't race the in Tour de France. So *chapeau* to you women of the Big Loop, you pioneers, you brave and determined cyclists. Thank you for every pedal stroke, every gasp of breath you took on top of those dizzying summits, for every drop of sweat and blood and tears you left on the asphalt and for the inspiration you gave to countless others to pursue their two wheeled dreams.

↔

It's easy to forget, in the afterglow of the experience of reaching the final big climb of the tour and the elation of accumulating all those miles, that there were three other epic climbs on stage 20, not counting the two unclassified mountains on the stage. Hey, a climb is a climb and they don't just disappear because the Tour De France doesn't officially acknowledge their existence. Somewhere in the roughly 10 months it took me to finish this narrative, I finally rooted out the fuzzy explanation and loosely-scientific system for categorization of climbs used during the Tour. Categorization seemed to matter most to the route makers and points givers. I always tried to not get too worked up about a climb's ranking during our daily rider briefings. Regardless of their categorization, we still had to get over the mountain if we wanted to reach the hotel. As you've noticed throughout my journal, I've written about official climbs and mentioned their rankings from the least difficult, a category 4, to most difficult, a category 1. The H.C. or hors catégorie, remember, is applied to climbs "beyond categorization" and was a term only applied in 1980. Remember they aren't necessarily referring to the mountain, sometimes just the pass around or between.

Don't think for a minute the mountains actually care about this arbitrary system. They remain as stone-faced as ever as we decide from year to year how hard we think they might be to climb them. Perception of difficulty is an important factor. One cyclist's category 4 is another cyclist's category 1 and so forth. There is an official level of difficulty, such as it is that attempts to rank mountains on a tangible scale. It is a whimsical at best:

Category 4: At least 4 kilometers, maybe more with a grade of at least 4% average.

Category 3: At least 4 kilometers, maybe more with a grade of at least 6% average.

Category 2: At least 5 kilometers, maybe more with a grade of at least 7% average OR a least 10 kilometers, maybe more with a grade of at least 5% average.

Category 1: Ranging from 5 to 10 kilometers with an average of at least 8% OR more than 15 kilometers with an average of at least 6%.

Hors Catégorie: At least 15 kilometers with a grade of 8% average OR less than 15 kilometers IF the average grade is greater than 8% AND the climb comes at the end of a stage with multiple climbs AND/OR occurs towards the end of the climbing stages of the race.

Bluntly, a climb is not officially recognized if it would muck with the points being awarded for more important climbs on the stage. For example, stage 21, the final leading into Paris, has barely a blip of a climb on the radar. Nevertheless, it gets to be officially categorized as a "4" because it's the last chance to accrue valuable "king of the mountain" points before the end of the race. The same might hold true for a smallish category 3 or 4 climb in the early stages of the three week event. As in, "it's the only hill for hours so we may as well recognize the darn thing". But given the smorgasbord of mountains in the Pyrenees or the Alps, on the days they come up fast and heavy, there are big-name climbs around every bend. In that case, only the really big ones (Category 1's, 2's and H.C.'s) might count for points and the lesser climbs on the same stage (3's and 4's) don't even bear mentioning. To make this more difficult to follow, when the route changes in a successive year and bypasses some of the bigger climbs, suddenly those lesser climbs become more important and thereby becomes necessary to "categorize" so points can be awarded for climbing them. Pertinent to the classification system is the position of the climb within the stage as well as the overall race. In other words, if the climb comes late in the stage it might warrant a tougher ranking. If it comes late in the race, the same rule applies. This explains how some climbs can morph between categories from year to year.

For example, the Col des Aravis has been ranked a category 2 climb for the great majority of its appearances in the Tour. Except in 1975 when it was demoted to a category 3 for appearing after the category 1 Col de la Madeleine on stage 17 and in 1991 when it was upgraded to a category 1 during stage 18. The Aravis is an epic stretch of road connecting the regions of Savoie and Haute Savoie and has been used by the Tour de France a whopping 40 times since its debut in 1911. In fact, it was the first Alpine pass to appear on course during the inaugural inclusion of the Alps. Until then, only the Pyrenees had been used to torture riders, utilizing the region's infamously treacherous unpaved roads and reliably temperamental weather.

In 1911, Émile Georget and Paul Duboc, both Frenchmen, would be the first to cross the Aravis. In 1912, the first to summit would be none other than Eugene Christophe, the man who seemed to be able to overcome any setback yet never win the Tour (though he did have the honor wearing the first yellow jersey). Perhaps Christophe and decades of riders, professional and amateur alike, took comfort as they passed the tiny chapel of Sainte Anne, whose 1867 *façade* is graced with the blessing *"Sainte Anne Protégez Les Voyageurs"*. The pretty little structure was founded in 1624 by the Lord of Flumet, whose residents made the pilgrimage along the range of the Aravis mountains to appeal to Sainte Anne to bring them rain. At only 1,486 meters high, the view of the towering Mont Blanc is pristine and both monuments are well-photographed by visitors.

Our next climb of the day was the horizon dominating Col de la Colombière. Since 1978 it has maintained its category 1 status for 18 inclusions in the Tour. It was climbed three times prior and ranked a category 2. Not to be confused with the H.C. category Grand Colombier of Jura fame that we climbed during stage 15, this col is all Alps. Stunning in its beauty, steep in its profile especially near the summit, steady was the way we rode the nearly 12 kilometer ascent. At a gradient hovering below an average of 6%, it was hardly a laborious effort. I remember loving this stretch of ribboning road, riding along the narrow strip of weather-worn tarmac as it coiled through grey rock and alpine meadow awash with flowers and flitting butterflies.

By then I had settled into a pleasing rhythm and Scott and I were enjoying riding two abreast guffawing at the enormity of the landscape. Traffic was non-existent. Besides the occasional motorcycle tourist or local resident, anyone looking for an efficient journey opted for the A40 highway instead of the slow going D4. I was happy to see few cars but disappointed to not

301

catch sight of the famous Alpine Ibex who frequented those sloping pastures. A member of the goat family, the *Capra Ibex* is an excellent climber and since it enjoys very little predation living above the snowline, lives a long life of defying gravity, succumbing only to old age.

I was beginning to succumb to the cumulative fatigue of a three week bicycle ride and the reduced energy of troubled lungs. It was a shame too, since the sky was clear and warm and could not have been a better day for climbing mountains. But I was tired. And tired of being tired. And tired of worrying about so much, like Scott's condition, my own condition, pissing off the staff, pissing off drivers, our shop back home, my horses, everything. Everything. I needed a moment where none of it mattered and I was allowed to be sick, unruly, belligerent, forgetful, irresponsible, selfish, disappointing and ungrateful. But at the same time I wanted to be happy and content. I guess I wanted it all. Just for the length of a single climb, if I couldn't ask for the whole of the day. And on the Colombière, I got that. Once I realized it, I felt utterly spent.

That's part of the reason we skipped the Col de la Ramaz. That and it had a tunnel. Actually I can't use that excuse because I didn't learn about the tunnel until after the tour. It just didn't make sense for us to tackle the category 1 pass when our hearts (and legs) weren't behind it and there was another difficult mountain left on the profile, one whose reputation had proceeded it as being a real beast. Besides, I knew nothing of the climb, no history, no stories, no impressions of it whatsoever so it wasn't hard to take a right turn in the village of Mieussy towards Tangines. The road there bent sharply upwards without warning as if to taunt us for being too cowardly to face the Ramaz. It wasn't cowardice at all but a desire to end the tour on a positive note, feeling like we came out on top with some strength left in our character and some pep left in our pedal stroke. I remember looking over my left shoulder at the base of the steep mound where the pass began and thought it just looked like another lump of grey rocks. There was no desire in me to reach the top, no spark to light the fire that usually propelled me to the summit and I knew the choice to ride past and not over was the right one. Dr. Julian had joined us and we three rode together, enjoying some lighthearted conversation between breaths before arriving early to lunch. Others would follow, arriving in dribs and drabs, relieved to have taken the detour themselves. Relief was fleeting as the pitch of the road increased by the kilometer. We wouldn't find the pedaling easy until the descent into Morzine and the sight of the last neon arrow guiding us home. It was the last time we'd lay our heads down as Lifers because tomorrow there was Paris and there we'd find the end of our tour.

↔

The sun on my face and bare feet felt divine. Scott was showering, rinsing the remnants of the road from his tanned legs and I was sitting in a plastic chair on our small balcony.

It was a lovely, comfortable hotel. I could see across the rooftops of Morzine and smell the mountain air and meadow mixed with wood smoke. As the church bells next door began to chime the hour, I was smacked hard by the realization that this perfect moment was ever so fleeting. When the last of those throaty tones echoed across the horizon and disappeared into the folds of the peaks beyond, I'd be a minute more removed from the wonderment of this day. Then I became terribly sad. It was a bitter-sweetness really and as equally as I was joyful for the experiences of the last three weeks, I began to lament that my future days would be so vastly different than the ones I had just lived, seeing the world from upon my bike. It was the emptiest I had felt in a very long time.

I confessed such feelings to Scott when he joined me in the slanting rays for a brief respite before setting out for a stroll. He made a promise that we'd return to these places again and see such adventures for all the years of our lives. I believed him and the empty moment passed, filling my heart and head with hope that comes with the expectation of making future memories.

STAGE 21:

Bleu, Blanc, Rouge

July 17th, 2016 ~ Megève to Morzine. "Does Paris know we're coming?" says a fellow Lifer upon boarding the bus the morning of the final stage.

"44.6 miles and 1,634 feet of climbing."

↔

Nothing. That's what I found in my diary for stage 21. Just the quote and distance I scribbled in the margin of the small, spiral notebook I had carried in my bag throughout the tour. It is hardcover and white with red polka-dots (like the climber's jersey). The battered little book did an honorable job of safely securing my carelessly scripted thoughts at the end of each tiring day. Except for the final one, where there was almost nothing on the last of those narrowly lined pages. That's because we were in a hurry to get washed and tidied and somewhat presentable for our last dinner together.

We were booked to take an after-dark boat ride on one of the famous Bateaux Mouches, wine and dine and receive our finishers' awards then enjoy the glittering lights of Paris as we cruised up and down the Seine. We'd arrived at our hotel late in the day, much later than expected with very little time to come down off the high we felt racing through the bustling city, dodging taxis and tourists alike. It was mayhem and nothing like navigating the busy streets in a car, protected from the cacophony of sounds and smells in relative safety behind a barrier of steel and glass.

Our late finish was due to an equally late beginning. And that was after an ingloriously long bus ride from Morzine. We departed at 5:30 in the morning and motored upwards of 8 hours, including the mandatory stop at a service station for our driver. I didn't mind that part one bit, what with my bizarre fondness for French gas station sandwiches (the kind with pickles and saucisson) and spicy paprika Pringles. Plus there were those magical automated espresso machines. Don't judge. We all have our peculiarities.

The long bus trips gave me a chance to see a greater swath of the countryside. Certain stretches of field and road looked so similar to the places I've called home over the years. And then my eye would fix upon the outline of a faraway chateau or the steeple of a medieval church. Then I'd be reminded of just how many miles, if not centuries, lay between what I called home and here, this land that was growing familiar.

306

As the motor and wheels of the big bus hummed along the wide lanes of the motorway, many of my companions slept, the early start and last few weeks drawing heavily from their stores of energy. Scott slumbered lightly beside me, eyes slitting open only when I felt the need to share something of note I saw out the window. The landscape morphed noticeably from one hour to the next. The dawn lifted slowly over the peaks of the Alps, tinting everything a golden-rosy hue and before the sun had melted away the morning, the mountains were already far behind us. We spent the next few hours driving with the nose of the bus pointed ever so slightly down, towards the rolling terroir of fertile wheat fields. Now plundered of their bounty, their sacrifice would be savored upon the altar of millions of tables, from the farm houses buried deep in the folds of these bare hills to the sidewalk cafés as distant as Paris.

Never satisfied to retain one shape over another, the landscape morphed again and we rose towards a horizon-wide plateau. The terrain here was at the mercy of an army of tributaries and feeder streams each funneling their life-giving waters to the mighty Seine. They carved and sliced their way through the earth, leaving fruitful soil in their wake where villages sprung up like wild mushrooms and spindly willows in the eons that followed. Villages were protected by them and nourished by them and sometimes even powered by them. Rivers have been our lifeblood since the dawning of civilization and how many had we cycled aloofly across as they continued to etch their way slowly to the sea, influencing not only native rock and flora, but modern man as well. This very country was compartmentalized by rivers, some lazily flowing, some mightily raging but all important enough to have departments named in their honor and delineated by their boundaries. The Dordogne, The Loire, The Lot, The Garonne and The Seine.

The Seine twists and writhes around a body of land called the Île-de-France, so large it not only encompasses Paris but a swath of country almost 4,700 miles in size and contains eight of the nation's 97 mainland departments. It also nourishes some of France's most prized forests including the two we were about to motor through; the Forêt de Fontainebleau, South East of Paris and the Forêt d'Halatte bordering Chantilly, our eventual destination.

The Forest of Halatte, I would later learn is a 10,000 acre labyrinth of woods with walking and cycling paths funneling visitors through stands of old growth beech and oak and subtle hints at ancient residents of this nationally protected forest. Long before Kings could claim the land and fauna residing in it as their very own hunting grounds, even before the Gallo-Romans could build a minor temple here in the very first century, there was evidence of habituation by Iron-Age tribes. They left stones and mounds to mark the eternal resting of their honored dead and some still stand today. Here it is the narrow brown river Nonette that influences the environment, and the land is marshy and the small, well-kept villages along its verdant banks have a strong medieval feel to them.

The delay came when we left the motorway to travel the last few miles to our departure point, where we would have a late lunch before setting off on a shortened stage into Paris. It was a Sunday and the organizers would have no prior knowledge of the town-wide rummage sale blocking our way through the suburbs of Senlis. The road was lazily blocked by two stanchions and at first our driver thought she might be able to pass through. Two kindly gentleman had removed the barriers for her and waved enthusiastically at us to continue our progression. Just as she stepped on the pedal, a frantically shouting woman with obvious authority halted our bus by standing directly in our path with her hands firmly planted on her hips.

Sitting in the front row as I was, I had a good view of the proceedings and thought we were about to all get an unpleasant earful. Though after a few matter-of-fact exchanges between the perplexed villager and our calm driver, the entire tone of the conversation changed. Suddenly, the two women were smiling and thanking each other in a polite, civil manner while a few extra villagers began to assist in our reversal. Astonishingly, the bus driver would have to drive the 45' long vehicle backwards down the road (of which we blocked the entire width). That meant reversing several blocks before we could safely turn around and try another way through. Because of the town *fête*, there were cars lining both sides of the narrow lane and pedestrians were ambling unhurriedly in all directions. It was the most harrowing slow-motion half-mile I've ever had the pleasure to be party to and half the fun was watching the faces of the crowd that had gathered along the way to witness the proceedings. They were all clapping as she adroitly maneuvered the wheeled beast to freedom. Such skill though couldn't be hurried and many slow minutes ticked by while she unstuck our caravan.

Back on track and progressing in a more forwardly direction, we finally arrived at lunch. Better late than never. It was a simple arrangement, long tables set under a large white tent on the lawn of a tired looking restaurant with equally overworked wait staff. They tried in earnest to satisfy our entire lot of road-weary and rather starving cyclists, denied our clockwork breaks for sustenance over the last eight hours. I felt lucky to have stashed away some cookies in my backpack or I might have begun to gnaw on my own appendages. Even still, my stomach was growling audibly by the time I stepped off the bus. We were all anxious to eat and get pedaling.

While the professional peloton would ride 70 miles including 8 laps of the Champs-Élysées, we would ride 44 with only a lap and a half of the cobbles between the Arc de Triomphe and the Tuileries Gardens. Picardy, the region our wheels were currently spinning through, was plump with photogenic villages and smooth as glass avenues. I had never before visited the equine-rich town of Chantilly or its suburbs, but along our route were the grandiose stables and fine horseflesh of the greatest of France's racing communities. Yes, it was the very place known for the cream and lace of the same name. While evidence of neither was apparent on our journey, one could still see protected lanes for horses, running parallel to city streets, covered with sand instead of pavement. The urban roads here were quiet and scenic and shaded well by the far reaching boughs of plane trees as the noble manors and manicured lawns spoke of the wealth of these neighborhoods.

The route was easy, navigating through attractive hamlets. There were no climbs to speak of until reaching the category 4 Côte de l'Ermitage. At barely a kilometer in length, it still packed a stinging punch at 7% grade and ever more so because we hit the base of it absolutely flying. I was sitting on the back of a spirited group that included Jaime and Sylvain, both capable of putting down serious power on the flat run to the climb. I was content at the tail of this speeding train and didn't think I'd mind getting left behind, figuring they'd go too hard for my tastes anyway given that I was more in the mood for a Sunday drive into Paris.

They dropped the hammer and made a significant gap. Considering this was the last stage, Scott seemed ready to let it all hang out and gave fair chase. I couldn't help myself. The blood rose in my veins and I was out of the saddle in pursuit. I had a lot of work to do to catch back up given my delayed reaction and no one was going to hang around and wait for me to get to it. The top of that hot little hill came and went and I hit the big ring and surged out of the saddle again for a half-dozen pedal strokes to make time on the descent. Back in the saddle, hands in the drops, back low and lungs demanding more air, I had already passed a few of the fiery group's slowest climbers and was gaining on one or two more on the descent. Descending used to be my nemesis, scared as I was of going fast downhill. Though once I learned how to get low and trust my bike as well as my own skills, I could cut through the air as well and as fast as anyone with twice my mass.

The front of the group had come back together without letting up on the throttle and before another dozen pedal strokes I had joined them. Scott looked over his shoulder to see who had caught up and whether he was surprised to find it was me I couldn't say. It was in that moment that I understood just how strong I had become, how strong we had all become.

For the length of the tour we had been keeping something in reserve every stage. We never quite knew what emergency energy we'd need to draw on due to the heat, rain, length of the course or difficulty of the climbs. But that didn't mean we hadn't become fit and quite capable of sustained endurance and bursts of power. I relished in the feeling and asked my legs for even more. They delivered and I surged forward, quicker and quicker with every pedal stroke. I seemed to find no bottom to this well and I wondered if I'd ever be this fast again. Probably not, I instantly realized as I shifted into a harder gear and pushed mysef with confident abandon.

↔

As we began to enter the outskirts of Paris, one thing became abundantly clear. The disparity between the wealth of Chantilly's neighborhoods and the immigrant heavy arrondissments was startling, though not surprising. I had driven through the outermost perimeters of the city in years past and seen the shift in quality of life and livelihood but from the mobile bubble of a bus seat. Sitting exposed on a bike, in the notoriously dangerous suburb of Saint Dennis, I was becoming an interesting spectacle at every red light. The hoots and hollers of loitering masses in the hot sun put me on point and delivered a whopping blow of reality and dash of vulnerability. The streets were littered and sticky with the remnants of late-night commerce and odiferous in the heat of the day. Cracked pavement, shattered glass, potholes like a minefield…this was no place to linger over a flat tire, so we picked our way carefully but expediently from one intersection to the next. These were the boulevards the tourists hardy ever saw but were just as much a part of true Paris as the famous promenades in their guidebooks. Saint Dennis was once the burial place of Kings and had seen human existence in many shades from the days of the Romans to modernity.

The traffic increased five-fold with each block that we pedaled closer to the pulsing heart of Paris. Scooters and motorbikes, taxis and rental cars were each vying for the same gap in the same lane sometimes splitting the lane between them. Familiar sights were coming into view and my heart was racing with the nervousness of riding among so many cars. Riding in a group was next to impossible. It was every cyclist for themselves on these streets. You had to stay hyper-aware of not only where you were placing your front wheel but choosing a safe line through traffic that was changing every second. Cars could appear without warning and open road was fleeting. Intense as it was, I'd still choose Paris over Montpellier any day. A few months before the tour I'd had the chance to ride through Brooklyn with Scott and our friend Chris Bishop, a still-practicing bicycle courier in Baltimore. Trying to hold onto his wheel as he wove his handmade fixed gear (sans brakes) in and out and between the bulk of delivery vans and buses was terrifyingly beautiful. Scott could hang, himself having grown up riding on the gridlocked streets of Washington, D.C. but I gave up after too many close passes and missed lights. I just didn't have the nerve.

I was going to need all the gumption I could muster to face the journey up and down the Champs Elysees. The famous bustling thoroughfare would not be closed to cars and if you've never had the chance to drive along its wide berth, it is a sight to behold. But first we had to get through the enormous intersection of the Place de la Concorde. Ideally we would have made the green light, settled into the flow of traffic, shielded ourselves between cars and carried-on through the massive stellar footprint of cobbles. But we pulled up just as the lights turned red. Like a six-armed starfish sharing the same smooth core, when the signal turned all the lanes would go at once and the motorized madness would begin. Cars would speed every direction, threading in and out of the axis, exiting and entering from six distinct lanes. Alex, a fellow Lifer, as kind as he was quick on the bike, joined us at the light. His energy was infectious and we shared a laugh at feeling like mice about to be flushed from their cover. We made a pact. We'd make a run for it, sprinting as fast as we could manage across the sea of slick lumps of well-worn stone to the safety of the bridge in the foreground. It was imperative to get across the center before the traffic could. The light turned green and Alex screamed go! go! and we three squealed with a mixture of delight and terror as we mashed on the pedals with all our might. We made it to the river safely and that brief moment became one of my favorites of the whole tour.

We regrouped briefly in view of the Eiffel tower for group photographs. We were encouraged to roll together down the cobbles of the Champs-Élysées insofar as possible with the congestion, but after a few blocks, the group broke up into twos and threes and were spread out like confetti. It was just as well because even on a hot Sunday in July, the avenue was pulsing with traffic and thick with exhaust. The cobbles were present but not an overwhelming force since they were well-worn with use and time and were sporadically covered in broad but interrupted patches of asphalt. Scott and I seemed to catch every traffic signal at its reddest, stuck behind cars three-deep and impatient. If we could have just carried a decent and consistent clip over the *pavé* instead of the awkward stops and starts, we would have found the journey more to enjoyable. When we finally reached the famous Arc de Triomphe for the first time, we were distracted by the neon arrow pointing to the right and veered its direction. That arrow signaled the way to the hotel, but it was too early yet to turn off. We still had a lap to go. There were other riders there snapping self-portraits with the arched icon in the background, some with their bikes held aloft in the popular pose of the two-wheeled conqueror. Sharing photo duties in between stop-light cycles, we each managed to snap a decent photo of one another with the triumphant arch in full view, without getting pummeled by the continuous wave of cars.

It seems every book I've ever read about the Tour de France contains an obligatory shot of the Arc de Triomphe on its cover. It's a token of gratitude perhaps to the towering challenge that is the Tour and most certainly a symbol of the triumph of man (and woman) over mountain. So on the back of this book you'll find the photo I snapped on the last day of my own tour, because it just felt wrong not to include it. Below the arc, cropped from view you'd have found me and my bicycle, grinning proudly under the French blue sky. I was existing, finally, in a moment I had hoped for but could never quite imagine. Now, I can picture myself there in that busy cobbled roundabout with complete clarity and my chest still fills with pride. It seemed like a lifetime had passed since Scott and I and the rest of the Lifers had taken that very first pedal stroke away from the bay of Mont Saint Michel, towards the golden wheat and towering mountains and all the secrets they held. No matter from how many different places the Tour chose to depart, they all ended up here, in *la Ville Lumière*. We had made it; more or less intact, more or less the way we hoped, sometimes clumsily but ultimately together.

↔

Dinner on the Seine was a touching affair. My hands were red and throbbing from all the applause. Each Lifer's name was read aloud to the group by our honorable leader Phil. As the volume of clapping maintained at a deafening decibel for the entire rollcall, we each accepted our participation trophy. Handmade by the very recipients of our fundraising, we all relished the engraved token and held on tightly to the small symbol of our accomplishment before returning misty-eyed to our large round banquet tables to the back-patting and hand-shaking of friends.

The mood was relaxed as the boat fleetingly navigated the dark waters of the fast-flowing river, passing the illuminated façades of the city's greatest architecture. We ate, we drank and we laughed despite the fatigue of the last twenty-three days and nearly 2,200 miles. We had ascended an astounding 148,500 feet and witnessed the world from the mighty crowns of more than fifty categorized peaks, passes and mountain tops; transcending many more without mention. Though it didn't mean we couldn't still be amazed by the most simple of sights.

A respectful but delighted gasp spread through the deck as we floated smoothly past the Tour d'Eiffel, lit up and glittering in the *bleu, blanc et rouge.*

↔

I slept like a stone at the bottom of a well. Dark and dreamless, absent from the mental noise and anxiety that another day of digging to the depths of my capacity could bring. Getting up each morning of the tour took resolve. To know that your imminent waking hours would bring adventure but also the physical strain of continuous and deliberate and often difficult pedaling and to do it through the power of choice and freewill alone…well, that was something. Then to desire such tempest, to crave it even, knowing another day in the saddle could be longer and more trying than the last…well, that was something else. So waking up without the necessity to cover half the country before nightfall was peculiar.

The last arrows we'd see guided the way to the breakfast hall, where we would get once last chance to say our goodbyes, some of them tearful with the occasional laugh to clear the air. We said *au revoir* to Jaime and Tom and Sylvain and the other members of this elite band of *rouleurs* and *puncheurs* and *baroudeurs.* These were the men whose wheels I trusted most and would miss lamentably in the months to come. Then we shared our final hugs with Indy, whose spirit was unflappable even during these painful farewells. We were all dispersing to our corners of the earth, most back to England, some to Australia and Ireland and a handful would remain here in France. We too would set off for our own small getaway, a few restful days in the countryside where Scott could put up his feet for a spell and I could exhale, nice and slow and we could both stay motionless long enough to put a little flesh back on our sun-tanned bodies.

Though I never had the chance to say goodbye to Phil, I imagined him stealing away in the wee morning hours, setting off to prepare for his next cycling conquest, that of a thousand of the most storybook *cols*.

RECOVERY:

A Cat Named Golden

It felt strange to have our time as our own again, to no longer follow the directive of an anonymous arrow telling us where to turn, when to yield and how to find our way to rest, lunch and shelter. While liberating, we also felt a little lost. And restless. Lithe and fit and sun drenched and confident, but somehow uprooted. Which was ridiculous considering there had been no time over the last several weeks to lay down anything resembling roots (except for our asses rooted heavily upon our saddles). But that was it exactly. That was what was missing from our new reality and it was stark and obvious and left us wondering how to behave with all this new found freedom. We had lived an engine's life, an existence consisting of sleeping, waking, consuming fuel and expending energy for 21 days that could have felt like 21 years if not an entire lifetime. Now we were free of the task of relentless pedaling and it felt as if a part of us had been lost, a plug had been pulled from the outlet, suddenly silencing the humming machine.

Determined to ease out of our rituals and back into the reality we knew before the tour, we had planned a few days of recovery time before flying back to the States. There, home and work were waiting patiently for our return. We had become addicted to riding our bicycles, cycling was our narcotic and like any addiction, we needed to detox, to gently shed our habitual skins. Participating in the tour had simplified our lives; eat, pedal, sleep, pedal. We had to prepare ourselves for return to "normalcy", a life drastically more complicated. The thought could be depressing if we dwelled to much upon it. So instead, we distracted ourselves for a few days by taking a proper holiday, to learn to behave like ordinary people do when they aren't traversing an entire European country on two-wheels.

We went to the Perigord, naturally. There, the sun was warm and the sky was bright blue and we could drown our sorrows in duck confit and cave art like millions of other tourists do every July. Before the tour we had booked a few days in Scotland to go mountain biking near Edinburgh, because who doesn't recover from a 2,200 mile ride over some of France's most daunting mountains by negotiating heather-strewn rock gardens and epic single track? We did, until it was suggested by the tour doctor that Scott avoid any strenuous activity for the next few months if he ever hoped to properly ride a bike again. Therefore mountain biking was out and we were scrambling to find a more suitable location that didn't require a ten-hour drive across two countries, toting two bikes and four bags and straining the abused clutch of our boxy little rental car.

Also out was any location where it might rain. We'd seen too much of that already. What we needed was a reliably sunny forecast, forgiving terrain for a few lazy bicycle rides and enough touristy activities to keep us occupied for a handful of days until we returned to Paris for the flight home. The Dordogne region sounded perfect. Not too far to drive, cuisine to indulge our appetites, dry heat and all those glorious pre-historic caves. We arrived almost five hours later, at Hotel du Parc next to the shallow Vézère river. It was a tidy, quiet place with a pea-gravel drive, the kind that Scott is so fond of. There were two creamy stucco buildings, built in the traditional style of the region. A terrace, shaded by mature trees, looked welcoming in front of what appeared to be the restaurant. After ringing a brass bell on the desk in an unoccupied office, we met Monsieur Dominic, unhurried in his manner and as he was welcoming in his greeting. He made us immediately comfortable and treated us like family right from the start. A retired banker from Paris, he had found his peace along the banks of the gently flowing river and took pleasure as well as pride in sharing that peace with his guests.

It was the perfect place for us to recover for a few days, waking late in the mornings and lingering over a simple breakfast before setting out to explore the treasures of the Perigord Noir. The area is known for duck and truffles, foie gras and pre-historic caves and was graced by the ancients with beau villages clinging to limestone hillsides, their chateau the envy of a number of fairytales. We toured the dark recesses of the earth and gave witness to the artistry of humans as old as history itself. We strolled along market streets, buying cheese made from the tangy milk of local sheep and washed it down with the chalky local wine. We picnicked along the clear waters of the Vézère, originating from the volcanic mounds of the Massif Central and filtering through the department of Corrèze before joining the Dordogne on its journey to the ocean. It was with the help of this innocuous river that there were caves here at all and without it dripping away at the earth for millennia, there would be no cave walls, no canvas on which the art of our ancestors defies our imagination still.

It wasn't all sightseeing and lazy days. We managed a few easy rides, 75 miles or so each. I realize that might not sound "easy" to some but compared to the distances we had covered the week prior, gently pedaling along the moderate hills in this region really felt like a recovery ride. Even when we were caught in a pelting but warm rain or took a wrong turn and ended up in a farmer's vast meadow. Once we had to pass through barbed-wire fence lines and hike with our road bikes slung over our shoulders through the fragrant oak forests better known for being the magical hiding place of truffles. One of my favorite memories is being stopped in our two-wheeled tracks by the overwhelming waft of fresh strawberries, growing on a farm along the roadside. They were more sweetly smelling than any berry I had ever known and hardly registered as natural. We lingered there, half-mounted on our bikes, sniffing the air until we were drunk with the aroma and lightheaded with the effort of inhaling.

In the evenings, we would return to the Park and enjoy a simple but satisfying meal served by Dominic and his companions. For starters there was a homemade country soup, clear broth with small bits of vegetable and other nourishing morsels. We sopped up our bowels with thick slices of rustic bread. Then an appetizer, usually local foie gras or confit. Followed by a roast chicken or grilled rabbit or a nice breast of duck with a side of fresh salad. We would sit back in our chairs, under the shade of a large willow tree, in the pleasant company of only two other tables, sipping on *noisette* liqueur.

It was on the first evening that I met Golden, named after the beer that Dominic stocked in the hotel fridge. She was an old scraggly yellow cat and her long coat needed a decent brushing. She wasn't necessarily fond of people, biting and clawing at them if given the chance, but was fond of the table scraps "dropped" at her feet when she turned those sad watery eyes in a guests' direction. A woman at the neighboring table was clearly not amused with her feline antics. Perhaps she was allergic, but nevertheless swatted at the elderly beast each time the cat muttered a hoarse meow. They were equally persistent in annoying each other, so I smooched under my breath to get the animal's attention as I simultaneously dropped a piece of duck near my chair. That accomplished two things; securing the cat's unyielding affections for the rest of the week and landing me in hot water with Dominic for encouraging such bad behavior.

I managed to discretely and covertly feed her over the next few dinner services (and breakfast too) and was only busted for it once more. I was given a stern look and a firm scolding but I caught the corner of a smile when Dominic turned to leave us to the rest of our breakfast. It seemed to also please the only other guest in the dining salon and I enjoyed her companionship and hearing her velvety bygone era silver screen voice. She was doted on by Dominic and treated with kind reverence, so she was either a repeat customer or somebody quite special. I figured he had forgiven me since on our last evening, we were invited to his family table to share a digestif with him and his friends. He was generous to a fault and would occasionally translate the rapid-fire commentary into English for me to understand. He and his companions spoke to Scott only in French and complimented his grasp of their language.

When it was finally time to leave, neither Golden or Dominic were to be found anywhere. I asked the fine matron at breakfast to say goodbye on my behalf and she agreed that she would. We bade each other farewell and *bonne journée* and I turned to leave, stealing a second glance in case either the cat or the proprietor appeared. They didn't. It was probably easier that way but my heart still ached to depart their easy company and the serenity of the simple hotel on the banks of that peaceful river. With our bikes disassembled and packed securely in their travel cases, we loaded the car and drove away from Thonac. In the rearview, a half-crumbling chateaux clung defiantly to the river bank.

↔

We returned to Paris a day earlier than our flight so we could witness our favorite teams of riders whizz past on the final stage of the Tour de France. Before Chris Froome came carving around the corner in front of the Musée du Louvre where we had stood for hours to secure a front row view of the race, we were entertained by the caravan of cars and floats and sponsors, honking and waving and dancing enthusiastically to blaring tunes. My favorite was the giant chicken on wheels. How can you not love a country that has such a fondness for poultry?

The publicity caravan was first introduced in 1930 by Henri Desgrange and had just three sponsors, including one manufacturer of chocolate. The glory years included the likes of sponsors such as Laughing Cow and Cinzano then Nesquik and BIC, until more recently the giants Carrefour and Vittel. But the caravan contains more than just a convoy of 170 sponsor floats throwing out upward of 14 million treats and trinkets like water bottles, keychains, caps, coffee, even saucisson (though sadly, no more cheese or chocolates). There are also officials and special guests, security and neutral support, team cars and most importantly, the race director. These days that's Christian Prudhomme, who can be seen grinning broadly from a red Škoda sedan. No, it is not a French car. I was also surprised.

When the last lap of riders came and went before barreling down the cobbles over the finish line, the winner of the stage was the powerful sprinter André Greipel who narrowly beat out fan favorite and infamous trickster Peter Sagan. As the *lanterne rouge* (the last finisher of the Tour) crossed the line, the heavily armed gendarmes gathered up the rider's discarded bidons, tossed a few to the begging crowds and started to assist the departing masses.

I had my sights on one of the official Tour arrows, a yellow and black sign marking the course, affixed high on a street light but couldn't push my way upstream against the tide of shuffling fans. Before I could arrive to shimmy up the post and steal away a piece of cycling history, a young man bearing his girlfriend on his shoulders pulled the arrow down and escaped in the receding wave of human beings. Damn it. I felt slighted. He hadn't just ridden up all those mountains! He didn't know those roads like I did! He didn't deserve to go home with that arrow! Pouting, I let myself get picked up in the flow of departing spectators and was delivered back to Scott. He put his arm around me and apologized for my missed prize and we ambled slowly back to our hotel. With no more arrows to guide us, we succumbed to the reality that both events, their Tour and ours, were really over. It was finally time to return home.

EPILOGUE

Perspective

Being back home was strange. I had just put myself through a genuinely life altering experience and it was still very fresh on my mind and body. Thomas Wolf wrote that "you can't go home again". After experiencing the world and all its wonders, he became disillusioned with his hometown. It turns out that you can, of course, go back to the place you once called home. You can also cross the same stream twice but the waters will always be different, won't they?

So then what did home feel like when we returned? It felt like a foreign place, full of foreign customs and foreign expectations. Only our work felt familiar; hands on our well-known tools, the aroma of our well-known coffee, the smiles of well-known customers and friends. Time has marched steadily on, but we still feel like foreigners in our own lands. The siren song of France and the gentle staccato of chain noise echoing off her endless roads calls to us from across the restless ocean. The sound has grown fainter to our ears, but the heartstrings that now bind us to her mountains are stretched as taught as they ever were and the memories of that summer adventure continue to pluck and pull at our very core. A desire reverberates through my bones to return to that country and ride and ride and ride until I am old and frail and can recall with pride how I rode them all; every road and every climb and every canyon and through every village square. It's as foolish as it is romantic and a little heartbreaking too. Writing this story has given me that chance to reminisce, with all the memories flooding back. Now that my retelling of events has come to a close, I feel emptied of them all over again and that saddens me more than I expected.

Which is why perhaps, about halfway through putting words to page, with Scott resting on our bed reading through what I had already written, I turned to him and asked if he'd want to ride the tour again. Without hesitation, he answered yes. I wasn't surprised at his response, only wondering how long he had been holding on to the desire and whether or not he would have ever shared it with me if I had failed to inquire. Pretty much since we finished, he replied, when I asked the follow up question. That's what I figured, I said. It made sense considering he had a score to settle with a few mountains and his own physical form. He wanted the chance to ride sound and painlessly tackle every single kilometer of the course. I wanted that for him too. And for me. So we agreed to ride again in 2018.

Like becoming parents of a second child, I hoped that we made all of our mistakes with the first one and our second attempt will be less stressful and more successful. Perhaps we won't fuss as much over the details and we'll rear our second adventure

329

with less fear and anxiety and more freedom and free-reign. Second children claim to have an easier childhood, don't they? At least I'll be able to sleep through the night.

It has been easy to wax poetically about the tour, conveniently forgetting the bad bits. Not all our memories and experiences were peachy, so it's important to keep things in perspective. When asked by the film crew at our final dinner in Paris if we'd ever ride the event again, we responded with an emphatically synchronized no. Not a chance, we went on to explain. Too much traffic, too many busy roads and too many close calls. Too much rain and cold and bad weather. Too many tunnels, I chimed in, not caring if there was really only the one.

Though, like the fading pains of childbirth reveal the desire to add another leaf to the family tree, we seem to have forgiven those trespasses while not entirely forgetting them. They still exist, those close calls and distracted drivers and as much as I can hope I'll never have to ride through the rocky guts of a mountain again…there will be those too. And if it isn't a rainy tour it will be a hot one. And if we aren't blanketed in a freak snowstorm along the brow of the Alps, we'll be blown off the side of Ventoux by the tempest. We'll shiver and sweat, curse and cry. Alas, I'll write about it in my diary and laugh about it in the months that follow.

Riding the roads of the Tour de France has taught me some valuable emotional lessons and rewarded me with irrepressible spirit. I've realized with sometimes uncomfortable clarity who I am at this very moment, though not who I was or even who I might become. Those are the me of a different time, influenced by a different adventure. I've discovered that the world is both quite small and quite surprising and still holds wonders yet to be realized. I've learned to quickly reset expectations, to keep myself shielded from disappointment. I've understood how determination can be an unyielding force, whether its physical or mental or both. I've seen limitless generosity and the power of positive thought. I've seen how thoughtless words and careless actions can chip away at others and even more so at yourself, especially if you are the one wielding them. I've learned that illness and injury can be a brute force when the only motor propelling you forward is your own. I have been reminded how little power we have over nature and our only defense is to respect her. I have also been reminded of our power over each other, to harm as well as to heal.

Then there were the unspoken lessons taught by my bicycle; that I got out tenfold what I put in. How to pedal smooth circles, not jerky squares even when I was painfully tired. How to keep my line steady and true, despite the rain stinging my eyes or the wind trying to blow me off course. How to trust another rider's wheel, even if I didn't trust my own. How to gratefully accept a helping hand on the side of the road or in a pace-line. How to spend my fair share at the front and to sometimes take more pulls than I expected. How to put my head down and get to work and let everything else become unimportant. How to take care of my body, feed it well, water it often and rest it when necessary. How to always take care of my equipment, because when I did, my equipment would always take care of me (thanks Dad). How I should always ride my own ride and nobody else's. How the view from the top of the greatest mountain was far better when I had someone next to me with which to share it.

Of course, these are not all the things the tour helped me realize. Some of them are impossible to articulate and others are simply private. The most important message is that bicycles can change lives. I watched them do it and I am ever grateful for the opportunity. Susan B. Anthony said of the bicycle, and I am paraphrasing, that it had more to do with the emancipation of women than any other tool of the 20th century. She wasn't incorrect but her words would not have been far off the mark if she had said the same about all of mankind. My desire to ride my bicycle, which I cherish, along the roads of France, which I adore, motivated me also to raise money for those less fortunate, whom I might never have known about, if it wasn't for the love of a bicycle. And if it sounds cyclical, as a finely tuned wheel traveling in a near-perfect circle goes around and around, it is. Thus contains its very power…to propel, to engage, to make us healthy and happy and connect us to each other as well as the greater world. The next time you pass a person on a bike, give them a smile and a wave. You never know, they might be in the middle of their own grand adventure.

The End

ACKNOWLEDGEMENTS

It Takes A Peloton

I would not have been born into a life full of adventure without my parents, so to them I say thank you for allowing me to explore the world in my own way, all the while keeping me safe as I forged my own path through life. You are tree from which this apple falls.

I would not have found cycling without my husband, so to him I say thank you for all the love in my life and for riding beside me faithfully and without fail, no matter where our wheels are rolling. You are the fuel for my fire and the wind in my ship's sails.

I would not have a story without characters, so to the Lifers and staff of Tour de Force, I say chapeau. Thank you for your care, your companionship and for sharing your own grand adventure with the likes of me and Scott. You are forever my two-wheeled friends.

There would be no Tour de Force without the Wates family, so to you I applaud you. Your vision to make the world a better place for the recipients of your endless kindness, especially in the memory of such personal loss is both honorable and humbling. You are my inspiration to ride for a cause.

And finally, to my friends, family, customers and generous strangers who donated their hard-earned money to help us reach our fundraising goals, without which we would never have ridden a single mile, I offer you a million thanks. You are the ones who made this possible.

APPENDIX:

List of Categorized Climbs of the 2016 Tour de France

Stage 1: Mont-Saint-Michel to Utah Beach Sainte-Marie-du-Mont 188 km

Côte d'Avranches ~ 1.2 kilometers at 5.7% **Category 4**
Côte des Falaises de Champeaux ~ 1.3 kilometers at 4.8%
Category 4

Stage 2: Saint-Lô to Cherbourg-en-Cotentin 183 km

Côte de Torigny-les-Villes ~ 1.4 ~ kilometers at 5.7%
Category 4
Côte de Montabot {D28-D98} ~ 1.9 kilometers at 5%
Category 4
Côte de Montpinchon ~ 1.2 kilometers at 5.9%   **Category 4**
Côte de La Glacerie ~ 1.9 kilometers 6.5% **Category 3**

Stage 3: Granville to Angers 223.5 km
Côte de Villedieu-les-Poêles ~ 1.5 kilometers at 4.4%
Category 4

Stage 4: Saumur to Limoges 237.5 km

Côte de la Maison Neuve {D25-D7} ~ 1.2 kilometers at 5.6%
Category 4

Stage 5: Limoges to Le Lioran 216 km

Côte de Saint-Léonard-de-Noblat ~ 1.7 kilometers at 5.2%
Category 4
Côte du Puy Saint-Mary ~ 6.8 kilometers at 3.9% **Category 3**
Col de Neronne ~ 7.1 kilometers at 3% **Category 3**
Pas de Peyrol {Puy Mary} (1,589m) ~ 5.4 kilometers at 8.1%
Category 2
Col du Perthus (1,389m) ~ 4.4 kilometers at 7.9% **Category 2**
Col de Font de Cère ~ 3.3 kilometers at 5.8% **Category 3**

Stage 6: Arpajon-sur-Cère to Montauban 190.5 km

Col des Estaques ~ 2 kilometers at 6% **Category 3**
Côte d'Aubin ~ 1.3 kilometers at 5.4% **Category 4**
Côte de Saint-Antonin-Noble-Val ~ 3.2 kilometers at 5.1%
Category 3

Stage 7: L'Isle-Jourdain to Lac de Payolle 162.5 km

Côte de Capvern ~ 7.7 kilometers at 3.1% **Category 4**
Col d'Aspin (1,490m) ~ 12 kilometers at 6.5% **Category 1**

Stage 8: Pau to Bagnères-de-Luchon 184 km

Col du Tourmalet (2,115 m) 19 kilometers at 7.4% **HC**
Hourquette d'Ancizan (1,564 m) ~ 8.2 kilometres at 4.9%
Category 2
Col de Val Louron-Azet (1,580 m) ~ 10.7 kilometres at 6.8%
Category 1
Col de Peyresourde (1,569 m) ~ 7.1 kilometres at 7.8%
Category 1

Stage 9: Vielha Val d'Aran to Andorre Arcalis
184.5 km

Port de la Bonaigua (2,072m) ~ 13.7 kilometers at 6.1%
Category 1
Port del Cantò (1,721m) ~ 19 kilometers at 5.4% -**Category 1**
Côte de la Comella (1,347m) ~ 4.2 kilometers at 8.2% -
Category 2
Col de Beixalis {CS210-CS310} (1,796m) ~ 6.4 kilometers at
8.5% **Category 1**
Andorre Arcalis (2,240m) ~ 10.1 kilometers at 7.2% - **HC***

Stage 10: Escaldes-Engordany to Revel
197 km

Port d'Envalira (2,408m) ~ 22.6 kilometers at 5.5% Category 1
Côte de Saint-Ferréo ~ 11.8 kilometers at 6.6% Category 3

Stage 11: Carcassonne to Montpellier
162.5 km

Côte de Minerve ~ 2.4 kilometers at 5.4% **Category 4**
Côte de Villespassans ~ 2.3 kilometers at 4.5% **Category 4**

Stage 12: Montpellier to Mont Ventoux
178 km

Côte de Gordes ~ 3.3 kilometers at 4.8% **Category 4**
Col des Trois Termes ~ 2.5 kilometers at 7.5% **Category 3**
Mont Ventoux (1,912m) ~ 15.7 kilometers at 8.8% **HC**

Stage 13: Bourg-Saint-Andéol to La Caverne du Pont-d'Arc 37.5 km

Time Trial Stage, no categorized climbs

Stage 14: Montélimar to Villars-les-Dombes Parc des Oiseaux 208.5 km

Côte de Puy-Saint-Martin3.6 kilometers at 5.2% **Category 4**
Côte du Four-à-Chaux3.9 kilometers at 4.2% **Category 4**
Côte d'Hauterives2.1 kilometers at 5.5% **Category 4**

Stage 15: Bourg-en-Bresse to Culoz 160 km

Col du Berthiand (780m) ~ 6 kilometers at 8.1%
Category 1
Col du Sappel (794m) ~ 8.8 kilometers at 5.6% **Category 2**
Col de Pisseloup ~ 4.9 kilometers at 5.8% **Category 3**
Col de la Rochette ~ 5.1 kilometers at 5.4% **Category 3**
Grand Colombier (1,501m) ~ 12.8 kilometers at 6.8% **HC**
Lacets du Grand Colombier {D120-D120 A} (891m) ~ 8.4
kilometers at 7.6% **Category 1***

Stage 16: Moirans-en-Montagne to Berne 209 km

Côte de Mühleberg ~ 1.2 kilometers at 4.8% **Category 4**

Stage 17: Berne to Finhaut-Emosson 184.5

Côte de Saanenmöser ~ 6.6 kilometers at 4.8% **Category 3**
Col des Mosses ~ 6.4 kilometers at 4.4% **Category 3**
Col de la Forclaz (1,527m) ~ 13 kilometers at 7.9%
Category 1*
Finhaut-Emosson (1,960m) ~ 10.4 kilometers at 8.4% **HC***

Stage 18: Sallanches to Megève 17 km

Time Trial Stage, no categorized climbs

Stage 19: Albertville to Saint-Gervais Mont Blanc 146 km

Col de la Forclaz de Montmin (1,157m) ~ 9.8 kilometers at 6.9% **Category 1**
Col de la Forclaz de Queige (870m) ~ 5.6 kilometers at 7.8% **Category 2***
Montée de Bisanne (1,723m) ~ 12.4 kilometers at 8.2% **HC**
Le Bettex (1,372m) ~ 9.8 kilometers at 8% **Category 1**

Stage 20: Megève to Morzine-Avoriaz 146.5 km

Col des Aravis (1,487m) ~ 6.7 kilometers at 7%   **Category 2**
Col de la Colombière (1,618m) ~ 11.7 kilometers at 5.8% **Category 1**
Col de la Ramaz (1,619m) ~ 13.9 kilometers at 7.1% **Category 1**
Col de Joux Plane (1,691m) ~ 11.6 kilometers at 8.5% **HC**

Stage 21: Chantilly to Paris Champs-Élysées 113 km

Côte de l'Ermitage ~ 0.9 kilometers at 7% **Category 4**

*Indicates a climb not attempted by author in 2016

ABOUT THE AUTHOR

Nicole Marie Davison is an avid cyclist who rides for the love of the climb and for delicious French cheese. She refers to herself as a recovering equestrian though still enjoys the company of two handsome horses she calls her "boys". She blames her fondness for handmade steel frames on her husband Scott who is happy that the *s-1 rule does not apply to their household. She and Scott and the horses dream of living in France someday, where they can pedal (and gallop) to their hearts' content. Until then, you might still be able to find them riding fun bikes and drinking fine coffee (and munching green grass) in Virginia.

*s-1 where s = the number of bikes
your spouse wants you to own.

Made in the USA
Columbia, SC
03 August 2017